NET VALUES

Nicole D. Peterson

NET VALUES

Environmental, Economic, and Social Entanglements
in the Gulf of California

The University of Arizona Press
www.uapress.arizona.edu

We respectfully acknowledge the University of Arizona is on the land and territories of Indigenous peoples. Today, Arizona is home to twenty-two federally recognized tribes, with Tucson being home to the O'odham and the Yaqui. Committed to diversity and inclusion, the University strives to build sustainable relationships with sovereign Native Nations and Indigenous communities through education offerings, partnerships, and community service.

© 2025 by The Arizona Board of Regents
All rights reserved. Published 2025

ISBN-13: 978-0-8165-5518-5 (hardcover)
ISBN-13: 978-0-8165-5479-9 (paperback)
ISBN-13: 978-0-8165-5480-5 (ebook)

Cover design by Leigh McDonald
Cover art by Lizette Inzunza
Typeset by Leigh McDonald in Warnock Pro 10.5/14 and Korolev Compressed (display)

All photos and map are courtesy of the author.

Library of Congress Cataloging-in-Publication Data
Names: Peterson, Nicole D., 1974– author.
Title: Net values : environmental, economic, and social entanglements in the Gulf of California / Nicole D. Peterson.
Description: Tucson : University of Arizona Press, 2025. | Includes bibliographical references and index.
Identifiers: LCCN 2024032674 (print) | LCCN 2024032675 (ebook) | ISBN 9780816555185 (hardcover) | 9780816554799 (paperback) | ISBN 9780816554805 (ebook)
Subjects: LCSH: Fishers—Mexico—California, Gulf of—Social conditions—21st century. | Fishers—Mexico—California, Gulf of—Economic conditions—21st century. | Marine resources conservation—Social aspects. | Fisheries—Mexico—California, Gulf of.
Classification: LCC HD8039.F66 M648 2025 (print) | LCC HD8039.F66 (ebook) | DDC 338.3/727091641—dc23/eng/20241227
LC record available at https://lccn.loc.gov/2024032674
LC ebook record available at https://lccn.loc.gov/2024032675

Printed in the United States of America
♾ This paper meets the requirements of ANSI/NISO Z39.48-1992 (Permanence of Paper).

Para la comunidad de Playa Tranquila, y las otras comunidades pesqueras de Loreto.

CONTENTS

List of Illustrations		*ix*
Acknowledgments		*xi*
	Introduction	3
1.	Rhythms	27
2.	Tourism Encounters	53
3.	Women, Work, and Moral Economy	77
4.	Being Good Children of the Sea	102
5.	*"Que hace el parque?"* What's the MPA Doing?	125
	Conclusion	155
	References	*163*
	Index	*185*

ILLUSTRATIONS

FIGURES

1.	Fishers mending nets on a windy day	31
2.	Tourists photographing a cultural dance in the central plaza of Loreto in the early 2000s	57
3.	Dorado sportfishing tournament in 2012	58
4.	The streambed has been excavated for dirt and stone for the resort	67
5.	Signs blocking beach access say, "Private property, no access"	69
6.	Fishing boat in front of a new resort in Baja California Sur	71
7.	Fish packing by the Hijas in 2010	79
8.	Laundry in Playa Tranquila under the mango trees	87
9.	Bread oven in Playa Tranquila	93
10.	An embroidered tortilla wrap from Playa Tranquila	99
11.	Workshop for drafting the management plan, July 2001	117

MAP

1.	Map of Loreto Bay National Park	7

TABLES

1.	Data Collection Timeline	20
2.	Timeline of the Loreto Bay National Park	113

ACKNOWLEDGMENTS

This book took a long time to write, and a lot of people helped me find the book in all of my messy data. For those who usually skip the acknowledgment section, just know that writing a book is both easier and harder, lonelier and more communal than you would ever expect.

It was easier because I got to finally tell more about people who became friends and collaborators in helping me understand the environment and fishing. For many years, I felt like I benefited more than the community I studied because this research helped me advance my own career. I tried to give back, bringing gifts and requests with me, teaching computer classes, building websites, and supporting education through donations. Most people were kind enough to accept these with the wish that I would just come back and visit them again. Writing this book has been in a sense an extended visit, a chance to share with them what I have learned and how this research might eventually do something to make it easier for them or others like them to get ahead. Each memory, each story connects to stories elsewhere and brings similarities and differences into focus. I cannot thank my friends in Loreto and its fishing communities enough for welcoming me into their lives and letting me write about them, and I think each of you can see a glimmer of yourselves in the pages here. I also want to thank Lizette, Adela, Graciela, Conchita, and Julie for making it easy to relax in Loreto. I feel like I wrote this book alongside my friends in Playa Tranquila and Loreto, but the story isn't mine anymore.

Writing this book was harder than I expected because it meant revisiting happy memories alongside discussions about the depressing state of fishing and the environment in Loreto. I hope I've found a good balance between hope and despair; if I thought it was useless to try to address environmental problems, I wouldn't have written this at all. I also struggled with revisions and perfectionism, making this process much more difficult than it needed to be. The first draft was years in the making because I kept rewriting everything, and even the last draft required me to incorporate some excellent suggestions by three anonymous reviewers in a short amount of time. They helped me connect the narratives I told more effectively to the work of other scholars, and I thank them and my editor, Allyson Carter, and the whole University of Arizona Press team for their suggestions and faith (and patience).

The conclusion was one of the most difficult things I've ever written because it meant saying goodbye (once more) to friends in Loreto whom I'll never see again. I also felt the absence of several mentors who helped get me to Mexico and beyond but who will also never have the chance to see this book, like Roy D'Andrade, Aaron Cicourel, Dave Krantz, Pancho, and my father. I can't thank you all enough.

As I wrote this book and related work, I found an immense amount of joy in thinking alongside other people; the references in the text give a sense of my debt to many other scholars. My other dissertation committee members, Ed Hutchins, David Kirsch, Joel Robbins, Shirley Strum, and Mark Spaulding, helped me understand how to study, think, and share ideas, as did their colleagues Nancy Postero, Tanya Luhrmann, and Michael Cole. Mentors come into our lives in many ways, and as I wrote this, I kept thinking about my first writing group with Julie Monteleone and Sharla Blank; you were with me in spirit writing this as well, asking for that next draft, as were Julia Offen, Greg Simon, Jon Bialecki, Brendan Jamal Thornton, Cage Hall, Liz Peacock, Bambi Chapin, and other friends from graduate school. I was very lucky to find some amazing colleagues at the Center for Research on Environmental Decisions and Columbia University who pushed me to think more broadly than anthropology and Mexican fishing communities, including Ben Orlove, Kenny Broad, Dan Osgood, Renzo Taddei, Sabine Marx, Angie Heo, and Paige West.

My research, including this book, has benefited from the opportunities to think alongside colleagues while we wrote special issues around participatory processes and rational actors, and I thank Kent Glenzer, Carla Roncoli, Cindy Isenhour, and Molly Doane for their conversations and support. The University of North Carolina at Charlotte has continued to support my intellectual growth through conversations about social sustainability with Brett Tempest, Robby Boyer, Helene Hilger, Jen Munroe, Beth Marino, Sarah Bell, Rachelle Hollander, Adjo Amekudzi-Kennedy, Paul Thompson, Sandra Santa-Cruz, and the many other Integrated Network for Social Sustainability participants. Other scholars have inspired me and my work as well, including Maria Cruz Torres, David Hoffman, Susie Crate, Kate Browne, Nora Haenn, Linda Whiteford, Keri Brondo, Sarah Lyon, Lisa Cliggett, Susan Andreatta, the late Carolyn Lesorogol, Erika Edwards, Cat Fuentes, Sara Juengst, Colleen Hammelman, Dena Shenk, Cheryl Emanuel, Lydia Light, Andrea Freidus, Carmen Solis, Jürgen Buchenau, Greg Weeks, Donna Lanclos, Kathy Metzo, Tina Shull, Caitlin Schroering, Janet Levy, and my inspiring students.

I was also very privileged to have been part of the Center for U.S.-Mexican Studies fellows program in 2004, with the generous and smart Carmen Maganda. I am also thankful for the other organizations that have supported this research, including the University of California Institute for Mexico and the United States, University of California San Diego's Department of Anthropology, the Center for Iberian and Latin American Studies, Friends of the International Center, the Earth Institute, and UNC Charlotte's Faculty Research Grant and the Department of Anthropology.

I want to recognize that this book would not exist in any final form if it wasn't for Poonam Arora, who helped me convince myself that I needed to finish it, building on so many of our discussions around economics and choice. Similarly, Sharon Watson helped me see that this was worthwhile and meaningful, pushing me beyond my doubts. Both of you are incredible scholars and people, and I'm always so amazed to have your support and friendship.

Finally, writing is also lonely in many ways, and even though it is never done in isolation from other people and ideas, it is often a lot of time with a computer and lots of documents. I'm very appreciative of friends like Emily Burns, Marti Kuern, Sam De Rosa, Michele and Matt Lemere, Lauren and Erik Schalburg, Mel and Matt Allen, and Heather and Kevin Gavagan, among other friends who always make things fun and keep me from getting too antisocial, including the dogs who needed to play catch and to go for walks. My mom, dad, and Amy have always been so supportive of me, along with Jimmy, Connor, and Alice; I am who I am because of you. Thanks also to Astrid, Lourdes, and Fatima who helped me finish this book, giving me a place to write and grace when I was late for lunch.

And, of course, I cannot thank Eric Hoenes del Pinal enough for his support for all these years and for the title (now we're even). Since I can't top his book acknowledgment, I can only say that I know we'll always be able to find days of enchantment and amazing food together, and that all's well that ends well to end up with you.

NET VALUES

INTRODUCTION

The beach was empty. A new chain-link fence asserted ownership, separating the Gulf of California and its beach from the latter's namesake community, Playa Tranquila.[1] Five years earlier, don Javier had greeted me there next to his palm-roofed house, smoking Marlboros under his jaunty white cowboy hat. Despite his age, he quickly stood to shake my hand, sunglasses reflecting the water behind me. The glasses also caught a few fishing *pangas* that straddled water and land, much the way don Javier's life also had. He was the patriarch of the community, a fisherman who had turned a fish camp into a permanent residence, bringing his wife and children from a community farther south to join him. His home was a cluster of several thatched-roof rooms almost entirely open to the breeze off the water. Along with the slight noise of the small waves breaking against the sand and the frequent cry of seagulls, we heard the murmur of several fishers as they talked and laughed nearby in the shade of the *palapa* next door, watching their neighbors and friends unload and sell their catch. On the other side of the *palapa* was where I would live, a

---

1. All personal and community names are pseudonyms, aside from published authors and the town of Loreto.

vacation house built by an *Americano* friend of don Javier.[2] But five years later, the beach is empty—the small houses, shady gathering spot, the boats and their mounds of nets and gas containers were gone. It was, as they say, *limpio*. Clean.

Don Javier's and his *Americano* friend's homes had been demolished to make way for a new tourist resort, which had claimed the beach as its own using a combination of Mexican law, intimidation, and cash. While don Javier had once shown me thousands of old (valueless) pesos in an attempt to impress me with his wealth, he now had that and more in real currency. He built a new concrete house almost in the center of the community near several of his children and next to his *Americano* friend's new walled compound, also built from money paid by the resort to ease relocation. Despite being centrally located, don Javier seemed unhappy and bored. Once at the center of fishing activity, he now spent most of his day alone. He often visited his nearby children to eat or socialize, but I almost always found him sitting at home under his new *palapa*, which was much smaller and simpler than before, smoking and gazing somewhere into the distance, at the hills or mesquite trees surrounding him. The fish buyer's representative bought fish next door to don Javier's home; fishers were no longer allowed to leave their equipment on the beach and thus quickly hauled their boats to Raul's for a quick sale.[3] Few hung around for very long, but don Javier did not seem to join them even for this quick exchange.

Don Javier said he missed his old home, as he sat smoking in front of his cement block home. He now lived next to two of his six children, one a fish buyer and the other a worker in the hotel that had displaced him. Other children, grandchildren, and great-grandchildren lived nearby, much closer than before, but don Javier said that they never visited. He also asked why I never visited, his sad eyes seemingly without the glint

---

2. Following local usage, *Americano* refers to U.S. citizens who reside in Loreto for any length of time; the usage is similar to "gringo" but without some of the negative connotations.

3. Although most people who fished in the Loreto area were men, a few were women, so I use the more gender-neutral term "fishers" throughout.

of mischief that usually accompanied the old joke about how I could visit more often if I moved to his home permanently.

Over the weeks of this visit to Playa Tranquila in 2012, I would see don Javier only two or three times, aside from brief glimpses of him at his granddaughter-in-law's kitchen eating breakfast or under a tree with an old friend. I ran into him at a few other homes when we were both visiting one of his children or when I stopped by his house. Heavily, he would sigh, as he always did when I came to visit. "Eh, Nicole. Why haven't you come to visit me more often during this trip?" My replies about work had never satisfied him, and we would almost always lapse into companionable silence for a while. Don Javier seemed to feel his age more and more over time, and sometimes he wasn't at home when I visited because he was at the doctor's. On this last trip, he seemed particularly tired and talked about moving permanently to a town a few hours away, where one of his daughters now lived. He often mentioned his health problems as a matter of age, but his life had also changed dramatically when he left the beach. He had to get a ride with someone to visit the family and friends who used to come to visit him in the course of their work or as part of a short trip to the beach.

Occasionally, I could goad him into joking with me as he used to about a party we went to or finding a girlfriend for him in Loreto. But now, even reminiscing about the past seemed to be less enjoyable for him, and he had not offered to talk with me about old fishing canoes or trips for a long time. Unfortunately, the years have brought many changes for don Javier, and I hated driving away from his cinder block house in the desert not knowing when I would return.

Don Javier had made a choice to sell his home on the beach, as had his friend, in exchange for money. Other choices were important for his life as well, including the choices to move to Playa Tranquila, marry and have children, and to fish for his livelihood. But I want to look closely at this word—"choice." It implies an agreement, in this case a transaction, taken rationally and with full ability to choose differently, if one wanted. Don Javier and his neighbors, as poor fishers, seemingly had choices about where to live (and whether to sell their land), where and how to work, and how to care for their families. Like don Javier, they could choose to sell, to fish, to send their kids to school, and could make many other big and small decisions. But the more I understood their experiences, the less these matched with thinking about decisions as originating in the lone, rational individual weighing pluses and minuses as they managed their lives. Did don Javier really have a choice in selling his home? For him, it was an inevitability that he would have to leave his home, given the legal gray area of Mexican beaches.[4] His best option, he figured, was to take the money rather than to be forced out. How do we understand these kinds of choices or decisions? A colleague of mine has written about "choiceless choices" (Mitchell Fuentes 2022), and this describes don Javier's quandary, and he feels constrained, stuck, and trapped with few options, similar to Matilde Córdoba Azcárate's (2020) research on tourism in another part of Mexico.

• • •

Over the course of my research, I heard about similar experiences around livelihoods, plans for the future, and even daily struggles to provide for families. But primarily, fishers in the community felt unsure about how fishing could both support their families and be sustainable, and where it would be in the future. Environmentalists and others in the nearby town of Loreto and from around the world also wondered why the fishers continued to fish despite the negative environmental impacts on the area. When I first arrived in Playa Tranquila, my naive belief, based on what I'd read about fishing and the environment, was that the fishers were unaware of the impact they had on the marine areas where whey worked. But the more I talked with don Javier and the other members of his community, the more I realized that awareness of their impact was not the only barrier to better care of the marine area, and in many cases, the fishers were fully aware of the impact fishing had, telling me about how they now fished for the "trash," the less valuable species of fish, because the others were gone, overfished over time.

Environmentalists also had ideas about fishing and its impact, and some had successfully pressured the Mexican president to declare the local area a marine protected area (MPA), creating the Loreto Bay National Park (Parque Nacional Bahía de Loreto) in 1996, a few years before I arrived (see map 1). As I talked with a variety of environmentalists, tourism business owners, and other residents in the Loreto area, I learned about

---

4. Beaches in Mexico are legally a federal zone and cannot be owned. A new law in 2020 reinforced this idea of public access by expressly giving people access to beaches.

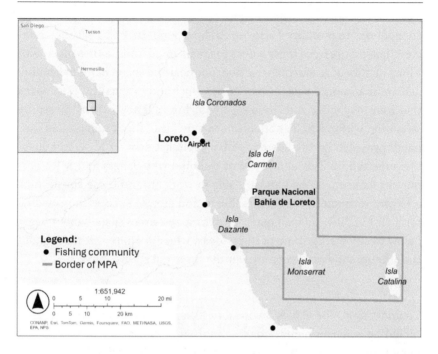

MAP 1 Map of Loreto Bay National Park, created in ArcGIS using Google Earth.

how they understood the issues facing the area and the blame they usually placed on artisanal fishing. As environmentalists once lamented to me, "they choose to overfish," and fishers are "not taking responsibility."

This idea of choice kept coming up in my twenty years of research in Playa Tranquila and the larger Loreto area. Don Javier and others in his community felt a lack of choices but also managed to find ways to fish, support their families, and enjoy their lives. Others, including the MPA staff, also felt constrained in their options. This ethnography is my attempt to capture the complexities of their lives and experiences, and to understand (1) why the fishers continued to fish despite the precarity of fishing, (2) how the MPA and tourism affected local people's livelihoods, and (3) why the environmental management strategies of fishers, MPA employees, and tourism initiatives largely failed to improve the environment.

To answer these questions, I compare the different values of fishers, MPA staff, tourism entrepreneurs, and other residents around the environment, work, and family, including their contradictions and connections to morality. I also look at how people use a variety of strategies that emerge from these values to create opportunities in a place with a long history of resource extraction, political and social marginalization, and an increasing focus on economic values and rationality. This means that I am engaging with theories about how agency is constrained by structure, with particular attention to how ideas about individual rationality provided by the current global capitalist economic system affect this interaction. This allows me to examine why fishers and MPA employees feel constrained and are able to work around these constraints, and why, ultimately, they are unable to find greater success in providing for their families and managing the marine resources sustainably. I begin below by reviewing some of these ideas, which I will revisit throughout the ethnography as I try to answer the three questions above.

• • •

To understand the values involved in fisheries and other resource uses, including environmental conservation and tourism, I have found it helpful to examine how these resources have been valued historically, since patterns of resource use often repeat and also provide the basis for current values, strategies, and conflicts. Chapter 1 looks at community experiences with resources and boom-and-bust cycles of resource use, in which discoveries of resources like pearls and fish led to large-scale efforts to extract them, followed by a period of economic depression in the region once the resources were overharvested or replaced by other discoveries in other places. Tourism appears to be the latest boom-and-bust cycle, given the steep decline in the wake of the 2001 terrorist attacks and the more recent COVID-19 pandemic; although rates of tourism recovered from these events, they revealed that tourism was not always going to be a reliable industry (Fletcher 2020). Values of independence, hard work, family, community, and the environment emerge from cycles of resource use and abandonment, which have also led to strategies for managing these cycles, including social networks and multiple livelihoods (see also Comitas 1964; Cruz-Torres and McElwee 2017). Fishing is also valued in Loreto and elsewhere for its contributions to the social structure, individual and community identities, and food sovereignty (Cisneros-Montemayor and Cisneros-Mata 2018; García 2020). Fishers also value dignity and interspecies relationships more than money in some fisheries (Viatori and Bombiella Medina, 2019; Saavedra Gallo et al. 2021), and also prioritize having a good life in many places (Córdoba Azcárate 2020; Fischer 2014; Calestani 2009).

Understanding the boom-and-bust cycles requires examining another set of values beyond those of the community: the economic values of resources, services, and labor that drive the overexploitation and subsequent crashes. Economic values have largely been taken for granted and viewed as "natural" but have also emerged from a social history; for example, the term "economy" only became widely used around 1950 (Mitchell 2014). Our modern understanding of economics was born from debates around whether economics is ultimately about individuals making rational choices to maximize their outcomes or about the society and institutions that enable societies to meet their needs (Çalışkan and Callon 2009, 2010). The former clearly has sway over economics at the moment; psychological and economic research tends to start with assumptions around individual rationality—involving almost complete awareness of options and their characteristics, weighed by their utility or usefulness to the decision-maker (Hastie 2001, 658). Çalışkan and Callon (2009, 2010) use the term "economization" to refer to the ways that economics and the economy are undertheorized, leaving their models often unable to predict outcomes. Taking economization seriously means we need to examine how economics is so influential in so many domains, including research in psychology, and also how it fails to describe the world as we know it. As a starting point, Skidelsky (2020) argues that economics has a weakness in generalizing from oversimple premises or assumptions, including the focus on individual rationality rather than social relationships, power, agency, morality, and even its own purpose. Despite this, the dominance of economic ideas in fisheries, natural resource management, and other domains leads to a focus on autonomous individual rationality, and it benefits us to ask about the implications of this as well as how scholars might better describe what people actually do when making decisions.

For example, it would be tempting to see don Javier's decision to move in light of these rational action models—that he was aware of all of his options and the value they held for him, that he decided to move because it would provide for his economic needs better. But this does not fit with what he's told me. Unfortunately, viewing don Javier's choice and that of his friends and family to fish only as economically rational can lead to the "naturalization of capitalist employment and monetary exchange as the only legitimate mode of sustenance" (Miller 2019, xii), leaving fishers and others feeling like they are not "full cultural citizens" as providers for their families (Viatori and Bombiella Medina 2019, 152).

Anthropologists and others largely reject models of rational economic behavior because the models don't reflect ethnographic data (Guest 2003; Garro 1998; Quinn 1978) and ignore the complexity and social character of decisions and decision-making processes (Mykhalovskiy 2008; Boholm, Henning, and Krzyworzeka 2013; Chibnik 2011). Psychologists like Herbert Simon (1990) began looking at "bounded" rationality, where choices were made within cognitive limits and with compromises, or "satisficing." This research also highlights how habits or heuristics, how people understand or frame choices, and the choice environment influence choices (Jungermann 2000; Gigerenzer, Todd, and ABC Research Group 1999; Ochs and Jacoby 1997; Hastie 2001; Weber, Blais, and Betz 2002).

From these perspectives, perhaps don Javier accepted moving next to his oldest son as the best acceptable option, without considering all of the other places he could live or how he could contest his seemingly inevitable relocation. We might also see deciding to move as a choice that is constrained both by past decisions to spend time with specific family members as well as a context in which politics and law can make things difficult for an older fisherman. Bringing the social context into don Javier's decision to sell and move allows us to see how his limited income might make him more susceptible to a buyout, how the history of changes in the community might convince him that being on the beach was less desirable, and of course how the available land near his son might be a good location to live. Similarly, community norms about caring for parents and the changes affecting the grandchildren and children who lived near him can also play a role in this kind of decision. However, given what I saw with don Javier and others in the fishing community, and in Loreto more broadly, it seems clear that context plays an even more important role in decision-making, yet few studies consider how individuals make use of their sociocultural environments to make decisions (Hutchins, 1995; Mullainathan and Shafir 2013; Shah et al. 2018; Dash and Gladwin 2007; Jaeger et al. 2013).

These economic assumptions about individual rationality persist, however, as part of a larger set of economic ideas and policies that influence fisheries management and economic development programs, among other domains. Economic policies are currently informed by what some refer to as neoliberal economics, which includes theories, arrangements, or policies in the global capitalist economy; the prefix "neo" marks how capitalism has become more entrenched in social and political institutions than earlier "liberal economics" (Harvey 2005). Ganti (2014) suggests that anthropologists and others portray neoliberalism either as a structural force that affects people or as an ideology of governance that shapes how people think about the world. In this book, I approach it as a form of governance that works through processes like privatization, deregulation, and liberalization of trade but also through ideas about individuals making rational choices and what free markets entail. However, given the importance of these ideas about governance in my case and others and the way that governance often happens without an apparent central actor, I argue that people also perceive neoliberalism as a structural force in itself and that this force becomes an important way to understand their relationships to resources and to each other.

In Mexico specifically, neoliberalism has come about through a long history of those boom-and-bust extractive cycles discussed above, as well as through land reform initiated with the 1910 revolution (Monteforte-Sánchez 2020). The 1982 debt crisis and other events encouraged greater privatization and public spending cuts, spurred changes to the *ejido* communal land ownership system, and led to a focus on Mexico becoming a source for cheap labor in the global economy (López Vergara 2022). Today, these reforms have increased the privatization of land and resources, including through tourism, removing them from public access to the benefit of large international businesses (Talavera 2019). The reforms have also led to a focus on resources like land and labor as commodities that can have economic value in the marketplace, which can lead to conflicts between private interests and citizens, especially when the environment is degraded (Toledo, Garrido, and Barrera-Basols 2013; Durand 2014). Morgan (2023) calls the process "touristification," describing how narratives around land favor investors and allow political power to transform public resources into private commodities. Córdoba Azcárate (2020) calls this "predatory tourism," emphasizing the ways that people become stuck both geographically and in terms of employment, where employment can be difficult to escape but also comfortable. In the state of Baja California Sur (BCS), tourism has been an elite project that removes citizens from what were public spaces (Morgan 2023), disrupting community life, displacing livelihoods, and creating conflicts as it privileges real estate values over use values (Bojorquez 2022). Neoliberalism and neoliberal projects are thus intimately entwined in power relationships; although the market is considered neutral in economic theory, it inevitably reconfigures relationships that can reinforce inequalities (Durand 2014; Apostolopoulou 2020), as described in the expulsion of don Javier and the fishers from the beach in the name of tourism development, as well as in other changes in Playa Tranquila described in chapter 2.

Environmental conservation is not immune to the influence of neoliberal economic ideas, as it usually approaches conservation through strategies that use economic markets, privatization, decentralization, deregulation, and commodification as ways to improve the environment, leading researchers to talk about "neoliberal conservation" (Fletcher 2020; Apostolopoulou 2020). Chapter 4 introduces the MPA that attempts to control commercial fishing through similar neoliberal economic strategies. Garrett Hardin's 1968 model of the common pool resource dilemmas, which has been a major influence on ideas about natural resources, is based on the ideas of self-interest and maximization, similar to the core set of individualistic assumptions underlying neoliberalism (Mansfield 2004). Hardin used the hypothetical example of two herders who share a pasture but who both keep increasing the size of their own herds because of the low immediate cost to themselves of doing so. As Hardin argues, the long-term cost is that the land becomes degraded through overgrazing. For Hardin, the combination of open land ownership (the commons) and individual self-interest prevented either herder from considering the long-term sustainability the land: "As a rational being, each herdsman seeks to maximize his gain. . . . Ruin is the destination toward which all men rush, each pursuing his own best interest in a society that believes in the freedom of the commons" (Hardin 1968, 1244). As long as resources can be "used up" (subtracted) and users cannot be excluded, Hardin argues that resource degradation is inevitable, a "tragedy of the commons," and that government restriction or private ownership are the only remedies. This publication is one of the most cited and taught in environmental fields (Janssen et al. 2019), and many resource management strategies depend on these ideas (Kraak 2011; Cashore and Bernstein 2023), though some argue that the approach may contribute to the behaviors it warns about (Maurstad 2007). The ideas of the tragedy and strategies to prevent it have been incorporated into other domains as well, including public health (Maaravi et al. 2021; Porco et al. 2012).

The tragedy of the commons model of human behavior has led to policies that attempt to restrict this self-interest or greed by changing property regimes. For example, those working from this model often recommend either government or private ownership, or creating management strategies that can overcome the tendency toward self-interest. Many protected areas, including the Loreto Bay National Park (LBNP), were created as an attempt to curb self-interested natural resource use through rules and regulations. In the case of many protected areas, private-public partnership between a government agency and a variety of nongovernmental organizations (NGOs) regulate specific areas, removing them from public and historical uses (Brondo and Brown 2011; Carrier 2001; Mansfield 2007; West, Igoe, and Brockington 2006). In addition, they bring in private capital through grants and funders to protect nature because they see value in conserving it. However, there is substantial evidence that management is often weak (Réyez 2016) and that part of the challenge lies in "predatory capitalist projects . . . obtaining the maximum profit as quickly as possible, even to the detriment of the natural resources themselves" (Talavera Martínez and Massieu Trigo 2021, 20; my translation).

In the decades since Hardin's article debuted, many have challenged his contention that land held in common will inevitably be degraded by showing how local resource management strategies can prevent the overexploitation of resources (Acheson 1988; Dietz, Ostrom, and Stern 2003; Ostrom 1990). Ostrom and others have documented many other similar kinds of management regimes and use these findings to challenge Hardin's assumption of self-interest: "Instead, a basic finding is that humans do not universally maximize short-term self-benefits, and can cooperate to produce shared, long-term benefits" (Vollan and Ostrom 2010, 923). This kind of work has led to new conservation strategies like participatory processes or community-based conservation in which community input is valued as a way to ensure conservation success (Dietz, Ostrom, and

Stern 2003). Ostrom's focus on local-led governance institutions remains an important aspect for conservation efforts, particularly when these are understood as nested within regional and national contexts of governance, economics, and other power-laden relationships (Ostrom 1990). Like Hardin's formulation, Ostrom and others are invoking certain ideas about individual behavior in their work, like incentives (Andersson and Ostrom 2008), but argue that social institutions and informal rules can influence the actions of resource users through social norms and other forms of "softer" influence. And as the tragedy of the commons literature makes clear, many hope that fishers and others might become rational and then change their behaviors "by appealing to economic rationales and altering values and ideologies" (Holmes and Cavanagh 2016, 206).

• • •

One solution to precarity and irrational use of resources has often been economic development, envisioned as bringing opportunities to poorer communities and in some cases to environments as well. In the 1990s, given various critiques of development (Ferguson 1994; Escobar 1995; Mosse 2004; Li 2007), efforts to improve communities were reimagined as "capacity-building," though with a clear focus on self-regulating, responsible, and market-knowledgeable subjects who self-transform with the assistance of capacity-building programs (Phillips and Ilcan 2004; Kacou, Ika, and Munro 2022; West 2016), where capacity is an "emergent combination of individual competencies, collective capabilities, assets and relationships that enables a human system to create value" (Baser and Morgan 2008, 3, in Kacou, Ika, and Munro 2022, 216). In effect, these efforts often take as their starting point "low-producing" groups that are deemed to exhibit "economic backwardness" (Ramachandran 2021), following distinct neoliberal ideas around the economic values of the environment, entrepreneurship, and responsibility (see also West 2016; Li 2007). Loreto-area communities experience capacity-building efforts from the MPA and other organizations; I highlight some of these complexities in chapter 4.

Similar discussions around fisheries conservation are "promoting the ideology that fishers had to demonstrate that they were entrepreneurial and responsible for themselves and the resources they used" (Viatori and Bombiella Medina 2019, 151). Responsibility is connected to ideas and values around work and morality, as well as explanations about why some people do better than others, which Viatori and Bombiella Medina (2019) show in their fascinating analysis of fisheries in Peru. The authors highlight the ways that neoliberal ideas around entrepreneurialism, responsibility, nature, and culture obscure how nature, class, and politics co-produce each other in particular historical moments, with a focus on individual efforts and results. This focus on individual responsibility and rationality can lead to excluding those who are deemed irresponsible (or irrational) and also encourages fishers to blame themselves for any exclusions, despite the fact that they recognize that they often had no other option due to structural constraints. The differences between economic and community values can lead to conflicts, especially when community values find economic values harmful or immoral, such as around labor exploitation or restricting resource access, contrasting a financial economy with a moral economy (Thompson 1971; Scott 1976; Peluso 1992; Edelman 2012; Córdoba Azcárate 2020).

Paige West's research highlights how conservation efforts in Papua New Guinea offered to teach Gimi how to correctly value their environment, ignoring existing value systems and culture: "What conservation-related actors never took fully into account, however, was that Gimi have a set of social relations with their surroundings that far surpass what outsiders think of as 'value.' . . . These social relations are not neutral and economic; they are familial and poetic" (West 2016, 92–93). Gimi themselves see the disjuncture between their ideas about nature and those of conservation efforts, theorizing that through rules and regulations, as well as by disregarding the knowledge and world-building of women, they experience a form of dispossession or loss of access. West (2016, 128–29) is careful to clarify that Gimi are not valuing the environment in the way that people often talk about value, since they reject the idea that one thing is valued more than another, complicating the simplification I have used to talk about values.

It is clear that how we talk about values matters and that even the words we choose to describe things have real effects on people, their experiences, and the policies created about them. West (2006, 2016) has long argued that nature and culture are discourses, or socially created representations of how we think reality is. Particularly for those communities without much power, dominant nonlocal discourses around nature and culture that ignore local ideas can further marginalize local people. When rules and regulations focus only on the economic value of nature or treat it as separate from culture, exclusions and enclosures can seem natural (Viatori and Bombiella Medina 2019). West (2016) uses the term "discursive dispossessions" to talk about how representations or rhetoric about culture and nature are used to exclude people from sovereignty (see also Miller 2019). Separating humans from nature through discourse is one way to justify appropriation and dispossession, as these ideas define appropriate or correct uses of nature by humans (Viatori and Bombiella Medina 2019).

The result of these environmental conservation processes of restriction, responsibility, and exclusion is often described as accumulation by dispossession (Harvey 2012) or accumulation by conservation (Doane 2012) in Loreto and other places. Other authors use terms like "land grabbing" (Brondo 2017) and "enclosure" (Grandia 2012) to describe processes of exclusion that often result from neoliberal conservation efforts (Monteforte-Sánchez 2020), particularly when local communities often lack the resources to contest these exclusions (Durand 2014). Exclusions from protected areas can take the form of displacement and criminalization of behaviors, and not being part of planning processes can exacerbate these due to power differences (Apostolopoulou et al. 2021; Kuymulu 2011; Maestre-Andrés, Calvet-Mir, and Apostolopoulou 2018). Tourism, particularly megaprojects, also uses accumulation by dispossession, leading both to environmental injustice and territorial imbalances (Ortega Santos 2021) as well as to poverty, vulnerability, and inequality (Ángeles Villa and López Vergara 2022).

Neoliberalism provides a useful perspective for understanding fishing, tourism, and environmental changes in terms of different values in play, as well as how configurations of capital investment and extraction continue to lead to dispossessions. Yet to understand how neoliberalism became a dominant set of values, it is also useful to consider the influence of power relations on fishing, tourism, and conservation. I have found political economy a useful lens because of its focus on power influences resource access (Roseberry 1988; Gudeman 2016; Harvey 2005). When the fishers experience constraints related to costs and prices, political marginalization, and global fisheries markets, political economy allows us to connect national, state, and global policies and practices to these outcomes. In addition, political economy allows us to see the MPA efforts in connection with political pressures and a larger context of international conservation, economic ideas, and politics. Relatedly, political ecology allows a more critical look at the broader formations of economics and politics, as well as social relationships and cultural ideas that shape and are shaped by access to natural resources (Peluso 1992; West 2006; Doane 2012). Understanding the MPA restrictions and their impacts on fishing and fishing communities is one way that political ecology adds to political economic analyses, as is examining the discourses around the environment. Feminist political ecology also helps analyze how gender shapes access through culturally appropriate strategies given gendered responsibilities, and the implications of access for gender roles, including ideas about family and strategies for success (García 2021; Cruz-Torres 2023; Peláez González 2015). Some of the women in Playa Tranquila I'll describe later struggle to get the resources they need for some of their livelihood strategies, many of which are connected to fishing. They inevitably must manage expectations tied to their gender, in terms of behavior and family responsibilities, and use a variety of strategies to do this. Understanding how gender structures resource access provides a critical perspective on their work in chapter 3.

Moving beyond individual rational actors to understand choice in Playa Tranquila, I also need a way to connect people and values to contexts and power. The final idea that I find helpful for understanding the lifeworlds of Playa Tranquila and Loreto is that of agency, which historically has been contrasted to the idea of structure; the latter includes the kinds of institutions and formations revealed through analyses using political economy, political ecology, and feminist political ecology. Thinking about agency means asking how people act within formations or contexts that constrain them. Here, I take agency to mean "the human capacity to exert some control over the conditions of one's existence" (Gomberg-Muñoz 2010, 297), though ideas of agency vary somewhat across the social sciences (Ahearn 2001; Comaroff and Comaroff 1997; Dove et al. 2008).

Researchers emphasize that ideas of agency vary cross-culturally and that we cannot assume we know what agency looks like, or how it will be expressed except by reference to specific sociocultural contexts (Ahearn 2001; Keane 1997; Münster and Broz 2015) or relationships of power

(Abu-Lughod 1990; Mahmood 2009). Because of the importance of context for ideas about agency, some theorists argue that agency originates with social interaction and is primarily relational in nature (Bunn and Lamb 2019; Sewell 1992) rather than simply possessed (Barad 2003). Given these characteristics, it is likely that "inequality differentially constrains the scope and effectiveness of agency" (Gomberg-Muñoz 2010, 297; see also Ortner 2006; Sewell 1992). Anthropologists have critiqued economic development programs for recognizing only certain forms of agency and, in some cases, attempting to engender a form of agency recognized as legitimate by the development agencies, irrespective of other forms that might be present (Everett 1997; Green 2000; Seckinelgin 2006). Claims about agency can thus take on moral valences, similar to a moral economy, depending on the values in play (Robbins 2007; Bordonaro 2012; Mattingly 2012; Dove et al. 2008).

Sherri Ortner and others have shown how neoliberalism has influenced ideas about agency in that the "model [of agency] is that of an essentially individualistic, and somewhat aggressive, actor, self-interested, rational, pragmatic, and perhaps with a maximizing orientation as well" (Ortner 1984, 151; see also Asad 2000; Bordonaro and Payne 2012; Gershon 2011; Harvey 2005). Neoliberalism brings specific assumptions and attributes of agency; ideas around freedom, choice, and responsibility are assumptions about the autonomous rational individual without much reference to the surrounding context of culture, institutions, and other structures, let alone social inequalities in access to resources and networks (Chen 2013; Ganti 2014; Pfeilstetter 2021). Particularly when ideas about responsibility, blame, choice, and control are involved, neoliberal ideas around agency can create what appears to be a level playing field, when the inequalities around resources and networks can create very different options for action (Chen 2013).

Yet researchers also find that ideas about agency can also be linked to new subjectivities, or ideas about one's own self, in which individuals change themselves to align with these ideas around choice, responsibility, and rationality through their discourses and practices (Bordonaro and Payne 2012; Türken et al. 2016; Urla 2019). For example, Arun Agrawal (2005), drawing on Foucault's ideas of subjectivity, explains how Indians engaged in environmental efforts will come to new ideas about their best interests, new relationships with the government, and new identities, naming this "environmentality." People in Loreto and elsewhere are engaging with the ideas about neoliberalism and its related values in different ways and using these experiences to understand their own beliefs about agency and their own identities in relationship to the environment, neoliberal expectations, and community values, among other influences.

The ability to define agency for oneself or others can thus be understood as a political act because different ideas about agency can lead to different policies (Dove et al. 2008). In the case of fishers in Peru, "paying attention to how people talk about these slow processes [of being deprived of rights or access] and to what or to whom they attribute responsibility or blame for their progression is a critical aspect of thinking about how dispossession works or is potentially blocked" (Viatori and Bombiella Medina 2019, 183). Unfortunately, much of the literature around environmental change ignores agency and leaves it underanalyzed in thinking about societal responses to change (Brown and Westaway 2011; Apostolopoulou et al. 2021). Seeing how people respond to neoliberal choice, including tactics used to circumvent expectations around maximizing economic benefits as lone individuals, can "help identify both the architectural cracks in neoliberalism and the emerging participatory resistances to it" (Kim 2023, 945; Certeau 2011). In one example, Hirsch's (2020) villagers build relational expectations into neoliberal development schemes as agentive tactics that could yield longer-term benefits for Caylloma villages.

Understanding how ideas of agency intersect with fisheries and other natural resources requires a closer look at how agency, morality, and behavior are contested by different groups, and what the outcomes of the contests mean for management decisions and outcomes. Richardson and colleagues (2024) suggest that one way out of commons dilemmas could be understanding the dynamics between resources, knowledge, meanings, and agency, with a focus on how agency is situated or embedded in particular contexts, which constrain opportunities for action but also allow communities opportunities to shape their futures. Likewise, Bryant and Reeves (2021) propose the idea of sovereign agency as a way to understand how agency and authority connect, or how communal desires are pursued with a goal of control over their own lives.

In considering how don Javier and his friends and family see themselves and their environment through experiences with institutions, conservation, and tourism, I examine how these experiences connect to histories, values, political and economic structures, neoliberal economics, and ideas about agency because these approaches help make sense of don Javier's new home, livelihoods in Playa Tranquila, and the challenges the staff of the MPA encountered.

Methods

Most research on choice takes place in featureless rooms on university campuses, where participants complete tasks set for them by researchers. This methodology seeks to remove personal, historical, cultural, and other contexts as variables. As I have explained, I see these contextual factors as integral to the choices people make. Thus, to understand the role of context in decision-making, I needed to get out of these "pristine" laboratory settings and into the "wild," as Edwin Hutchins (1995) calls it. My methodology follows the cognitive ethnography approaches developed by my mentors Edwin Hutchins (1995) and Michael Cole (1998) for studying cognition in context. I used ethnographic methods to study decision processes, immersing myself in the daily lives of participants by visiting their homes and places of work and supplementing this with interviews over several decades (see table 1). I spent countless hours with don Javier and his family as well as members of other families in Playa Tranquila and Loreto and with the MPA staff. We talked and I would

TABLE 1 Data Collection Timeline

Date	Fieldwork activities, noting any important activities
2001–2003	Resided in Loreto, BCS, with travel to Playa Tranquila and other communities
2008	Visit to Playa Tranquila and Loreto area, interviews with women
2010	Visit to Playa Tranquila and Loreto area
2011	Visit to Playa Tranquila and Loreto area, economic census
2012	Visit to Playa Tranquila and Loreto area
2012–2022	Online connections to community
2023	Visit to Playa Tranquila and Loreto area

often help them with their work; sometimes we just sat and watched the sea together. Every life and individual who participated in this research was unique; yet over time, commonalities and patterns emerged to produce a portrait of a fishing community and the MPA. As a qualitative study, this work describes the contours of the lives of many people gleaned through careful observations of the patterns that emerged from responses to my questions and the choices they had to make on a day-to-day basis. From my experience, other fishing communities in Loreto were slightly different, but again, several issues appeared across them, and these dominate the analysis presented here.

Fieldwork is an intensely personal experience, dependent as it is on relationships, and another researcher would inevitably have different interactions than the ones I had. But over twenty years of experience and comparing Playa Tranquila to other communities around the world reveals that the major arguments here are sound and replicable. In this way, don Javier with his distinctive hat, sitting under a *palapa* he built along a stretch of the coast of the Gulf of California transcends the anecdotal. His experiences and perspectives help support broader arguments about value in fisheries, economics, and environment; even though his voice is but one in a survey of thousands, the brilliance of his denture-white smile shines through the crowd.

I explicitly approached this research as an exercise in grounded theory—I wanted to let the observations and data help me frame the outcomes and develop hypotheses and theories about what was happening in Playa Tranquila. As it turns out, most people have their own theories about their lives, relationships, and events, and these are also useful ways to understand field observations. For me, being an anthropologist meant being open to the many ways to understand the field experience, including those held by its residents. When someone said, "It's all politics," I saw this as an opening to understand what kind of theory they had about their world, including what they meant by politics.

However, after leaving Mexico, I searched for ways to interpret the data I had collected, particularly the ways that the residents of Playa Tranquila and others in Loreto had understood their lives and experiences. I was looking for a theory, or several theories, that would help explain their lives. But decision-making theories alone were not quite as useful in explaining what I had seen or what people had experienced as I had hoped.

Understanding cognition in a cultural context involves studying how choice occurs in real-world activities in addition to an "interview context," which can alter the activity under study. For example, during interviews in Loreto, I collected descriptions of characteristics people thought were important in building social and professional relationships and compared them with what happened in interactions and informal conversations. The interview data were fairly consistent among different groups, including a women's organization, international and local NGOs, the national park, and fishers, among others. They all emphasized trust, reliability, and respect. Yet in practice, these characteristics were almost absent from what I observed. For example, certain interactions seemed to be predicated on *dis*trust—individuals were unsure of what the others were doing and thus were constantly checking up on their activities. Given the frequency of comments about disrespect in different situations, the idea of respect seemed like an unreachable ideal on the one hand and an impediment to good gossip on the other hand. Likewise, under certain circumstances, unreliability could easily be ignored, and a relationship could continue with seemingly no ill effects. So, then, how to account for this gap between people's clearly stated values and what they actually did?

Ultimately, cognitive ethnography has allowed for a more complex understanding of the role of sociocultural context in decision-making. By starting with a larger unit of analysis than a single choice and instead focusing on how individuals engage with the environment around them, this approach leads to a deeper appreciation for the ways that individuals use their cultural beliefs, social relationships, and experiences to find solutions to a variety of problems. In sum, my approach is not to isolate the choices people make from their contextual variables but rather to see those variables as integral to the choices people make.

Plan of the Book

This introductory chapter has highlighted the main themes of the book, and each chapter takes up part of the argument here while grounding them in the experiences of the residents of Playa Tranquila.

The next chapter describes the rhythms of the fishing community in order to examine the community's livelihoods and the values of independence and hard work that fishing provides, as well as how it helps support their families and community relationships. Yet for people in Playa Tranquila, fishing also connects to uncertainties of weather and the widely acknowledged decline in the local fisheries, which is linked to historical boom-and-bust cycles of resource extraction and collapse going back to the seventeenth century. This chapter thus also examines the strategies that those in the fishing communities have employed to mitigate change over time, including migration, investments, developing new skills, and relationships with those from outside of the community.

Chapter 2 examines some of these external relationships in how tourism has changed lives and livelihoods in Loreto and Playa Tranquila over time with its own cycles and rhythms, exploring both the value of tourism and the barriers of entry for certain forms of tourism, which are often tied to class. When the boutique hotel near Playa Tranquila became a resort, the differences between forms of tourism and values were brought into stark relief, including reimagining tourism as an economic activity and community members as economic actors, despite locals' attempts to retain a focus on social relationships that had characterized earlier tourism arrangements. The resulting commoditization goes beyond dispossession of resources and land to interrupt community strategies for adapting to a broad set of changes via social capital and networks.

Chapter 3 takes us into the household-based small businesses that some of the community's women engage in, such as selling tortillas, opening restaurants, providing manicures, and exporting tropical fish to the United States. As fishing and tourism have waxed and waned in economic importance, the women of the community have been building micro-enterprises in their homes to help adapt to the uneven incomes from these industries. These efforts align with some of the values examined in chapter 1, yet also complicate them by introducing how gendered expectations and responsibilities can alter people's access to resources. To develop and maintain these businesses, women in the community have adopted several strategies seen in previous chapters but also take advantage of the invisibility of domestic work, the support of their husbands, and social networks to find ways to earn money. Women's multiple livelihoods in Playa Tranquila are not without controversy or contradictions, but they also reveal how work, agency, and culture can interact to enable activities that reach beyond the usual understandings of alternative and moral economies.

Whereas the first three chapters focus primarily on the experiences and strategies of those living in Playa Tranquila, chapter 4 foregrounds the LBNP, an MPA initially conceived by environmentalists in Loreto as a means to better manage the water and islands near Playa Tranquila and reverse the decline in the local fisheries. In this chapter, I compare the multiple narratives about the creation of the MPA, with attention to how ideas about economic rationality, profit motives, and the tragedy of the commons led to a focus on responsibility, blame, and greed. Even the supposedly participatory process led to exclusions of fishers through the logistics, language, and process. In addition, discussions about blame and greed overshadowed any recognition of the economic and political context in which fishing happens and the values that fishing has for local residents beyond economics. The resulting management plan(s) assumed individual maximization, and the MPA's policies were thus focused on values of exclusion and control, with tools like restrictions, incentives, and fines, in line with a neoliberal outlook on conservation.

In the fifth chapter, I look at how these policies played out in practice after 2001. From 2001 to 2003, communities awaited the publication of the final management plan, but the MPA still had the option to enforce national-level laws. This chapter attempts to answer what fishers and their families always asked me during this period: "What's the MPA doing?" I focus on the MPA staff's efforts around policing use of the MPA, monitoring species levels, educating people about natural resource use, and creating capacity-building programs to create alternatives to fishing. I show that all of these areas of effort illustrate some of the core problems of resource management in their mismatch with the larger context in which they were implemented. I examine why monitoring and education were much more successful than policing, and how capacity-building efforts shifted over time to reflect community interests and concerns as well as MPA priorities. In capacity-building activities, the MPA staff worked with local communities to develop alternatives to fishing but continued to draw on specific ideas about agency and morality that were largely focused on individual actions and motivations rather than the larger context of natural resource management. Looking at policing also brings attention to how the MPA staff understands its own ability to act in the postplanning context, as well as the agency of the fishers and others. The continuing inability to manage the area successfully also reveals the limits of conservation efforts built around economic-focused models. While blame is still put on the "social problem of fishing," or the political unpopularity of prosecuting local fishermen, the apparent impossibility of the coexistence of conservation and fisheries in Loreto has deeper connections to the state's deep neglect for the concerns, needs, and values of fishing communities and political participatory processes that are superficial at best. These management challenges reveal that structure, agency, and neoliberalism are deeply connected in terms of how ideas of economic rationality set the stage for not just dispossessions and prosecutions but also for how motivations, values, and the ability to act are understood in different contexts and even weaponized.

The conclusion to the ethnography revisits the three questions posed at the start of this introduction: (1) why the fishers continued to fish despite the precarity of fishing, (2) how the MPA and tourism affected local people's livelihoods, and (3) why the environmental management strategies of fishers, MPA employees, and tourism initiatives largely failed to change what they wanted to in the area. Drawing on ideas around economic rationality and the consequences of this for tourism and marine management in Playa Tranquila, I also suggest how we might avoid dispossessions, conflicts, and environmental degradation through a more context-sensitive or holistic approach.

CHAPTER 1

RHYTHMS

After I met don Javier on the beach in 2001, he invited me to live with his family in a palm-roofed house facing the bay. Don Javier's grandchildren, Magdalena and Memo, had lived with him since his wife died a few years earlier. Magdalena cooked and cleaned while attending high school, and Memo had all but left high school to fish. Although Magdalena was unique among her peers in her responsibilities to her grandfather and brother, each morning had a specific rhythm that resonated with those of the other homes I visited in the community over the years. These rhythms highlight some of the key aspects of life in the fishing community of Playa Tranquila, including the uncertainties of fishing, the role of relationships with both neighbors and global industries, and the cooperation among households and families. They also introduce some of the central values for most community members, including the importance of family, social relationships, work, education, and the local environment. What follows is a description of community life in Playa Tranquila in 2002, with some notes about important updates throughout.

One of the rhythms in the community was set by the fishing schedules, which started with rising before dawn (and even before roosters began their morning alarms). Fishers grabbed their clothes and equipment while others in the house prepared bottles of water and coffee, and tacos, sandwiches, or other food. The fishers tossed this into a bag, swung up into trucks or the *pangas* (boats) behind them, and bumped along the pitted dirt road through the quiet community to the nearby beach with two or three brothers, cousins, or friends. At the beach, the fishers loaded their *panga* with piles of nets, buoys, bottles of engine oil, and a radio and launched it into often glassy waters, startling gulls and small schools of fish. The fishers headed toward their favorite locations, recognized by how the hills or other landmarks lined up against the horizon or sometimes using GPS or sonar. In some seasons, fishers set nets in the evening and checked them the next day, while in others they preferred to fish with thick nylon line wound around old blocks of wood in place of the higher-priced rods used by those in sportfishing tourism outings. Several communities in the area prided themselves on using only fishing lines because of the lowered risk of bycatch, but Playa Tranquila was not one of them. However, by 2023, fishermen were required to use lines to fish due to new regulations (see chapter 4).

Other fishers fished primarily at night, illegally spearfishing so they could find their fish prey asleep and sluggish but with a greater ability to catch only certain species. Other divers focused on clams or sea cucumbers on the seabed, with or without the required permits. Diving with scuba tanks was rare; most free dived or used a gas-powered compressor. Divers filled their net bags with the catch and brought it to the waiting boat at the surface, relying on years of on-the-job learning to avoid the danger of exhaust from the compressor entering the air line. A few men of the fishing community have died while diving over the past decades, and this rare event was devastating for the family, both emotionally and economically, as well as for the larger community. Widows were cared for by families and neighbors, and many were first in line for community work opportunities, like in local tourism efforts.

When the fishing was better farther out in the gulf, fishers sometimes stayed out for several days and camped on the islands. But usually, the fishers returned to the beach to sell their fish in the afternoon, meeting back up with the owner of the boat and the fish buyer's representative, Juan, waiting for them at the beach. In Juan's refrigerated truck, kilos of yellowtail (amberjack) and sea bass were covered with crushed ice for transport to Loreto (thirty minutes away) or Ciudad Constitución (about two hours away). Accounts were settled in the fish buyer's notebooks; after subtracting for the cost of gas and oil, the fishers received money they would split equally among themselves and the boat's owner and sometimes also got a little ice for their coolers to take home for refrigerating milk, meat, cheese, or fish. The fishermen often lingered to chat for a while and then returned to their homes for a late lunch or early dinner, cleaned or repaired their equipment, and then relaxed with their families and others in front of the evening soap opera.

Over the course of the season, winds or rain could alter this schedule, leaving the fishers on land to mend nets, repair boats or cars, or chat. In winter, harsh winds interrupted fishing more often, sometimes for weeks at a time. Other times, fishing was poor for other reasons, and boats came back with only a few fish to show for a day's work. Scarce fish near the shore pushed the men farther out, and fishers often complained about the decreasing amounts of "high quality" fish over time, which meant they had to catch more "trash" or low-quality (and lower value) fish to earn the same amount of money. Because fishing was usually the main source of income for a family, the swings in work created uncertainty for buying food, fuel, or other needs. Some of this was absorbed by a limited amount of store credit offered to all families; everyone carried a notebook to the stores to record credits and payments.

Fishing seasons brought not only different weather patterns but also different species. The summer-warmed water invited squid to the area some years, depending on the El Niño weather pattern. The nocturnal feeding habits of the squid meant that fishing started at sunset and continued into the early morning, often drawing on the labor of older children and others to hook the squid with fluorescing lures and haul them into the boat without being pinched by the sharp beaks or inked by other defenses. Squid fishing paid much less per kilo than other kinds of fishing, but fishers could fill their boat until the rim was just above the water, ensuring more profit than any other kind of fishing. One family of five used several seasons of squid revenue to build a house, finally moving out of their small camper. I was able to join a squid fishing outing in 2002, enjoying the cool air and seemingly hundreds of *pangas* visible only with lights hung to help bring the squid into the boat; I left soaked with seawater and squid ink, my arms the sorest they've ever been, and without one of my contacts, but I will remember that experience forever, even though the squid haven't come to Baja California Sur since 2007 (Armenta-Cisneros et al. 2021).

Despite these uncertainties, most fishers told me that they loved the independence of fishing. They could set their own schedules, decide where to fish, and once on the water, enjoyed time to sit and chat or just the quiet. The hard work of finding, catching, and hauling the fish in also provided them with a sense of hard work with tangible results. This work intersected with ideas of masculinity such as independence and hard physical labor, adding value for the male fishers, who were the majority. Even during slow fishing times, the work repairing nets, boats, or other equipment was demanding but still allowed for time to sit together and talk, such as at don Javier's home before he moved.

Aside from the uncertainties of weather, storms, and diving dangers, fishers also risked being prosecuted for illegal fishing. If caught using illegal methods like spearfishing, catching endangered species like sea turtle, or fishing without a permit, fishers could be fined, have their boats impounded, and even spend time in prison. Technically, every fisher without a permit was fishing illegally, and many used photocopies of permits to try to evade this issue. With the establishment of the LBNP in 1996, fishing regulation enforcement shifted somewhat, as described in chapter 4, but primarily brought more attention to the issue of permits and use of resources.

Unlike Maine lobstermen or others, fishers in Playa Tranquila did not have territories exclusive to specific groups (Acheson 1988), nor did they have a history of creating social norms or community rules for sharing the fishing resource (Ostrom 1990). The small groups of fishers had favorite locations and managed to avoid each other in the water. In the late 1990s, several groups of fishers organized into cooperatives as a way to interact with the local MPA (chapter 4 focuses on the MPA). However, these cooperatives were widely regarded in the community as a formality only and, with a few exceptions, had little impact on fishing or livelihoods. Fishers largely dismissed the cooperatives as unimportant for them, pointing out that they did not fish for very lucrative species like the lobster and abalone on the other side of the Baja peninsula, where cooperatives played more of a role in management and markets, using dues from members to support these larger roles. Besides, several fishers said, we see on the other side how the cooperative president is corrupt and takes all of the money, and we don't want leaders like that here. Instead, most fished in groups of two or three, plus the boat's owner, usually all related through blood or marriage. Small-scale cooperation was essential

FIGURE 1 Fishers mending nets on a windy day.

for fishing, even if community-wide or regional management strategies were less formal or acknowledged in the community.

High costs for gasoline and low prices for fish compounded the stress of the uncertainties around fishing. Overwhelmingly, fishers reported that fishing was getting more expensive and more difficult over time, as prices for boats and supplies increased, the amount they could earn for each fish decreased, and the relative quantity and quality of fish also declined. With the requirement to fish using lines, fishers in 2023 also complained about the cost of bait. The fish buyers had a monopoly on prices, and unless fishers could transport their catch themselves, which would take several hours each day, they had little choice but to accept the rates offered. In addition, many were already indebted to a fish buyer for equipment or supplies and had to continue to pay off what they owed with a percentage of their catch each day. In terms of the supply of fish, decades of fishing by large industrial boats and migratory fishers from other parts of Mexico had added to the stress on the fisheries (see also Armenta-Cisneros et al. 2021). These external pressures by the economic and political contexts tended to lead to overexploitation. No one was sure what a sustainable fishery would look like, but they knew that what they had was unsustainable. Even younger fishers could rattle off the changes in the fisheries, as higher-quality fish became rarer and lower-quality "trash" fish became more marketable and fishing happened farther away in the gulf.

If one spends any time at all in a fishing community like Playa Tranquila, it is likely that talking about fishing quickly takes on a gloomy tone. Fishers complain about the declining number of fish and prices for them, the increasing costs of equipment and supplies, and the prosecution of illegal fishing by government agencies. Almost every fisherman I knew in Playa Tranquila saw no future in fishing and wanted their children to work in a different industry. Household surveys and economic diaries reinforce what fishers told me about earnings: fishing was barely enough to support the family's need for food, gas, school, and other basics. Those fishers who fished illegally (diving, primarily) were a little better off but not by much. Although not everyone in Playa Tranquila depended on fishing as a primary livelihood, this industry provided the majority of most household incomes, except for those relatively rare families who owned stores, worked in tourism or government, or ranched (each of these came with their own risks, as I discuss below).

Given their gloomy view of fishing, I asked some fishers why they fished. Those whom I knew well explained the inappropriateness of this question through their own anger at what seemed to them to be a catch-22: "What else can we do?" one lamented. "We have no education, no skills except to fish." Lacking postprimary education, most older fishers had few skills beyond basic writing and math and fewer resources to invest in new equipment or materials. Some of the younger fishers did attempt to move into sportfishing or other forms of tourism but struggled to learn English, buy better boats and equipment, and compete with the more established and well-financed Loreto businesses (as described in chapter 2).

Despite the apparent hopelessness of fishing, each year, more young men in the community left school to fish. I watched as each class of students got closer to graduation while many of its young men dropped out. Most departed to contribute to their family's income, transforming school expenses into fishing income, however minimal. But the young men had also grown up in the community, fishing on weekends and vacations, seeing the men in their lives embody a certain kind of masculinity through the physical toil of fishing and enjoy a specific form of male sociality through fishing partners (*compañeros*) who were often brothers or cousins. The male fishers I knew from Playa Tranquila were often reserved and quiet, except in the company of other fishers, creating behavioral norms for their sons with deep social ties to fishing.

Once young men left school, their options narrowed, making an escape from fishing even less likely. A few young men did leave the community for more education or work in medical or law enforcement fields once they completed high school, but most returned within a few years to fish, citing family needs or personal desires. Even more worked for a while in local tourism as security for the new resort or day laborers; within a year, they tended to leave these jobs for fishing, claiming these jobs were low paying, exploitative, or just didn't match the independence of fishing (see chapter 2 for more detail). Most of the young women graduated high school, though many married their now-fishermen boyfriends and started families in the fishing community. By 2023, some young people had gone to college, while others became parents and grandparents, staying in the community to fish.

Fishing wasn't making anyone in the community rich; when fishers came back in with their catch, they paid around a quarter to the boat's owner, a percentage to repay the fish buyer for the oil, gasoline, and fishing permit he had provided, and the rest was divided by the fishers to take home to their wives, who then repaid part of the grocery store credit and school expenses. What was left was used to buy what could not be put on credit, like gasoline, water, and car payments. And some weeks, high winds or storms kept fishers on land without any income at all.

The rhythms of fishing, despite variation over the seasons and changes over time with new technologies, show the strong importance of work, community, family, and environment. Economic values are still crucial, driving fishers to continue fishing in what was perceived by all as a dying industry and encouraging children to fish as a way to supplement household income. But money isn't the only reason that fishing continued as a primary livelihood; values of independence, hard work, community, and family drew fishers back from other industries and encouraged young men to prefer fishing to tourism, ranching, or other occupations, even when these might provide a less economically precarious livelihood (see also Viatori and Bombiella Medina 2019).

The choice to fish or not to fish was not really a choice in Playa Tranquila, at least not the way I had come to understand decision-making. Individuals were not weighing several options, considering the utilities of each, or comparing long-term outcomes. Were there real options outside of fishing? The "choiceless choice" (Krzyworzeka 2013; Mitchell Fuentes 2022) of whether or not to fish includes options about how to fish, with whom to fish, and others. The choices to fish, to fish illegally, or to fish certain species instead seemed to emerge from a context that blended economic need with availability, opportunity, and skills; individual preferences with cultural norms and expectations; and risks of prosecution with the uncertainties of making enough money to eat. The choice to fish was not an actual choice, and decision-making in this context appeared both effortless and directed by the economic, social, and cultural contexts.

Older fishers were resigned to how their lives had led to their fishing and their sons' lives as well. Grandchildren like Magdalena and Memo were encouraged to go to high school in hopes that they would find new careers. But life on the land was not always easier.

Rhythms on Land: Education and Relationships

In the community, the rhythm of the school day joined the uneven patter of fishing, as the children and young adults in the household from five to their early twenties got up and ready for school after the fishers left for the beach.[1] In don Javier's kitchen in 2002, Magdalena prepared a breakfast of handmade flour tortillas and dried beef or fish, called *machaca*, for her grandfather, brother, and the visiting anthropologist, with a side of coffee and beans. After this, Magdalena and Memo dressed carefully, following norms to dress up when leaving the community. Magdalena pulled her hair into a neat and tight ponytail and put on a little makeup while Memo donned his newish tennis shoes and a clean button-down shirt and slicked back his hair jauntily. When the white van pulled up to a nearby house, the two joined about eight other students to ride to a high school (or *prepa*) in Loreto, from where they would return in the afternoon. Previously, the students had attended a *teleprepa* in the community, a form of high school in which lessons are given over televised programs; most students had found the *teleprepa* insufficiently challenging. Magdalena and Memo joined others in school, and like others, their interest in and commitment to education varied. Some students seemed to be in school because it was expected, and many ended up leaving to fish or work elsewhere. Others were able to use high school as a way to get a degree that would help them find work in tourism or earn college admission. Parental expectations varied similarly, though most parents said that they wanted education to be a way out of fishing and possibly the community for their children. By 2010, a few older children were in colleges around the state through the support of a foundation started by two U.S. citizens and administered by a community board. The foundation was also responsible for the high school van, computer classes, and eventually, a dorm for students from more rural areas (though this was open only a few years), and a community library, which was still open in 2023. By 2017, even more children had entered teachers' colleges, technical schools, or other forms of higher education, and in 2023 many continued to plan for college. Although most college students or graduates

---

1. High school was only available for the community starting in the early 2000s, and for this reason the early classes included many students over eighteen who had not been able to attend previously. While I was there from 2001 to 2003, a donated van took students to Loreto for high school; some parents took them in cars earlier than this or continued to do this, especially when the van broke down.

were women from the community, some men were also able to use this educational route to leave fishing.

In households with smaller children, mothers or older siblings helped children into school uniforms, brushed and styled their hair, and prepared breakfast and lunch for them. With their backpacks filled with homework, snacks, and bus money, the uniformed kids ran out to catch the secondhand yellow school bus donated by a sister community in California, which took them to the elementary and middle school in the community. The younger students returned from school for the midday meal in the early afternoon, for which women in the household usually prepared a fish filet, beef stew, or chicken with rice, with more flour tortillas. After changing out of their uniforms, the students worked on their homework or played around the house until they ate a light snack and went to bed.

In addition to the pulses of activity from fishing and school, other activities filled the day. Household chores like laundry, dishes, and cleaning often happened in the quiet mornings, and occasionally a neighbor stopped by to stay for a while or just to wave hello. When the neighborhood store opened midmorning, several women took their youngest children to get groceries for lunch. When their husbands camped on the islands, the women and children often spent much of this time with sisters or mothers instead of at home.

Aside from general housework, some women took their embroidery or other projects on their visits, while others helped mothers or sisters with other kinds of work around the house, like sewing or baking bread. In addition, if a rare quinceañera or even rarer wedding was coming up, family members helped create centerpieces, sew dresses, or coordinate the events. Several women in the community helped each other start and run restaurants, stores, or other businesses, while two groups formed cooperatives to create more externally focused projects like tropical fish exporting or aquaculture projects (chapter 3 has more details on these efforts). A few women also participated in a *cundina*, a local rotating savings and credit association, which met weekly. In these meetings, each participant put MXN$100 into the organization, and one member took home the resulting amount (for a group of ten members, this would be MXN$1,000, for example) for an upcoming expense. Because banking was nonexistent in the community and difficult to access in Loreto while

I was there from 2001 to 2003, the *cundina* was a way for these women to accumulate larger amounts of funds that otherwise might be spent on food, drink, or miscellaneous household expenses (see also Vélez-Ibáñez 2010; Delgado Ramírez 2021; Zambrano et al. 2023). Overall, women often talked about the value they found in keeping busy.

Children too young for kindergarten joined their mothers throughout the day, more or less kept out of the way through the deft corralling and attention by the various women present. Some days, the women called relatives in other parts of Mexico using the cellular phone at the community store; a more reliable cell tower was built in the late 2000s, allowing personal cell phone use. Like the rhythms of fishing, those in the homes and schools depended on values of work, collaboration, and family. Days were filled with tasks and appointments, and community ties provided resources and support.

Similar values were part of other livelihoods in the community. Older men and those who didn't fish also worked around the community, either helping with bread baking or taking care of goats or chickens, depending on their livelihood. A few other people worked for local government, as store owners, in a small boutique hotel near the community, or assisted expatriate U.S. citizens with domestic work or a variety of projects.

Ranching also involved some uncertainties, as this industry also fluctuated over time depending on the availability of water and the cost of feed and often was one of several livelihoods for a family. One of my most memorable days with don Javier was going with him in truck, boat, and on foot to find his lost cow. This cow, like other livestock in the community, was left to wander on its own to ensure it could find enough food in the desert. Inevitably, free-range cows could be stolen, hit by a car, or lost, as this one had been. But after trekking over beaches, hills, and rocks, we found it and brought it back to a closer area. Other community members were also often searching for their cows, goats, or horses, selling them, or trying to find food or water for them. Buying animals was an investment and one that could be lost with drought or sold for cash but involved a different and potentially complementary set of risks to those of fishing.

A few families ran local grocery stores, or *mini-supers*, that provided fresh and packaged food and drink to the community and those driving on the highway. The success of stores depended in some part on the local community economy, because if their clients could not afford groceries, the store's income decreased. In addition, as more families got access to cars, especially after 2010, they could make the short drive into Loreto to buy cheaper groceries, and some would drive several hours to Ciudad Constitución for even better prices. However, stores were still relatively lucrative businesses, and owners, who were primarily women, were among the wealthiest in the community, which meant they often could afford better goods and services, including health care and education; the store on the main highway had electricity at least a decade before anyone else in the community.

A couple of people were employed as teachers or government workers, like the community representatives or the men who drove the community garbage truck or maintained the community water system. Because the government pay was usually a dependable source of income, these were good jobs and supported some of the wealthier families in the community. However, getting and keeping these jobs was difficult in a fluctuating political climate. Mayoral elections often ushered in a new political party every three years, with their own people to reward. In addition, local and federal government pay could be withheld under budgetary crises, and at least twice during my time in Playa Tranquila, government workers went several months without pay.

Nonfishing livelihoods were thus also subject to uncertainties, and fishers often used these uncertainties to justify fishing, which they felt was less uncertain overall. This perception of uncertainty was largely a result of the different timescales of uncertainty—building up tourism, ranching, and stores were long-term investments in equipment, animals, land, buildings, and other elements. Yet these investments could be lost, in the case of animals, become outdated, in the case of tourism equipment like boats, or even the tourist destination itself could fall out of favor, seasonally or more permanently. Stores also depended on community incomes to repay credit. Working in government was likewise uncertain, potentially lasting only one administration. Even though fishing had some shorter-term uncertainties like windy days, the seasonal lulls could be covered by fishing different species like squid or sea cucumbers in the summer, and the longer-term trends in the fisheries were not yet perceived to be insurmountable.

Some weeks brought a government or NGO representative to the community for a meeting, and a doctor visited the town on alternate Wednesdays. In addition, a Catholic priest visited infrequently for baptisms or special saints' days; however, his visits became more regular once a church was built in the community in the mid-2000s. These events required more attention to appearance, prompting post-breakfast bathing, more professional clothing, and additional time on hair and makeup. Likewise, attending a party, horse race, or other event in the community also required more careful preparation, often taking hours to shine shoes and create elaborate hairdos. Parties often provided an excuse for new clothes, which generally were only purchased or sewn for a new school year or Christmas until clothing became cheaper in the 2000s.

Evenings brought stillness to the community. Before most homes received electricity around 2011 when the new hotel ran electrical lines through the community to the hotel, families and friends gathered in the patio of one of several houses with a gas generator to watch telenovelas. For an hour or two, those present chatted a little, supervised children who still had energy, and watched the dramas about other places in Mexico unfold. Generators, government-provided solar panels, or car batteries also powered washing machines, small fans, lights, or other electronics. By 2012, almost every family had electricity, a television, and a subscription to the Sky satellite service; those who watched telenovelas often did so in their own homes. As the evening turned to night, children and some adults ate a light dinner of milk, bread, or other snacks before going to bed. Eventually smartphones, tablets, and computers connected them to the internet, especially once the new hotel set up Wi-Fi the community members could access in 2012. In the hot summers after 2011, those with air-conditioning slept indoors, while those without it opened windows or slept outside, in one case on the roof, sometimes using a small fan powered by a car battery to circulate air, as the families did for decades before electricity.

Over time, interactions shifted—more televisions in the community allowed people to stay home to watch in the evenings, while educational opportunities connected them to more people and other communities. As I'll show in more detail in chapter 3, small-scale business opportunities connected households through provision of goods and services but increasingly connected them to other places. Families expanded in size and over space, as children moved to other houses or communities for jobs or marriage. As in fishing, work remained a central feature of lives on land, as women and other relatives found moral value in cooking, sewing, washing, caring, selling, learning, and building businesses.

Here, as with fishing, options were limited. The choice to shop in the more expensive local store was often made because going to Loreto or Ciudad Constitución was either too much time or too expensive in terms of gas, assuming one had access to a car. Similarly, one could use credit at the local store, which was often an important economic concern. Sending children to elementary school was made easier by the availability of bus transportation and the advantage of getting them out from under foot. Parents also valued the reading and math skills, among others, that students learned at school. Domestic chores were seemingly unavoidable, though the company of family or friends often seemed to lighten this work, and I always enjoyed being around the groups of women who were cooking, cleaning, or sewing together, as they laughed about jokes or discussed the current telenovela or gossip. The ease of habits, social relationships, and the values of keeping busy made the choices to shop, educate, cook, clean, and sew seem emergent rather than made each day anew. Could the women have done something else? A few of them did. But seeing these activities as decisions misses the ways that they are very rarely seen as a choice that is made, in the way that someone might choose to cook chicken or fish for lunch (though this also depends on what is available; beef was often for guests).

Ranching faced some of the same choiceless choices as fishing—animals required water, feed, and care; obtaining these was not always easy. Investments beyond the animals included land, which was not easy to secure, water tanks, feed for when the desert land didn't provide enough food, as well as veterinary care when needed. Markets for goats and other animals were also fickle and far away. Although the ranchers in the community had generations of ranching experience in the area to rely on, they often seemed to struggle against uncertainties, risks, and the lack of choices they had if they wanted to survive.

Overall, while fishing is the primary livelihood in Playa Tranquila, the community engages in multiple livelihoods because the precarity (Tsing 2015) arising from the uncertainties in livelihoods meant that just one livelihood would not support the family's needs at all times (Comitas 1964; Trouillot 1992). Economic precarity is endemic to artisanal fishing worldwide, given disparities in catches (Ramachandran 2021) and a lack of protections, insurance, or economic value given to labor (Viatori and Bombiella Medina 2019; Crespo Guerrero and Nava Martínez 2020).

Fishers attribute this precarity to a variety of causes, including these larger structural constraints, as well as competition from industrial fishing boats (Viatori and Bombiella Medina 2019), high prices for fuel and gear, lack of fair market prices and permits, and nondemocratic processes for regulations, as in other parts of Mexico (Cisneros-Montemayor and Cisneros-Mata 2018; García 2020). In addition, the Mexican state has neglected the fishing sector for decades, leaving them without support available to agriculture or other sectors (Alcalá 2003; García 2020). As in other places around the world, "loss of control over resources and the absence of basic material assets are identified as factors leading to a lower level of aspiration among societies exposed to uncertain economies" (Ramachandran 2021, 124).

In one study, 23 percent of fishers in Loreto said they earn between US$100 and US$200 per month, 51 percent earn between US$250 and US$400, 11 percent earn between US$900 and US$1,500, and only 2 percent earn up to US$2,500 (Armenta-Cisneros et al. 2021). Given this, many fishers in Loreto (39 percent according to Armenta-Cisneros et al. 2021) diversify their activities to increase family incomes, including through ecotourism or sportfishing. Those who do not work in other industries cite a lack of resources or interest to diversify or that they find it easiest to continue fishing (Armenta-Cisneros et al. 2021).

As a result of this diversification, multiple livelihoods appear to be a distinct social entity from single livelihoods, with different structural arrangements, including more social relationships (Comitas 1964). Cruz-Torres and McElwee's (2017, 138) survey of research across Latin America and Asia likewise suggests that livelihood diversification is critical for improving quality of life but can also be a way to "resist and respond to the risks and opportunities imposed by globalization upon their livelihoods, often in innovative and surprising ways, such as in the formation of new institutions, social relationships, and management practices for resources."

Uneven Rhythms

With some variation, the daily rhythms I described above were taken up by each household. Over twenty years, I also saw how these daily patterns shifted with new technologies or opportunities, including electricity and other home improvements, as well as changes in opportunities and employment. Many of these changes came from outside of the community in terms of new economic opportunities or through relationships with new residents. As an example of changes coming with new markets, many of these changes corresponded with shifts in the local tourism market, which brought a period of relative wealth in the 1990s, followed by more difficulties in the late 2000s (see also Ángeles Villa, Gámez Vázquez, and Bórquez Reyes 2017; Juárez Mancilla et al. 2020). However, as Playa Tranquila was about a thirty-minute drive from Loreto, drawing tourists to the area could be a challenge even in good seasons, and local hotels had to provide vans to bring people to the area. But the new hotel in 2012 brought important infrastructure changes to the community, as discussed above and in more detail in chapter 2.

Another example highlights how relationships brought in new resources and infrastructure that complicated local relationships. Resident U.S. expatriates invested in a piped water system for the community in the 1990s, which meant families no longer had to bring their water from the nearby spring or buy it from a truck. However, this system was unpredictable, and parts of the community were often without water. Different uses drained the available water at different rates, and homes at the end of the lines could be left without water for weeks, as happened to don Javier and myself in 2002. System breakdowns and limitations created conflicts among families, and additional maintenance and governance (informal and formal) were not entirely successful in preventing these. The addition of a large hotel at the end of the water line in 2011 also changed the character of these conflicts; while the hotel was supposed to use a saltwater-filtration potable water system, suspicions about the ability of this to provide the necessary amounts of water persisted in the community. And in 2012, conflicts over water reached a new high; every interview I conducted that summer was preceded by complaints about not having water available. Although I was unable to determine the precise cause of water scarcity, complaints about water hoarding, leaky lines, and the increased demand from new community members and the hotel were common. Given that the water system in 2012 included switching between two community water lines on a schedule, confusion over which line got water and when was a constant concern.

Further in the past, other changes in markets or relationships brought new resources, opportunities, dispossessions, and strategies to Playa Tranquila, setting the stage for the rhythms I observed. Past experiences also established the cycles of boom-and-bust that provided a larger context for these rhythms, which were inevitably embedded in resource valuation, exploitation, and depletion.

The pearl and oyster industries were the first to show these boom-and-bust cycles. As early as the 1590s, sailors near the peninsula were reporting pearl discoveries (Gerhard 1956), including rumors of a pearl worth MXN$150,000 that was sent to King Philip II. The possibility of riches drew more people to the peninsula from mainland Mexico, some of whom hired native divers, though local populations were excluded from the profits in the pearl industry and others (Cariño and Monteforte 1999). Although mission priests discouraged pearl diving, seeing it as a "fertile root of all the evils of the world" (Barco 1980, 251), people continued to dive until the industry declined around 1685, likely as a result of overfishing (Gerhard 1956). The discovery of pearls in northern parts of the peninsula in the 1740s reignited the industry until the beds were once again exhausted after two decades (Barco 1980; Gerhard 1956). The oyster shell itself became valuable in the early 1800s, creating new markets, and in the 1870s, compressors allowed divers to reach new oyster beds for pearls, reviving the industry again through the 1920s, when either resource exhaustion or alleged Japanese sabotage ended the industry (Irigoyen 1943).

Other industries experienced similar boom-and-bust cycles, including whaling from 1846 to 1875 and fishing for sharks from 1940 to the 1950s, tuna from 1925 to 1970, and sardines, which have continued as an important industry (Cariño and Alameda 1998). The cycles of these industries, like pearls before them, were tied to external market demand and economic recessions, changing patterns of investment in fisheries, and species declines due to overfishing or natural causes or, in the case of sharks, the industrial production of vitamin A, which used to be harvested from shark livers. Technological changes away from rough-hewn canoes and oars to fiberglass boats and gas motors and from ice coolers to refrigeration led to the growth of the local fishing industry.

Artisanal fisheries in the area peaked in the 1970s and 1980s, and many fishers refer to this period as a "golden age" of fishing. Playa Tranquila, like some of the other fishing communities in the area, began as a seasonal fish camp where fishers from other areas would stay for days or weeks at a time. Starting in the 1990s, the fisheries have been in decline, with decreasing yields and prices (see also Armenta-Cisneros et al. 2021), and fishers have moved on to new species like squid and sea cucumber and new industries like aquaculture, perhaps signaling the start of new cycles of boom and bust.

Several species, like squid and the locally important chocolate clam (*Megapitaria squalida*), have already seen massive declines; squid fishing is no longer an option. Chocolate clams had a high market value and low catch rate in the 2010s (Armenta-Cisneros et al. 2021), as well as important local values around recreation, history, and identity (Pellowe and Leslie 2021). The town holds an annual chocolate clam festival on the *malecón* (beachfront sidewalk), though by 2023, it appeared that the catches were no longer abundant. Fishers reported they had been banned from fishing these clams for six years but saw no sign on them on dives. Rumors suggested the clams for the 2023 festival were brought in from other states. In Mexico in general, García (2020) reports a 92 percent decrease in the species during the 2010s (see also Arizpe and Verdugo Partida 2020).

These cycles were not limited to the sea. On land, salt, silver, and copper mining and agriculture also saw booms of investment and busts due to resource depletion or droughts, low returns, or global competition. In many if not all of these cases, the resulting unemployment after the "bust" led workers to the beaches to fish (Martínez de la Torre 1998a). While all Baja Californians were affected by these economic changes, those who physically labored as pearlers, miners, farmers, or fishers in the employ of an owner or permit holder were often left without economic, social, or cultural capital needed to endure the periods of economic bust. As Jordán (1995, 134) writes about the end of the shark liver industry, "the misery of these people is physically overwhelming. There are few times when they have anything to eat." In particular, closing the marine trade routes led to isolating the communities and "killing them with hunger" (Jordán 1995, 136).

In addition, the economic benefits of boom times often corresponded to environmental degradation, which depleted local resources that could have helped buffer the impacts of periods of economic bust. Fishers showed me piles of oyster shells left from pearling and other uses and told me that shark carcasses litter the bottom of the gulf, killed for their valuable livers (in the early 1900s) or fins (more recently). The number of fish has declined precipitously over the past decades according to almost everyone I interviewed (see also Armenta-Cisneros et al. 2021), while water pollution has increased with the population of residents and tourists (CONANP 2000). Tourism, heralded as a more sustainable industry, also suffered from cycles of investment and disinvestment, most notably in the post-9/11 and COVID-19-era global tourism market declines (see the next chapter for details). None of these changes occurred without the involvement of community members and others, and most were accompanied by controversy and even occasional disasters, entwined as they were with broader changes in economic opportunities, political parties, social programs, medical programs, and land reform.

Throughout each of these boom-and-bust cycles, individuals and companies realized the dangers of overexploitation and attempted to control the resource extraction through government intervention. Padre Kino explained the crash in 1685 as a result of overfishing (Gerhard 1956), and Esteva (1865, 26) proposed regulation in 1865 "because of the fear that one day this branch of the public wealth will become extinct." In the last boom period, contracts for the pearl industry included a requirement for reseeding the oyster beds every two years but were never successful (Cariño and Monteforte 1999). More recent efforts include those of the LBNP, discussed in chapters 4 and 5.

There are at least four elements in common across these boom-and-bust cycles: natural resource demand, innovations, external relationships, and adaptation. The resources and the ability to extract them seem central to understanding these cycles, particularly with something like pearls. Loreto's experiences highlight the importance of global demand, whether through consumption or taste, which can create or revive industries like fishing and tourism as well as salt and copper mining. Each of these industries also relied on innovations to protect or revitalize its use of these resources, like motors or scuba gear. As resources were extracted, industries declined unless new technologies allowed for easier access or expanded areas of extraction. In addition, the degradation of natural resources can lead to an industry's self-destruction, as the resource on which the industry is based disappears, such as with pearls, squid, and chocolate clams. Overall, however, these experiences highlight the importance of the broader political, economic, and social contexts for these cycles, particularly the roles of external relationships and inequalities.

External relationships have influenced Loreto industries through the external control of local resources, often through monopolies. In addition, the nonlocal or even global demand for certain commodities or goods can be an important driver for local industries like fisheries and tourism. Seafood caught in Loreto is still shipped to other parts of Mexico or the world. For example, the summer squid fishery was run by a Korean company, and a Japanese group revived the sea cucumber fishery, to the confusion of fishers who wondered who would eat the furry sea creature. Mexico has a long history of giving concessions to foreign companies who pay for permits and provide local employment, as it did for the pearl industry. The history of neoliberalism in Mexico is visible here in the concessions for local resources, especially to foreign companies, who extract them as commodities and often use the labor of local residents in the same way. Industrial fishing and fishers from other states were the most visible of these external resource users for the fishers in Playa Tranquila, as local resources were taken in a form of dispossession that mirrored the previous boom-and-bust cycles.

As suggested above, these boom-and-bust cycles often left local populations with few resources. Although community members contended with downturns through several strategies, there was always a threat of real poverty and hunger when money became scarce. Fortunately, households could rely on fish, but other resources could be difficult to get in the desert. Doña Carmen, one of the oldest people in Playa Tranquila, described the difficulties of living in the community in the 1940s, when few goods arrived from Loreto and her family subsisted on goats they raised, wild deer, dates, dragon fruit, and seafood. She lamented that the rains were more predictable then, but in the 2000s, piped water allowed for papaya, fig, lime, and other fruit trees or garden produce, in addition to the occasionally picked dragon fruit. For those who could not fish or garden, this meant having to rely on others. I often heard about an elderly man in the community, who had died before I arrived, who ate a porridge of grass because he could not fish or afford food, as an example of the potential for deep poverty in the community. When his neighbors learned of this during a visit, they began cooking for him, helping him get to appointments, and providing for his other needs. Like the end of the shark liver industry, most of these livelihoods included the risk of "misery [that] is physically overwhelming" (Jordán 1995, 134).

Yet the end of each industry also reveals adaptation—moving to or adding fisheries or other livelihoods, migrating, changing which species are fished, learning new skills or investing, finding new opportunities, and relying on relationships. Work, community, family, and environment are important themes underlying these adaptations. For example, managing uncertainties in water, livelihood, and other resources required a flexibility that meshed with the independence and work ethic described before. Responses to uncertainties and change draw on strategies that are often familiar from or similar to previous efforts. What was once occasional fishing becomes more reliable than agriculture or ranching and so becomes a new livelihood or one of several livelihoods, as men join their cousins on the water to earn more. The ability to shift to new species or techniques also adds flexibility, and social relationships and new technologies assist with this. Other strategies have also been important buffers against livelihood change or uncertainties. But rather than see them as choices or decisions at one point in time, they appear more like old habits that emerge to cover needs that emerge from socionatural changes.[2]

Strategies

Completing a community census in 2010 was challenging because the community was growing fast. New residents had cleared new spaces in the desert for their homes, and children of community members were starting their own households. Some of the workers from the hotel had elected to stay in Playa Tranquila once their contracts ended; while some stayed on to work at the hotel, others started fishing, building relationships with their new neighbors to help them fish. They joined a

---

2. I use the term "socionatural" here to recognize that many "natural" changes are due to human activities and that the social and the natural are cocreated (Swyngedouw 2004; Peluso 2012).

community of people who had migrated to the area after jobs in the mines or building the highway ended or when agriculture or fishing in other areas yielded too little for their families. Periods of lower employment have led to migration—primarily into fishing, but there is also some movement into towns and even a few people use social networks to find work in the United States.[3] Playa Tranquila was born and grew from migration toward what people thought was a better life. While weather, winds, and decreasing yields can make fishing unpredictable, those who moved to Playa Tranquila from the ranches and agriculture believed that fishing was easier and less risky.

For example, Alfonso, like many others, moved to Playa Tranquila from "the valley," where agriculture takes advantage of the more arable land of the peninsula to grow wheat, corn, and beans. He talked about that life with a bit of sadness, mentioning the difficulties when things change every year, good year following bad. After four years in the fishing community, he finds fishing much easier: "There is work (money) all year here, and one can work only three days a week if one wants." He said he did not miss the seasonality of farming, which could leave someone without income for up to seven months at a time. The unpredictability of farming was also troubling, especially when crop losses and high expenses made a bad year disastrous, or dishonest buyers never paid for produce they received. Alfonso shrugged as he admitted that many farmers have started to sell their water, since the costs of production were so high as to make it more profitable to sell water than use it. "It's not a lot of money, but a little can make a difference."

Migration is only one strategy that residents have used to handle changes in industries. However, it has become increasingly difficult to find new places to live, and residents who have finally gained legal title may be less likely to move (though they may sell part of their land to someone else, which is an infrequent strategy). Other strategies have become important in the community, including investing in assets like construction or cars during boom times, gaining new skills, and probably

---

3. Migration from Baja California Sur to the United States is relatively low, and research focuses on in-migration from other parts of Mexico or Central America (Ganster et al. 2007; Ganster et al. 2020).

most important, developing relationships with people from other places. In many ways, these strategies provide more than quick income or opportunities in the face of industry downturns. Although these crashes have been devastating, they have also led to creativity and resilience, and the emergence of new ventures and values drawn from community beliefs, experiences, and relationships.

Investing in Playa Tranquila is not about bank accounts or even well-hidden money, though some residents use these at different times. Around 2003, many households started building or rebuilding and buying appliances, cars, or other goods using money from their work at the boutique hotel and other sources. I watched old wooden homes tumble down, to be replaced by new government-funded concrete block housing. Some people missed the air circulating through the palm frond roofs, but most enjoyed not having to replace the fronds and didn't miss their resident scorpions. Some residents used money from their hotel work to add rooms to their homes or to paint or add other decor. Others bought newer-model used cars, gas-powered generators, washing machines, televisions, or other electronics. Once the boutique hotel closed, I watched as these items aged, in need of repair or replacement. The relative boom time of the small hotel had helped create opportunities for investing in household goods. Some community members were able to use washing machines or other new items to create home businesses, like washing clothes, making tortillas, or others (see chapter 3).

A similar boom in consumer buying occurred when electricity entered the community, a by-product of the resort construction. In this period, people had started working for the hotel and also were able to take advantage of payment schedules, like before, so that they could acquire refrigerators, air-conditioners, and other appliances. The strategy of spending earnings on homes, cars, and appliances ensured that households had necessary working basics and that they could replace degraded goods. These strategies help protect against periods of lower income when debts are accumulated (such as at the local grocery store or more recently in credit for appliance purchases), cars grow older or are sold, and paint on homes slowly fades under the desert sun. Credit at local community stores, with the government or permit holders, or with the new appliance businesses allowed community members to invest at lower initial costs and to pay over time. Although these payments could be challenging during periods of low pay or unemployment, residents had a history of paying credit back slowly and when possible.

Another important strategy has been to enter new industries by learning new skills, such as those migrating from agriculture or developing tourism businesses. Other residents applied skills like diving to new industries like aquaculture or building microenterprises like bakeries and tropical fish exporting, discussed in chapter 3. While starting tourism businesses was a challenge for the reasons discussed above, many in the community worked to gain skills through courses in English, computers, cooking, or hospitality as ways to enter the tourism workforce. Some women in the community took handicraft or sewing courses to likewise develop new sources of income, and the 2020s also brought workshops around small business management.

Similarly, residents adapted to difficult periods by diversifying their livelihoods, as did many in the community through stores, restaurants, and selling crafts, often building on new purchases made with money from tourism or other boons (see chapter 3). The ability to earn income through a variety of sources buffered the uncertainties of most industries. While tourism and fishing were both slow in the heat of the summer, many families worked in the squid or scallop fisheries, sewed school uniforms for community members' children, or worked on handicrafts. Beyond fishing, some residents also raised goats or cows, though as I noted above, the latter could disappear as they roamed freely in search of scrub or in unfortunate run-ins with neighbors or cars. Some wealthier residents cared for horses that they would race for prize money or other winnings. Tourism was another source of income, either through occasional fish cleaning services for resident U.S. citizens or fishing outings, or as part-time work, supplemented by fishing.

However, by far the most popular and potentially most effective strategy was to develop relationships with individuals or groups external to the community like government officials, tourism business owners, or even tourists. These relationships could help with migration, new skills, and even new opportunities, facilitating the strategies above. Residents of Playa Tranquila were not just responding to these relationships; they were focused on building relationships and possibilities with those in many places. These relationships, I argue in chapter 3, are a central strategy for "getting ahead" or even "getting by." In tourism, we see some of the same dynamics, described in the next chapter. Looking at these in the context of the tourism industry, we can see more nuanced ways that these relationships are so crucial but also have limitations as a strategy, given the current state of tourism in Loreto.

Conclusions

The rhythms of Playa Tranquila follow from the uncertainties of fishing and other industries, the importance placed on education, and the value of social relationships both within and external to the community. Social relationships across and beyond the community help buffer these irregularities with fishing partnerships, store credit, savings, and additional work. These strategies have developed over decades and provide some protection against the unevenness of livelihoods.

A model of individual choice in livelihood ignores the variety of connections the local fishing economy has with other parts of Baja California Sur and the rest of the world. As part of a global demand for resources, foreign companies or organizations have a long history of claiming land or other resources for production (like the salt mines at San Ignacio), dispossessing local residents of local resources. What this means is that local control and management of resources has been eroded by global economic processes that reward large-scale investments with increased control over areas like Loreto, simultaneously making it economically and politically difficult for locally owned and smaller-scale businesses to survive. The consumption of these goods through global markets also connects Loreto to other places, though these connections can be powerful drivers of local inequalities, as with tourism and other industries, as well as tenuous links that can dissolve with market fluctuations, as with pearls, shark livers, and other goods.

The rhythms also reveal strategies that people in Playa Tranquila used to *salir adelante* (get ahead or make ends meet), which were tied up in the values they shared and the relationships they had with other people, places, and organizations. The daily life of the fishing communities over time shows how precarity born of uncertainty and "making do" is not a new experience but one that many communities have experienced periodically or even continually. Similarly, understanding how don Javier and others work within this precarity shows how other values become critical resources and motivations, creating greater security for some time at least.

While there are important economic aspects of fishing and other employment, there are many other values involved as well, including the importance of family, work, and collaboration, ideas about independence and masculinity, and other cultural and social expectations, which connect these strategies to the community. For example, we see here the importance of work as a moral imperative for most in the community—beyond income, it provides not only a sense of belonging but also independence and moral uprightness. Examining fishing and household occupations in this chapter has supported other research that suggests that social norms and culture matter for understanding fishing and resource use more generally, though the experiences in Playa Tranquila also suggest that we should think about community, family, and collaboration more carefully beyond just the social norms and expectations to understand how decisions emerge from group interactions, and from a larger historical, political, and social context rather than just from individual minds. In addition, we start to see the ways that community members understand their relationships to global markets and local economies (see also Li 2007; Hodgson 2001). As consumers and producers of commodities tied to marine resources, residents negotiate relationships with other people and places to create value and meanings for themselves (see also Appadurai 1986; Miller 1994; Bestor 2004), as changes brought new ideas and values about livelihoods, economics, and the environment to the community, as the next chapters explore in more detail.

CHAPTER 2

TOURISM ENCOUNTERS

Tourists who happen upon Playa Tranquila or similar fishing communities in Baja California Sur usually don't go looking for them. Like me, many get lost looking for the sea and stop to ask for directions. We end up finding conversations and, potentially, friendships. Even for those with limited Spanish, gestures and a few hesitant words get you fairly far, particularly with residents who know a bit of English. Other tourists may moor off the shoreline in the clear topaz water, and come onto land for a chance to put their toes in the sand or to hunt for increasingly rare seashells. They might eventually run into local residents on the beach, too. Some even hear about the beaches from friends or find them on the internet while looking for an out-of-the-way hotel or campsite. Most times, these encounters happen in the fall or spring, when neither the frigid winds of winter nor the intense summer heat are an issue.

Most visitors want to stay longer than they had planned and either bring back more supplies from town or ask for directions to the local mini-super convenience and grocery store, where they're likely to meet more people. Non-Spanish-speaking visitors will often test out their limited Spanish or, less likely, learn Spanish idioms and accents from other parts of the world. In any case, tourists quickly learn to say, *"cerveza,"* *"compa"* (short for *compadre*, loosely used between male friends in BCS), "*pinche*" (lousy), or "*picop*" (pickup truck), particularly when their visits lengthen, stretching from days, to weeks, to sometimes months, and in a few cases, into years or decades. Some visitors will receive embroidered tortilla wraps, shell jewelry, or other gifts from residents when they regretfully leave the beaches. Many tourists will say that they yearn for another visit, but the reality is that lack of time or money may mean they won't be back often, if ever.

On the other hand, some tourists avoid entanglements with locals, coming only to be blissfully isolated on the beach except for supply runs. During *Semana Santa* (Holy Week), the beaches are often packed, as inland Mexican residents flock to their favorite seaside spots. More recently, resorts have opened near some communities, drawing people through all-inclusive plans and elaborate websites. These visitors don't usually make it into the communities themselves, letting their taxis or vans take them past homes they may not even see, in air-conditioned comfort. Sometimes campers form new tiny tourist beach communities that last from a few days to years. Those tourists who reside in the area for months or years at a time can fill their days with activities with other tourists including fishing, art classes, cookouts, and social visits, and so interactions with local residents might be limited to store clerks, restaurant staff, weekly house cleaners, and the occasional handyman.

And what do local residents think of these visitors? How do they understand tourism and its possibilities? One of the things I heard repeatedly from environmentalists and others who opined that fishers should and "could do something else" is that tourism is a promising alternative to fishing. The fishers and their families also had an interest in working in tourism, so why wasn't everyone joining this industry? This chapter attempts to answer these questions. First, it helps to understand what forms tourism has already taken in Playa Tranquila and Loreto and how that connects to tourism around the world.

Tourism has become an important field of study, often focusing on impacts on residents and environments. Relatively recent reviews in sociology and anthropology highlight shifts in how tourism is approached (Cohen and Cohen 2019; Kaaristo 2018), revealing a focus on tourism encounters and tourist experiences in the former and on impacts of tourism on tourists and locals in the latter. An earlier review argued that scholars should focus on the interactions of tourists and locals beyond ideas of empowered tourists and disempowered locals (Stronza 2001), echoed in Kaaristo's (2018) review, who also notes a tendency toward interpretive rather than economic and political theoretical paradigms. Stronza (2001) encourages greater attention to local perspectives like Jamaica Kincaid's (1988) and a focus on why local people choose involvement in tourism to give more depth to research on economic changes including wage labor and wealth stratification, and social and cultural changes around identity and commodification. Córdoba Azcárate (2020), in examining how tourism creates and destroys in the Yucatán, also deepens social science engagements with tourism through an analysis of how neoliberalism re-creates spaces, labor, and morality through government efforts that include urban planning (see also West 2016; Fletcher 2020). This chapter responds to Stronza's challenge to focus on local perspectives but with some insights into tourist perspectives that suggest why tourism isn't an easy or obvious livelihood in Playa Tranquila. I start by examining some of the different forms tourism takes in Loreto, following Kaaristo's (2018) recognition that the lines are often blurry between tourism, migration, and owning second homes, as well as between niche, lifestyle, alternative, and "eco" forms of tourism.

A Few Hours or Days in Loreto

The cruise ship floating in the Gulf of California loomed large when one saw it at the end of Loreto's Calle Salvatierra, out of perspective with the rest of the town. Up close, the ship took on normal dimensions, shrinking without the frame of the city, like a full moon breaching the horizon. In front of the marina, the trash still lined the *malecón* from Mother's Day, but a truck with its masked garbagemen was making the rounds and would get it all soon. At the marina, double lines of taxis waited for the cruise ship passengers; their drivers chatting uncomfortably in the humid summer air. The golf and tennis club representative waited in the shade, hoping to lure people to the resort in nearby Nopoló, while four horses waited for riders on the other side of a restaurant. The English students would arrive later, with maps and information, wearing their language school's emblem on a T-shirt. The man with his loud English and constant offers of tours and information would also be around in a few minutes. The police were out early, posted on corners and along the "tourist route." At least they lacked the intimidating machine guns that security officers often carried in the local banks.

Along the street that connects the marina to the central plaza, people were setting up their wares on tables, like wooden figures, plates, or jewelry. I got a "good morning" and a few anxious glances as people hurried to be ready. In front of the El Indio restaurant, tables were set up and a pony was available for photos for one U.S. dollar, complete with a comically large sombrero for the intrepid tourist to wear. In the plaza itself, a small display of paintings covered a few freestanding walls. The central plaza acts as the tourist hub of the town, and picturesque cobblestone streets radiate outward from the town hall. Several hotels, restaurants, and curio shops surround this main area, which also includes the homes of several older Loretano families; I lived in one of them for a while, getting a bird's-eye view of the central tourist spot in town.

· · ·

The tourists arrived slowly to the central plaza, in fours or fives, though some were being led by guides giving historical tours of the city. A few had escaped to the islands on boats or to other locations in buses or taxis, but the majority wandered into town at about 9:00 a.m. for three hours of shopping and entertainment. The usual quiet of the plaza was interrupted by the youngest group of costumed and bedazzled schoolchildren, who twirled and shimmied to music on the platform in front of town hall as the tourists arrived (see figure 2). A trio of local folkloric musicians played during breaks between the dancing acts, waiting for the next group of children to move to the stage. People seemed inclined to wander away to the shops and restaurants when the older students performed folkloric dances. To one side, a beer stand with tables drew a crowd later in the day, especially during the dancing. An improvised horse-drawn buggy, simply a flatbed cart with roof and chairs, circulated with or without passengers. Some visitors took the time for a quick visit to the mission church and museum to learn about the over three hundred years of Loreto history. Wandering in town, these tourists, like others, looked for deals on T-shirts, pottery, or blankets (and perhaps ignored

FIGURE 2 Tourists photographing a cultural dance in the central plaza of Loreto in the early 2000s.

that they were produced in mainland Mexico or even farther away). They will usually note that their peso buys them less here than in other parts of Mexico, on a peninsula far from where most food and goods are produced, and if they discuss this with locals, they will learn that residents often bring things from the United States, where they can buy staples, clothes, and electronics much cheaper.

The show in front of the town hall was over by 1:00 p.m. or 2:00 p.m., and the tourists lugged their bags of souvenirs back to the ship with them. I talked to a few of the tourists as they wandered through the area, and most said they enjoyed Loreto and would like to come back to visit when they had more time. As several local people told me, these cruises gave a taste of different places, and each place, like Loreto, put an effort into showing them what they could experience if they were to come back another time for a longer stay. Those who organized exhibits or sold handicrafts found these days exhausting; fortunately, they were relatively rare at the time, but by 2023, almost twenty thousand cruise passengers arrived in Loreto each year (Gobierno del Estado de Baja California Sur 2024).

Sportfishing and Other Attractions

Most tourists, short and long term, come to the area because of the fishing, hoping to spend days on a boat with their fishing lines dangling in the water, waiting for a telltale pull on the line. In BCS, sportfishing generates a large part of tourism to the area, bringing people to tourism providers, hotels, restaurants, and shops selling fishing equipment, particularly in Loreto, which ranks among the four main destinations in the state for sportfishing (Hernández 2023). There are tournaments and sportfishing companies that cater to those who want to take a boat out with a fishing rod and beer and catch jurel, yellowtail, dorado, or other fish (Hernández 2023). Returning to the dock, the visitors proudly heft their coolers filled with fresh fish over the railing and onto their trucks to haul back to their homes or hotels.

May is the start of sportfishing in the area, and the early summer includes tournaments, fishing trips, and other ways to get visitors out on the water. These bring people into the Loreto area to compete over the

FIGURE 3 **Dorado sportfishing tournament in 2012.**

size of fish they can catch, especially in the popular dorado tournament, and the city of Loreto is transformed by the sudden influx of sportfishers and their families, particularly in July (SECTUR 2024a, 2024b). After their days on a boat, most sportfishers head to the international airport with coolers packed with frozen fish for the trip back home.

Other tourists come for swimming, snorkeling, diving, kayaking, golfing, or just relaxing. March is another important tourism month (SECTUR 2024a, 2024b), when a few come to whale watch, avoiding the larger crowds in the more developed industry on the west side of the Baja peninsula. A few other attractions, including the chocolate clam festival and some off-road races, also draw people. But most tourists and locals will agree that the view of the bay and the islands from the waterfront *malecón* is beautiful and worth the trip. Tourism brings many people to take in this view, and residents, even if they may grumble about the traffic and trash that more people bring, usually understand why thousands of people want to come visit their town.

From Dirt Roads to Cruise Ships

Loreto-area tourism developed in an area that lacked paved highway access until 1972. Early visitors from the United States or other parts of Mexico arrived via a meandering dirt track through mountainous desert by car or horse, by boat, or in private planes on an unpaved airstrip. Older residents told me that they themselves worked to complete the highway or came to fish as tourists. By the 1950s, the area was known internationally for its sportfishing, and the first hotel opened in 1959 (O'Neil and O'Neil 2001). By the time I arrived in 2001, tourism was still relatively young, especially compared with fishing and ranching, but had accelerated in the 1970s with government investment in a golf course and resort in nearby Nopoló, which officials hoped would draw tourists like Cabo San Lucas and Cancún (O'Neil and O'Neil 2001), and a deep-water marina in Puerto Escondido. By 1990, 22 percent of the workers in the state of BCS were employed in tourism, and the industry drew substantial immigrants from many other states in Mexico (Martínez de la Torre 1998b). In the late 1990s, the number of hotels in Loreto tripled (FONATUR 2003), and the number of tourism businesses increased to 120, including 105 registered sportfishing businesses together employing more than 225 people (CONANP 2000). Some sportfishing businesses reported serving more than five hundred clients per day before I arrived in 2001.

Tourism is a major industry in BCS, generating between 40 percent and 80 percent of the state's gross domestic product (Ángeles Villa, Gámez Vázquez, and Ivanova 2009; Ivanova et al. 2017). The number of passengers arriving on flights has grown from around 28,500 in 2000 (Gobierno del Estado de Baja California Sur 2005) to 32,000 in 2016 to almost 80,000 per year in 2023, after a dip in 2020 (SECTUR 2024b). Currently, Loreto has 37 hotels with a total of 1,170 rooms (usually 56 percent full). In 1998, Loreto hotels hosted 59,856 visitors, rising to about 64,500 in 2003 (Gobierno del Estado de Baja California Sur 2005); 185,711 people visited Loreto in 2023, slightly more than half of them Mexican residents (Gobierno del Estado de Baja California Sur 2024). Around five hundred people worked in hotels and restaurants in 2000 (Gobierno del Estado de Baja California Sur 2005); in addition, many Loretanos drove taxis, cleaned rooms, cooked food, or worked in shops that catered to short-term tourists, adding to the economic importance.

Tourism in Playa Tranquila

Guero had his own tourism business in Playa Tranquila in 2002, marked by a painted wooden sign in front of his house advertising fishing and boat tours. But Guero was a little down on tourism, telling me, "It's more a thing for Loreto, since it's so inconsistent, being only a few months a year." Guero was proud of taking a few groups to fish or boat each week during the high period but also says, "Tourism doesn't have a future here in Playa Tranquila. Too many Americans bring their own boats, so they don't need mine. Only a few out of a hundred want to go out [with me], so it's more fight than it's worth." Guero clearly enjoyed taking people out, listing for me some of the different vegetation tourists could find on the different islands, bragging about his low prices compared to elsewhere (around US$20 for five hours, rather than over US$100 elsewhere). He smiled about tourists who add a tip on top of his price. I wondered if he thought I was a potential client, though he still smiled as I walked away without booking a trip. I quickly lost sight of his sign as I drove to the highway and was glad he saw as many tourists as he did, tucked into the community.

Those who stay longer in these fishing communities will inevitably build relationships as they construct homes or the structures intended to protect their campers from the sun, wind, and rain. Some stays will become residencies, and U.S. or Canadian citizens sometimes apply for Mexican citizenship, returning to their homelands only for medical care or family visits. Those from other parts of Mexico also find new places to call home. These transplants find work in tourism or fisheries-related occupations, telework, or simply retire to fish or relax.

• • •

One day, I was sitting with a young fisherman's wife, Blanca, catching the breeze outside of her cement block house while her kids played nearby. "Do you know Shelley and Ken?" she asked me as part of some questions about my life back home. When I said no, she explained, "Shelley and Ken come down here to visit. They're retired, but we haven't seen them in a few years. I hope they're doing OK." When they had visited, Shelley and Ken parked their camper at the nearby beach and invited Blanca's family down to swim and eat dinner. Blanca also pointed out her grill, propane-powered refrigerator, television, and curtains as gifts from Shelley and Ken. Blanca and her kids laughed as they told me about the phrases they learned from Shelley and Ken and asked me how to translate "See you later, alligator; after a while, crocodile" into Spanish since they didn't know exactly what it meant.

The relationship with Shelley and Ken was important for Blanca's family despite the language differences. This was true for many others in the community as well as in other fishing communities. Occasionally, I met some of these long-term American friends at quinceañeras or other times, when the families I knew got very excited, cleaned their homes, and put on their best clothing. There is an ease to these relationships, from what I saw, despite the preparations—the tourists would visit, have dinner, share jokes and beers. Talking with some of the tourists, it became clear that even short visits were meaningful, and memories of them often bring them back for another visit. Some of the visitors also emphasized the value of the relationship for the locals, who benefited through goods and money, while also expressing their own benefits from having friends.

As with some of the American tourists who visit BCS, these friends chose to bypass the hotels and restaurants to camp on the beach and make friends with the locals. For some, visits are often at the same time each year, though schedules can shift unexpectedly. Before there was internet and reliable phone service in the community, notice of an upcoming visit could be minimal or nonexistent, and dear friends might just appear one day to hang out for a week. For special events, like quinceañeras or weddings, advance planning allowed for well-timed visits and gifts like dresses from the United States for those visitors named as *padrinos* (godparents).

When these visitors depart after a few weeks or months, they can leave chairs, curtains, grills, computers, refrigerators, generators, or even cars or campers behind as gifts for families they meet. I heard endless stories of the generosity of these absent friends, who might come down again this year. Talking with some of the visitors to Playa Tranquila, they focus on companionship and friendship and view their gifts and contributions as part of these relationships. Many visitors said that they were leaving behind things that they no longer needed or that they didn't want to take back. Others explicitly mentioned a need of the family receiving the items, and their desire to help address this need. Local residents reciprocated with handicrafts, sewing projects, fishing trips, or just good food and company. Residents talk about gifts and employment as evidence of friendship, not as its necessary outcome. The value of tourism for local residents is not primarily economic, in my experience, but in building these friendships.

I usually heard about these relationships when someone pointed out a gift or asked if I knew a friend of theirs, or when something I did or said reminded them of these friends. But over time, some of these friends have stopped coming as often, marking these reminiscences with a longing or melancholy of absence. By the 2000s, many of the tourists-come-friends were traveling less due to health or age, and there seemed to be fewer campers on the beach for new relationships. My own experiences in the community were no doubt colored by these American friendships, and I learned to bring gifts back from the United States but, more important, to return when I could just to enjoy friendship.

Tourists provided other important resources for the community. College educations for youth in the community were funded in part through an educational fund that provided around US$100 per month. While a local committee of both Mexican and non-Mexican community members administered the fund, much of the money came from U.S. or Canadian donations.

Resident tourists and others also helped provide the financing for the community's school bus, the van to take older students to the high school in Loreto, and computer classes, to name a few. In addition, resident expatriates brought employment and training opportunities as they hired locals to work with them on projects like hotels, fishing-related enterprises, or assistance with household tasks. These expatriate residents also contributed financial and physical resources to community infrastructures like running water, road upkeep, buildings like churches or schools, and fences. Yet they also sometimes lent money to their neighbors, taught English or computer classes, or offered other kinds of support, which was reciprocated in kind or in other ways.

• • •

Tourists (who could become friends) were drawn to the area because of the beach, where most stayed. Fishing, swimming, hiking, kayaking, and other activities were often shared with residents, along with food and time. As tourism in the abstract is valued for its potential livelihoods, tourists who are friends bring a personal perspective to tourism. While locals may wonder how their friends can afford to vacation for so long so far from home, they also share with them an appreciation for the beach, water, and other resources. Most residents enjoyed the beach and gulf in their free time, but I think it meant something that people came from far away to enjoy it as well. In these ways, tourism in Playa Tranquila goes beyond the short-term visits most people think about as tourism. Whereas brief visits happen much more frequently, the long-term relationships in Playa Tranquila and elsewhere provided a different kind of support and connection to other places in the world.

• • •

Tourism in Playa Tranquila developed a few decades later than Loreto, though it still saw some visitors arrive by boat or other means. When she was young, don Javier's daughter Isabel opened her first small storefront on the beach, selling food to tourists who came by boat. Don Javier later worked with an American woman who gave boat tours, provisioning the tourism groups with equipment, food, and other needs when they arrived at Playa Tranquila's beach. With the highway, new kinds of tourists came, bringing their camping equipment or campers to stay on the beaches near Playa Tranquila, and more people came by boat as well. With the international airport, visitors began arriving by air but would need to hire a taxi or rent a car to reach Playa Tranquila and other communities away from town or, if they were very daring, join the locals on the frequent bus between Loreto and nearby towns.

Sportfishing provided a large amount of income to the Loreto area, and those in Playa Tranquila were well aware of this. Given that most of the men in the community were fishers by profession and enjoyed fishing, many people assumed that they would have been able to transition into tourism-related sportfishing. The fishers already took their visiting expatriate friends (including anthropologists) out in boats to fish on lazy days where food, drinks, and fishing filled any silences after running out of shared Spanish or English words. A few people tried to build on these experiences, encouraging their friends to recommend them to other tourists or even hanging signs advertising sportfishing tours in front of their homes like Guero.

But despite having fishing skills, knowledge, boats, food, and drink, there was seemingly little interest in a guide from the community. In part, this was because their signs were often on their houses, far from the highway, and few people actually saw the advertised services. But there were other challenges, too (see also Gómez Pech, García Silberman, and Barrasa García 2022). The fishing equipment was often older and less tourism-oriented; the *pangas* were simple boats without awnings, cabins, or cushioned seats, and few were equipped with GPS or sonar. Their fishing tackle was usually nets or fishing line, not the expensive rods and reels expected by visiting sportfishers (though many brought their own). Finally, tourists from the United States or Canada often spoke limited Spanish, and local residents spoke little English, making these interactions challenging and limiting contacts that might bring new clients. A few younger men were working to invest in tourism equipment and to take English classes, hoping that this might shift some of the tourism revenue their way.

Other opportunities have also developed, though to a lesser extent. Ecotourism activities like kayaking and camping could be done on the cheap, but this meant that there weren't many opportunities to sell lodging, food, or services, and guides faced similar constraints as fishers around equipment, language, and contacts. In one case, resident Americans connected youth in the community to a fishing tournament; young men and women cleaned and fileted dorado caught during the competition (figure 3). While the longer-term relationships described above were personally important for many residents of Playa Tranquila, the masses of tourists were important for their livelihoods, and many in the community were trying to find opportunities with them. One major opportunity has been through hotels in the community or nearby.

Tourism Growth and Challenges in Playa Tranquila

U.S. expatriates Dan and Jessica were well loved in the community and were invited to every baptism, birthday, quinceañera, and wedding in Playa Tranquila, often as the *padrinos* or sponsor of an element of the event. As for other community members, these supporting roles were a show of community and personal support and also added financial, creative, or labor resources to the events. Dan and Jessica had arrived in Playa Tranquila as tourists in the 1980s. In the 1990s, they had opened a small hotel on the beach of Playa Tranquila, leasing the land from the owners, who lived in another part of Mexico. As longtime visitors to the area, they knew the families and politics and were careful to hire those in most need of the work, like widows or single parents, and employed someone from most of the families in the community. Their small hotel hired several men and many women in work maintaining the grounds, buildings, and equipment and providing food, cleaning, and tourism services to the hotel guests. While several people were permanent full-time employees, the majority, primarily women, were part of a rotating work schedule that meant that they worked a few shifts a week. Jessica created this arrangement so that more people could earn money working for the hotel, and although this lowered the ability of individuals to make full-time income, all workers reported that they were happy with this system, as their family and friends also had an opportunity to work. Only a few people ever complained to me about not being included; most understood Jessica's reasons. However, those women who did not work shifts in the hotel were able to sell handicrafts or tortillas there, providing some additional income, and a few men were also hired occasionally for fishing, diving, or other activities.

Dan and Jessica's relationships with community members were similar to those of other resident expatriates in Loreto-area fishing communities, if not closer, and many in the community were heartbroken when they sold the hotel and moved to another country in Central America in the late 2000s. Dan and Jessica had sold their lease on the land to an investor who promised many more jobs. However, the transition from the small hotel to the resort was a major change for the community. While it would take more than a year for the new resort to open, community members took advantage of opportunities in construction, security, and feeding the workers. In addition, to support the resort, the new owner brought electricity and internet to the area. Homes that had run washing machines and televisions on generators could now have refrigerators and air-conditioning as well, and residents bought or leased these on payment plans. Suddenly, the younger generation was on Facebook and messaging apps, even when cell phone service was still spotty. Jobs, electricity, and the internet were definitely important additions to the community. However, other changes also came with these new possibilities for work.

• • •

Everyone could see the new road going in. The completed segments dug into the side of the hill that rose above the houses on one side of the community. The machines and trucks interrupted the usual hubbub of daily routines as they slowly and loudly dumped gravel onto newly cleared and cut roads. But the noise was not the major complaint despite its volume and persistence. The concern people raised was about the old road, which bisected the community and for years had been the only link between Dan and Jessica's hotel and Highway 1. Months of moving heavy equipment and additional traffic from the construction had degraded the gravel road so that driving it meant going painfully slowly or dangerously fast to avoid a tooth-rattling and axle-straining series of continuous jolts, like fingers over an old laundry washboard. Even a fresh layer of gravel every few months couldn't stave off the effect for very long. Homes along the road closed their windows to avoid the dust cloud that followed every passing vehicle, and parents kept their children away from what was no

FIGURE 4 The streambed has been excavated for dirt and stone for the resort.

longer a safe place to walk. Once the hotel started work on its new road that would bypass the community entirely, repair of the community road ceased despite the continuing hotel traffic.

In addition, construction of the road and buildings required large amounts of dirt and other materials, which the company was mining from the nearby arroyo, or streambed. The streambed was usually only wet during the rainy season, when hurricanes and other storms dumped massive amounts of water into the desert mountains; the water then flowed to the sea through these streambeds, sometimes taking trees, bridges, or cars with it. Residents expected that the massive alterations to the streambed would create bigger problems for the whole community once these annual floods arrived. One young woman worried that the loss of gravel and sand "might lead to houses being demolished." Still another issue arose around the water system, already overused and fragile. The new hotel's plans had included a saltwater desalination plant, but many suspected it was still using the community's water supply, leading to concern.

However, the most contentious act of the new resort owner was when he seized control of the beach in Playa Tranquila around 2010. Those who lived on the beach, like don Javier, were offered what they thought were sizable sums to move and built small houses in the middle of the community, away from the fishing area. Fishers were also no longer able to keep their boats or equipment at the beach. Without the shelters at the beach and the cluster of equipment and boats nearby, fishers no longer had a location or reason to hang out at the beach. The fish buyer's truck moved into the middle of the community, next to the buyer's house, and trucks towed boats to the water, then turned around to head back home.

Some homes that bordered the beach area were surprised to find a fence in front of their homes, blocking their access to the beach. Two new gates blocked the two beach access roads, and eventually a lock was placed on the one fishers used to launch their boats, while the other had a new guard's post to monitor traffic to the resort. After weeks of locking fishers away from their beach, and only when a local politician came to the area, was the gate opened for fishing access again.

Land ownership was always a complicated topic in the community; few residents held the deed to their land despite long-term (sometimes lifelong) residence on the land. Yet as one community member asserted, "Possession matters here." Despite not having formal claims to land, several residents like don Javier were paid to relocate. To connect to the electrical system, residents needed to get deeds to the land from the absentee owner in Mexico City unless they were on *ejido* land, which was owned by a group of people from the other side of the peninsula. Some families claimed ownership through a relationship to the landowner, and others had purchased their land from the *ejido*. Others had to get their paperwork in line. At least one resident went to the governor of the state for assistance, pleading decades of living there and a letter from the owner allowing residence. Eventually, most residents were able to buy their land and tap into the electricity, while others ran extension

FIGURE 5 Signs blocking beach access say, "Private property, no access."

cords from neighboring homes or continued to use generators or solar panels. Several residents offered part or all of their land for sale hoping to make some money, putting up "For Sale" signs with phone numbers. Although a few workers bought these plots to stay once construction on the resort finished, most land went unsold. By 2023, almost all homes had access to electricity, if not deeds to land.

Once the hotel opened, many in the community were employed cleaning rooms, cooking meals, tending plants, or keeping watch on the property. At one point in 2010, there were over five hundred workers at the hotel making MXN$1,000 (US$72) per week or more; twenty-three cooks were paid MXN$1,500 per week, though this was then lowered to about MNX$1,250 per week, while security guards were paid about MXN$2,000 per week. This brought income to a community for which fishing was no longer enough. However, many men returned to fishing after less than a year of working in tourism, complaining about the low amount of pay, the schedule, or the instability of the work. In addition, although many community members were employed to help build the hotel, they were let go once the primary construction phases were completed. Younger women and community members felt they were let go most frequently. Some did stay on, saying, as one resident told me, "I don't like it, but it's a job."

For a while, many women continued to work in the kitchen of the hotel, most cooking for the staff. Although a few quit, most continued to work despite some complaints about the pay or the hours, which can mean very little time with family and few days off. One young woman left the kitchens for health reasons, suggesting that a hernia and general illness were a result of repeatedly lifting heavy pans in a hot kitchen. A few other women also left for health reasons, some complaining that overwork, slippery floors, or heat caused their medical problems. Most I talked with complained about a lack of breaks and long hours that started before sunrise and ended late in the afternoon. One cook explained that at the hotel, "they have different ideas about cooking," which led to food quality problems, "like too much meat." A hotel worker in Loreto expressed many of the same complaints about money, health, and work expectations as those in Playa Tranquila:

> I want to quit working at the hotel, since I'm not getting my full pay [*nomino*]. The records for the state don't reflect what I'm actually paid, and my employers owe me 2,000 to 3,000 pesos for the year I've worked. I spoke with an accountant who was supposed to help me quit but has not. There is a lack of help for me and other workers. It is too much work, I am expected to do everything perfectly, like get every last fly in every last corner. I forgot to wash off the outside table one day, and went in early the next to do it. I should also get paid time off for medical problems and not have to put up with my boss's attitude about paying me, as if it was not a normal expense and instead was a withdrawal from his personal bank. My employers will pretend to not understand me when I talk with them about this [despite speaking Spanish with her regularly]. I have other options that are beginning to look better and better.

In an interview, the hotel owner in Playa Tranquila suggested that community members were just not able to do the kind of work he needed for the wages he offered, and so he instead brought in workers from other areas of Mexico. Francisco explained what he had brought to the community in terms of "ninety types of jobs," pay, and infrastructure like water, electricity, trash, and computers in the local library, as well as support for medical care when needed, like heart surgery. Francisco also mentioned additional benefits of pride, skills, and environmental sustainability. He claimed he had "no problems with fishers" aside from trash, fish, and oil on the beach and that "the community is well" (*la comunidad esta bien*). He believed that the issue was with resistance to or fear of change or the unknown, of "very difficult men" (*hombres muy maduros*).

The community members still fondly remembered Dan and Jessica, the boutique hotel owners, who had become part of the community. The new owner was rarely around and seemed to actively avoid the community both by his absence and the physical attempt to bypass the community with the new road; he was not upholding the standards of social interaction and exchange with the community. Conflicts with landowners were not new but usually did not include constant construction noise just outside one's kitchen window. In addition, jobs in tourism, retail, and government were often unable to meet the needs of the community members despite greater financial benefits and more predictability in

FIGURE 6 Fishing boat in front of a new resort in Baja California Sur.

pay. Many felt that the pay was not sufficient given the hours, physical labor, and unsafe working conditions. In addition, labor needs fluctuated as the hotel entered new construction phases and occupancy. During my visit in June 2011, many residents awaited for news that they were to lose their jobs, claiming that hundreds had been fired from the hotel since December; fortunately, most did not lose their jobs.

Other Changes

The new resort was far from the only change in the community. I started my research in Loreto in November 2001, cringing at my own questions around tourism given the clear absence of tourists in the wake of the September 11 terrorist attacks in the United States, which grounded flights and led fewer people to fly. Those in the tourism industry reported devastating changes to their businesses, though some tourists continued to drive or fly to visit. The 2001 decline was not Loreto's first experience with dramatic fluctuations of an industry in which a partial collapse followed a strong period of growth, as discussed in chapter 1. Like other industries, growth was occasionally punctuated by downturns that were often tied to national or global events, like 1982's peso crisis (Martínez de la Torre 1998b), recessions, or COVID-19.

In addition, the tastes and preferences of tourists have shifted with time, leading them to abandon prior tourist "hot spots" for places that are perceived to be more exotic, less crowded, or that have other desired values (Fletcher 2020). Tourism trends lead to overly optimistic investments; Puerto Escondido, imagined as a key natural port for tourism in the area, was ringed with vacant lots for decades, kept alive by a gas station, grocery store, and RV park. Similarly, Nopoló seemed to struggle with occupancy rates and worked to reinvent itself through private development, as many other projects in the area did. Whereas tourism may grow as an industry globally, local areas can see disinvestment and decline, even in the absence of major events like natural disasters or economic recessions.

Other areas can likewise bloom. As with the pearl industry in the previous chapter, innovations like ecotourism can bring new kinds of clients, and investments in hotels, beach construction, or infrastructure can also attract visitors. Repackaging an area as historical, cultural, or natural is also a valuable strategy, as is broadening media campaigns, such as radio ads I heard about Loreto in San Diego. It seems that new innovations are as valuable for tourism as they were for other industries, creating new cycles of prosperity. Loreto became one of 132 Pueblos Mágicos in 2012, which recognizes an area's culture, history, and charm (SECTUR 2019).

In some cases, the popularity can lead to environmental degradation that can repel tourists unless it is somehow concealed (Stonich 2021). Like in marine industries, tourism has played a large role in changing the local environment, constructing hotels and buildings where desert ecosystems once thrived, taking water from the local system and raw materials like sand, and bringing more people and more waste to the area (García 2020). Any visit to Loreto's airport includes seeing many coolers taped up for transport—filled to the brim with frozen fish to accompany their sportfishers back home. Although artisanal fishing captures more fish, sportfishing's impact on the area is still non-negligible. Tourism also introduced new conflicts about who could control land, water, and other resources and what this meant for communities, individuals, and the future (see also Bojorquez 2022). Importantly, sportfishers and artisanal fishers capture many of the same species, introducing conflicts. In addition, some local environmentalists also have sportfishing businesses, complicating relationships among these interests.

Yet tourism opportunities required resources. Tourism in Loreto was dominated by larger, wealthier businesses that were almost always run by people who had moved to Loreto from other parts of Mexico or the United States. Many were very well educated and had come to Loreto with a history of investment and significant financial resources gained through these efforts. Their education, wealth, and experiences in investment also connected them to a wide network of potential clients or investors. Some had attended years of international boat shows or had worked to connect to international sportfishing groups to advertise their businesses. Those in tourism also worked to improve the reputation and infrastructure of the Loreto area, both as part of a business strategy and out of an altruistic interest in their new home. Part of this effort led to the creation of the MPA, as described in chapter 4. The same educational and networking skills that allowed them to create their tourism businesses also allowed them to influence the creation and management of institutions like the MPA.

For local residents, tourism like fishing was susceptible to fluctuations in demand and availability of resources. Tourism thus promises greater income but often at the cost of stable, year-round work (see also Vásquez-León 2012) and can require specialized skills like English competence and computer skills. In Loreto, the hot summers and windy winters are low seasons for tourism and can leave workers in this industry without income for months at a time.

Changes over time, both annual patterns and longer cycles of boom and bust, lend tourism important uncertainties that were familiar to residents. Local responses to industry cycles reveal a set of robust strategies for adapting to uncertainties and inevitable industry declines.

Community Engagements with Tourism on Their Own Terms

The question, often posed around fishers living near a tourism area, is often why fishers and their families don't engage in tourism instead of fishing. What we see in Playa Tranquila is that this is not the right question to ask. As this chapter has shown, tourism is complex and multifaceted, and reasons for engaging in it reflect a deeper history of tourism and opportunities, and the question ignores an entire set of relationships around land, resources, and networks that are unavoidably tied into the power and privilege of those already succeeding in tourism, including land and resource dispossession and "touristification" (Morgan 2023) where "political authority doesn't govern for the whole of society, but only for a select group of people" (Morgan 2023, 43; my translation). Assuming fishers can access these is naive at best (Gómez Pech, García Silberman, and Barrasa García 2022). As Paige West (2016, 42) suggests about surfing in Papua New Guinea, the sea has been transformed into a place for the display of wealth, and its residents have become commodities (see also Córdoba Azcárate 2020). These dispossessions and restrictions limit the opportunities for community members (Roseberry 1988), including when these ideas are internalized (Carpenter 2020) or values and moral expectations conflict, as we see with the resort owner's disinterest in community relationships in Playa Tranquila.

Understanding tourism as a set of relationships, expectations, and potential futures reveals how economic benefits, while important, are often not the primary drivers of local engagement in tourism. If tourism is imagined as a large-scale effort, we can miss Playa Tranquila's efforts entirely. Similarly, understanding tourism as an entirely economic activity conflicts with how tourism in different forms has supported the community socially, politically, and health-wise. A focus on economics (Çalışkan and Callon 2009, 2010) misses how losing resources and relationships can disrupt strategies for adapting to change and can lead to conflicts in moral expectations tied to labor and resource exploitation.

Given the various uncertainties and challenges, residents of Playa Tranquila have continued to engage with tourism on their own terms, using strategies that have worked for them in the past. This includes relying on social networks and personal relationships that have led to repeat visitors, some connections to Loreto-area tourism outfitters, and collaborations with friends and family more locally. The change from personal relationships to wage work highlights the importance of class differences between owners and workers under neoliberalism, particularly given differential access to resources, conflicting moral economies, and the resulting dispossessions and commodification of labor (Durrenberger 2011; Thompson 1971; Scott 1976); Jamaica Kincaid (1988) and others similarly argue that tourism reflects colonial and racial projects across the world, visible in the many non-Mexican tourists and owners, and marginalization of Indigenous people in other areas of BCS (Wilson, Gámez Vázquez, and Ivanova 2012).

In addition, fishers, ranchers, and others engage in tourism as part of a set of strategies, part of their multiple livelihoods in response to the uncertainties involved in many of these industries (see also Armenta-Cisneros et al. 2021), despite the difficulty of developing multiple livelihoods in BCS (Marin-Monroy and Ojeda-Ruíz 2023). As Trouillot (1992) argues for the Caribbean, multiple livelihoods encourage flexibility or movement within different occupations, not just between livelihoods. Overall, these strategies connect to ideas of work as more than labor or economic value and to the value of relationships as resources.

The new road around the community, like Highway 1 before it, created both opportunities and risks for the community. It was an outgrowth of tourism, which like many other industries has created employment for the area. It also signaled certain kinds of relationships between the hotel and the community in terms of plans for the area and who gets to make them. Finally but possibly most important, the road, like Highway 1, connected those in the community to new people, places, and goods, which could also bring benefits or problems. Similar opportunities and risks also arrived with many of the past industries, many of which left when they ran out of resources or demand. However, this road also circumvented the community, as did many of the opportunities for improving livelihoods, relationships, and the local environment. In addition to the direct dispossession of the beach and other land, there was dispossession of the local environment, both in terms of infrastructure like roads and the damage to the natural flood control system. The opening of the resort signaled new growth in tourism, but the effects largely bypassed the community. In their wake we found Baja Californians finding ways to live in the faded desert on the edge of a sapphire sea, as they had during past boom-and-bust cycles and as they will in the future.

CHAPTER 3

WOMEN, WORK, AND MORAL ECONOMY

The smell of mangoes still makes me a little sick. One summer in Playa Tranquila, in 2002, I ate five to ten mangoes every day. I would arrive at someone's house for an interview or just a chat, and they would hand me a mango or two. Anxious to get started asking questions, I would eat the fruit quickly, dripping yellow, stringy syrup onto the ground, constantly licking my fingers, and stealthily pulling strings of mango pulp from between my teeth. Inevitably, once I finished those, I was handed more. I learned to set them aside for later or risk eating my weight in mangoes every day.

I was staying with Dalia and her three teenaged children. Shaded by mature mango trees, the half-finished walls of her block house dwarfed the three-roomed wood residence next door. Dalia's husband was a fisherman, which meant that his income was unpredictable, and progress on building the house was seemingly permanently stalled. The perpetual construction stages were common in the community, and walls got higher only when some extra money allowed their owners to buy a little more cement and concrete block. Those rare people who owned stores or worked for the government were some of the few whose houses were both complete and painted, at least until a government housing program built a few homes.

One morning, Dalia asked me to help her take some mangoes to the other side of the community. We put several buckets of them into the back of my pickup truck along with two of her kids and started off. I was happy to help her transport them to what I assumed would be a relative's house. However, after she asked me to stop a few times at different houses, I began to realize that I had become part of her door-to-door mango business. I was likely selling the same mangoes that I would eat in my next visits. Dalia was determined to sell them all, and we continued to stop at one house after another. People were giving me strange looks, and I was concerned that they thought that I was showing preference to one family over another. By the end of the day, I realized that people were simply amused that the gringa anthropologist was selling mangoes, yelling with the kids, "Who wants [to buy] mangoes?" (*¿Quien quiere mango?*).

The money Dalia, her friends, and family raised by selling mangoes, tamales, Popsicles, and other foods didn't go toward supplementing household incomes. Rather, the women engaged in these small-scale forms of "penny capitalism" (Tax 1953) to invest in developing a cooperative that would earn money through clam aquaculture and exporting tropical fish. Dalia and her other five cooperative members started the cooperative Hijas del Mar (Daughters of the Sea) in 2000 and worked very hard over a decade to learn new skills and develop social networks to support their efforts (Peterson 2014b). This took long hours of work and required balancing their projects with household responsibilities and their husbands' and families' gendered expectations of how they should spend their time. The women went from selling mangoes, Popsicles, and tamales at community events to shipping colorful *cortez, nariz de gringa*, puffer fish, and other sea creatures to pet stores in Los Angeles. I was fortunate to meet them in 2002 when they were just joining an expatriate U.S. businessman's tropical fish exporting enterprise and watched them acquire a permit to capture the fish, learn the logistics of an export business, and start a female-run international company.

Eight years after I first met the Hijas, in 2010, I was in the community once again observing an evening of packing tropical fish. The Hijas were now the ones in charge and operating the business themselves from their relatively new workroom next to their boats, a van, and other equipment

FIGURE 7 Fish packing by the Hijas in 2010.

needed to run the enterprise. Around once a month, the women employed family, neighbors, and a biologist to catch, pack, and ship the fish, providing supplemental income to many in the community. Their work has inspired another women's cooperative in a nearby community and potentially others in Mexico through their contacts and even media appearances.

The Hijas cooperative was unusual in its women-only membership and its international reach. As an anthropologist, I was drawn to the cooperative in 2002 as an interesting case study in community economic development and have published on the strategies of the cooperative in reaching some of its goals (Peterson 2014b). However, after more than a decade working with the fishing communities near Loreto, I came to understand that the work of the Hijas was only the most visible example when it came to understanding alternatives to fishing and work in general in the community.

I found that many of the women in the community were involved in small businesses based out of their homes that sometimes included their family members and children. Other women in Playa Tranquila sold embroidered napkins, shell jewelry, bread, tortillas, or other things or provided services, including restaurants, stores, laundry, cleaning, and sewing services. They ranged from the formal businesses like local convenience stores to informal enterprises like the woman who does everyone's nails. The majority, though, tended to be informal businesses that occupied some kind of space in or next to the home.

Besides the women's cooperative and the stores, these enterprises were practically invisible in the community, particularly to outsiders (see also Arellanes-Cancino, Ayala-Ortiz, and Nava 2022; Delgado Ramírez 2021). In addition, few of the business owners claimed to see any real income from their work. Given that several women's cooperative members mentioned that their husbands and other family members discouraged them from doing this kind of work, I wondered why any women worked at all in these kinds of small enterprises and how they maintained their businesses in the face of competing household demands and disapproval from inside their homes.

The answer is a complex story, with many threads to untangle. I found that the reasons why women work are tied to many social values they share with each other and the fishers, including the importance of family, morality, and gender expectations. These values have encouraged certain kinds of approaches to work, including domestic-based projects, relying on family collaborations, and deliberately making the work invisible to outsiders, which connect to these values. As I discussed with reference to the fishing and tourism industries in previous chapters, here I show that the role of these small-scale domestic enterprises in the community goes beyond economic value to encompass specific kinds of moral engagements with work. The women understood their work efforts in terms of a moral obligation or correct behavior that creates value for themselves and their community, both in terms of the services they provide and their own sense of self-accomplishment. As with the previous chapters, we see several different elements of a livelihood model: cooperation and collaboration across the community, meeting the needs of family and kinship obligations, and mindfulness of the environment. As before, we see that work and economic relationships are deeply entwined with other social relationships, with a strong emphasis on interactions within the community. Below, I examine some of the influences on these small businesses, including gender expectations.

Barriers to Working: Gendered Expectations

Fishing communities around the world historically have had distinct gender roles for men and women, though this has shifted over time (Burton 2012; Abrams 2012; Cruz-Torres 2012, 2023; Cruz-Torres and McElwee 2017). In addition, women in fishing communities are increasingly involved in fisheries and a variety of other activities (Cole 1991; Nadel-Klein and Davis 1988; Burton 2012; Mendoza-Carranza, Paredes-Trujillo, and Segura-Berttolini 2024), and women in Mexico have been increasingly present in workplaces, either through formal or self-employment (Chant 1994; Cruz-Torres 2001; Parrado and Zenteno 2001; Gavaldón and Fraga 2011). The reasons women give for why they work, their ability to work, and their ability to access the resources needed for their work are all heavily imbued with gendered relationships and norms and include supporting their households (Anderson and Dimon 1998; Benería 1992; Cruz-Torres 2023) and increasing relative bargaining power, personal consumption, and/or the range of socially acceptable behavior (Benería and Roldán 1987; Eber 2000; Hirsch 1999; Mills 2003; Montaño Armendáriz, Pérez Concha, and Martínez Sidón 2022).

In Playa Tranquila, we see many of these same patterns in women's work and justifications given for it, and we also see a complex interplay between community gender expectations and norms and women's actual work. As in other places, gender norms can still limit the kinds of work women do, the strategies and other behaviors that support their work, and even the outcomes of the work for the women and their families. While the values and orientations toward work as well as some of the strategies they employ are similar to those discussed in the previous chapters, gender norms and expectations have led to an emphasis on different values, including downplaying the visibility of the work and a higher importance of collaboration and noneconomic values. These differences become ways to negotiate gender and work. Household and community relationships play some role in these negotiations, as do status and personality differences, particularly when women push the limits of gendered work norms.

In interviews, women often brought up their husbands before I got around to asking about them. They would typically affirm that their own husbands were very supportive of their work and explain that most other women didn't work because they thought or knew that their husbands would disapprove. Machismo is often used as an explanation in Mexico for male control that can lead to different forms of abuse or lack of support (Chant 1991, 21). Although many have noted that gender norms in Mexico are changing, women are still concerned about their husband's (and others') expectations, particularly jealousy, and women brought up machismo or similar ideas throughout the interviews. Several women I knew in the community claimed that their husbands kept them from working or from growing their businesses due to machismo. Lupita kept delaying formalizing the restaurant she had successfully been running for around three years for just this reason. She felt that she could not depend on her husband for support since he "changed his mind often," and this led her to be afraid of asking him for more time or money lest he remove his support entirely. Yvonne told me that she chose not to work at all, aside from some embroidery work that largely ceased when the boutique hotel closed and she no longer had a place to sell her handicrafts: "He doesn't let me work. What am I to do?"

Doña Ana, one of the leaders of the women's cooperative, believed that with respect to women working, "it has a lot to do with whether husbands support what we want to do. Machismo has a big effect when their husbands don't let them work or follow their dreams." Another cooperative member put some of the burden on the women themselves, explaining, "They continue with this mentality that their husbands are jealous. Mine is jealous, but I had a time where I had to work to earn my own money." Several of the women claimed that their husbands had started out being jealous but, over time, had learned that supporting the businesses would help the household by bringing in money.

For women working in the cooperative, the increased income seemed to assuage any spousal concerns of inappropriateness. The women, particularly those in the cooperative, were careful to avoid any behaviors that could be misconstrued as inappropriately attentive to other men, and they often arrived at work with other women or worked with male relatives to prevent this. Yet a few of the women were divorced or separated from their husbands (which was very unusual in the community), suggesting that the women's work was uncommonly stressful on marriages.[1]

However, women who worked to provide for their families also risked violating a community expectation of women not working outside of the household. Women and men in the community often critiqued the women in the cooperative for working, arguing that the women inappropriately leave their homes or are too bold in how they violated the expected domestic-public dichotomy (see also Worthen 2012; Tiano 1994). This certainly led to some complex gender dynamics with husbands and others. The women's cooperative, for example, was occasionally critiqued for being "shameless" (*sin vergüenza*) in creating business connections outside of the community (Peterson 2014b) or "crazy" for the kinds of masculine work they were undertaking (see also Cruz-Torres 2023). The ability of most of these women to run their businesses out of their homes was one means for defusing this; cooking and other activities were recognized as feminine across the community. The Hijas' cooperative was unusual in its members' tendency to embrace the criticisms of their publicly visible work, arguing that their efforts were "simply work" and any critique was just gossip (see Peterson 2014b).

Husbands' expectations that women should not work outside the home was not the only gender norm that affected the women's choice of work. Their motivation to work was often influenced by their roles as mothers providing for their families. As restauranteur Lupita said, "I look from one way to another to get my family ahead. I have to find the way to get us ahead." Paulina similarly baked bread because she felt she "had to work because I'm the one who has to maintain the house," given her husband's illness. The idea that mothers need to provide materially for their children was thus an important motivator for seeking to work outside the home.

However, while navigating gender expectations might be difficult for the working women, their activities may have opened up more possibilities for themselves and other women. For example, a younger cooperative member mentioned that she'd been motivated to join the cooperative

---

1. Domestic violence is another potential outcome of women entering the labor market but not something I encountered (Moser and McIlwaine 2000).

because she'd seen the other women working in it (Peterson 2014b). By 2012, many women in the community were involved in one or more microenterprises, making it increasingly difficult to find women who were not working at all. The community elected its first female representative in 2010, and a second women's cooperative had been established by 2012 as well. Although gender roles and expectations were important for these working women, they were by no means insurmountable.

Invisible Work

In 2010, after I'd finished asking about income and expenditures for the community census I was completing, Magdalena and I sat chatting near her recently acquired washing machine. She mentioned that she was washing some clothes for one of the workers at the hotel. I asked her why she didn't include that as income, and she laughed. She said it was so little money, it didn't matter. I tried asking another way, having her estimate the cost of washing the clothes and the amount she charges, but it still didn't add up to anything more than a few pesos a week. Aware now that I might have missed some of the small or microenterprises while conducting the census, I returned to reinterview some of the other women I'd surveyed, determined to find out how their businesses affected their household income. However, I found that most women had also left off their own household businesses for the same reason. Maria even laughed when I mentioned earning a profit from selling tortillas, saying, "Ay, no, Nicole! It's just enough to buy the flour and the gas." The more I learned about these businesses, the more that most appeared to contribute little if anything to household income. Yet these micro-scale businesses, barely visible even to the anthropologist, have persisted over time (see also Neilson et al. 2019; Arellanes-Cancino, Ayala-Ortiz, and Nava 2022; Mendoza-Carranza, Paredes-Trujillo, and Segura-Berttolini 2024; Delgado Ramírez 2021).

If proceeds barely paid for the expense of the business, then why did Magdalena launder clothes or Maria make tortillas in the first place? Despite their relative success in developing a bigger and more expansive business, Dalia and the other cooperative members have yet to see much profit for themselves in the decades I have known and been working with them. For several years, I attributed the lack of income to the costs of a new business. Yet year after year, despite the lack of real earnings, the women continued to work on the projects. How can we understand this as economically rational? If there is little to no economic benefit, perhaps we need to consider other motives for working.

Because the women downplay their importance of their microenterprises for the household economy, and because the work almost always happened in the women's spare time (and when I visited them that work ceased), the microenterprises had been both economically and physically invisible to me as an ethnographer. But this was seemingly contrary to what business owners would want in terms of profit and demand. Why was invisibility so pervasive to the women's microenterprises?

Money still mattered for these women despite the inability to report earnings. Most women claimed that the income helped their household (see also Cruz-Torres 2023). Almost every woman I spoke to talked about being motivated by earning money (see also Anderson and Dimon 1998; Benería 1992; González de la Rocha and Escobar Latapí 1991). When I asked why the women started the cooperative, they said, "One reason was to not be lazy and also to help the household and earn a bit of money." A few of the women were proud to provide some money for the family, such as one who said, "And now my money is what is valuable here in the house. We would be stuck if I didn't work" (see also García 2021; Ramachanran 2021).

A few businesses like the stores did provide a large proportion of the income for the family, and those business owners were able to talk with me about income. Paulina supports her family through bread-making and said, "To earn a little more money because we have the expenses. When there is wind, I can't make bread and I have to look for another form of work. Every day, I have to earn for the food, my girl who goes to school, and to pay for the bus. I work in what will bring me more money." Clearly, some of these businesses financially support the household in the absence of other income sources (e.g., from fishing) when husbands are absent or unable to work. But calculating income from the business was still difficult, and few women really wanted to talk about what they earned from their work.

Invisibility may have value for the women because it allows them to meet some of the gender expectations discussed above. When activities remain largely at home, there is less chance of censure and jealousy. The invisibility (and low levels of income) of the microenterprises might be a strategy to keep a low profile from family and community members critical of women working. Similarly, many of these women had built their current businesses from previous activities, investing prior earnings into new ventures. While Dalia's mango sales made sense as a way to compensate for her husband's bumpy fishing income, especially in the slow summer fishing season, she was primarily investing in a new business, using her earnings to create new businesses with the women's cooperative.

Another reason for the invisibility of these microenterprises was the small amounts actually earned on a daily basis. The women themselves had a hard time identifying any money that was not reinvested into the business (either as a cost or next-stage development). Net earnings are just too small for these women to include in their household accounting. Relatedly, these earnings may be absorbed into household expenditures without clear accounting. Most of the women did not keep a separate business account and instead bought groceries or other things with money from the same wallet where they kept their earnings, sometimes at the same time that they paid for business expenses (e.g., materials for Popsicles would be purchased alongside food for making lunch). Similarly, tortillas and meat initially bought for one's restaurant could become dinner for the family if they weren't sold to a client. Perhaps in this and other cases, women's earnings are incalculable because they are constantly integrated into the household economy, peso by peso, rather than as a lump sum at the end of the shift or pay period. This can further contribute to the invisibility of the work and its outcomes. In many cases, invisibility follows from capitalist and patriarchal logics and reveals that simply integrating women into work cannot overcome deep inequalities (Delgado Ramírez 2021).

In the first chapter, we saw how fishing was unpredictable and poorly remunerated but nonetheless met many of the needs and values of people in the fishing community. Learning about the microenterprises and other household activities led me to the realization that understanding household economies in Playa Tranquila required a more in-depth form of economic survey, moving beyond income and expenditures to a variety of other values and even economic principles that shape livelihoods. To understand why fishers fish or women sell mangoes required more than a financial analysis, and understanding what might reduce pressure on fisheries resources required a similar kind of perspective, as we see in the next chapters.

Values of Working

Most women in Playa Tranquila found that their small businesses met a variety of other needs, like moral correctness, maintaining social

FIGURE 8 Laundry in Playa Tranquila under the mango trees.

networks, relative bargaining power within the household, or mobility (also see, e.g., Benería and Roldán 1987; Eber 2000; Hirsch 1999; Mills 2003). In the case of Playa Tranquila, these needs have a social component, whether it is caring for families or following cultural norms for women's behavior. Evaluating other motives for work will reveal these values and help us understand the whole context for work, particularly the gendered component.

Anthropologists have long argued that livelihoods and exchange systems have multiple sets of overlapping and coexisting values. While I reviewed some of these approaches earlier, the women's microenterprises suggest specific kinds of values and how they intersect with their lives and community.

Moral Correctness

Doña Ana is a vivacious leader of the women's cooperative, a great-grandmother who still helps process and package the tropical fish for export, and someone who is essential for the organization of the cooperative. Like the other cooperative leaders, interviewing her meant finding a time when she had no other responsibilities and then getting down to the topics quickly. Interviews with her were efficient, but she was also quick to smile about the cooperative and its efforts, and she was particularly animated about her reasons to help start the cooperative. Doña Ana told me that she joined the cooperative because she did not want to be lazy (*floja*), she wanted to earn money, and she wanted to be healthy, or as she put it, "one feels old if one wants to feel it." She went on to say that she worked "to not be stuck without doing anything. You come out of your monotony, and you have to get active because if not, I would get older quickly." Her words were factual, but her tone was light and conversational, with an undercurrent of laughter. She seemed to see the value in work but also to enjoy it.

In talking with women about their microenterprises, many justify their work as a way to stay active or to avoid laziness. Building the business was seen as personally rewarding for other cooperative members, even if the rewards were not financial. Many spoke about the "restlessness" (*inquietud*) that led them to want to start a business. In 2002, the cooperative members declared, "We want to do something more than housework" (*queremos hacer algo más que casa*), and they have continued to create opportunities for themselves. Other women also spoke of their desire to work. Bread maker Paulina explained, "I have always liked to work. Before I was married, my father would take me to the fish camp and taught me that we should work and help. This is why I do this." In general, women talk about working as a moral good—as a way to prevent laziness, as a lesson from their fathers. The women also seem to judge those who don't work as lazy. Beatrice, who made quilts in her home for many years, criticized those who did not work, calling them lazy for not wanting to make money. The criticisms reveal a moral economy around work in the community, which of course not everyone follows.

For these women, work is a way to provide for their families and to avoid laziness, boredom, and health problems. Despite these reasons, it also has a moral valence, given the criticisms of the women I interviewed toward those who do not work. The ideas about work have a very gendered focus—few men I spoke with discussed work as a moral calling in the same way, though they did talk about supporting families. Some of the moral valence may be an attempt to justify work that goes against women's social norms, particularly criticisms that the work is not appropriate for women. Validating this work as a moral obligation toward family or oneself may be one way to counter any claims of immodest behavior. In addition, while women rarely explicitly discuss the value of their work for those outside of the household, the efforts also have tangible benefits for their community and extended families.

Community Connections

Maria makes flour tortillas daily, and I spent many mornings talking with her as she mixed the wheat-based dough, rolled it into balls, and flattened each ball to place on her *comal* to cook. A regular stream of visitors came by to chat for a minute and pay MXN$10 for a packet of tortillas sealed in a plastic bag with a staple. While some in the community got store-bought tortillas imported from another town, Maria's family and friends enjoyed them fresh and often warm with their lunch.[2] She often

---

2. When I started my study of Playa Tranquila, every grown woman made flour tortillas at home, but over the decade of the study, this fell out of favor as it has

joked that I needed to come early or risk leaving without tortillas, and this happened to me on occasion. While Maria efficiently went on with her work, I was able to talk with her about her family, her tortillas, and her other sewing and laundry work. Denying that her tortilla business made any profit at all after the costs of supplies, Maria was still happy to sell tortillas to her friends. While one might mistake her stern personality and demand for cash each day as a mark of a profit-seeking entrepreneur, she both enjoyed making the tortillas and seeing her friends take them away; her labor was compensated by the value she added to their meals as well as the coin it added to her purse. Other goods produced by the women's small businesses circulated throughout the community in similar ways, as community members went to their friends and relatives for bread, manicures, haircuts, and sewn garments like school uniforms. Most of the microenterprises supported local needs like these, including the stores, and often allowed purchases on credit to allow friends and family flexibility in tough economic periods. However, at least one woman found that she had to stop extending credit because she needed the money to buy the materials for creating the goods to sell.

Other practices within the community support this reading of the women's enterprises as community support. The community has a long history of collaboration and shared resources and childcare (see also Rothstein 1999; Cruz-Torres 2023; Delgado Ramírez 2021). For example, when a young woman in the community turns fifteen, the costs of the quinceañera are spread among her relatives and friends, as one becomes the "godparent" (*padrino/a*) of the cake, another of the dress, shoes, music, centerpieces, or location. Recipients of these titles of honor, godparents can spend hundreds of dollars on their contribution. Similarly, when someone in the community falls ill, others contribute money to a fund to send them to the specialist, sometimes in mainland Mexico.[3] Finally, the women themselves participate in a rotating credit association called

---

become too time consuming and hot in the heat of the desert. Now most buy them either at stores or from the few women who make them as part of a microenterprise.

3. Although many medical expenses are covered by the Mexican health plans, expenses for hotels and food, especially for accompanying family members, require additional funds on the part of the patient.

a *cundina*, as described earlier in chapter 2 (see also Delgado Ramírez 2021; Vélez-Ibáñez 2010; Zambrano et al. 2023).

Beyond creating goods for other community members, some businesses created jobs or income opportunities for others, even when the women running the businesses did not receive income from it themselves. The women's cooperative hired other community members to help them capture, sort, and pack the tropical fish. These noncooperative members were paid about MXN$400 to dive and capture the species and half that to sort and pack (out of the tropical fish sales). The women's cooperative had little money left after paying these wages as well as that of the biologist and the costs of the equipment, but the practice provided a source of income to other members of the local community. As one young cooperative member insisted, it is the community that needs to get ahead, not just individual people or families, for real success.

Other projects in the community also contributed to community employment. Restaurant founder Adela employed her mother and sister, and store owners tend to hire their relatives and children. The terms "wage" and "employ" are perhaps not quite appropriate for describing how these relationships are mediated since family members and others contribute not only for their own financial gain but to support those running the businesses.

Of course, a careful look at who in the community is supported challenges the idea that "community support" is wholly egalitarian. Even in a community as small as Playa Tranquila, there are conflicts and divisions among households. Most support is given within families, including close kin, and among close friends (often with *compadrazgo* relationships and other less formal friendships). A women's cooperative member expressed a view common within the community to explain why most cooperative members were related by birth or marriage: "With family, you get along better" (*Entre familia, se lleva mejor*). The tendency for women and their husbands to work with family in businesses or fishing, respectively, highlights the value of these relationships.

Where these relationships are lacking, results can be uneven. I interviewed a few women who either did not work or whose businesses closed. Although they often shared an interest in work and were motivated to avoid laziness, they also had very insubstantial or tenuous relationships with others in the community. These women married into the community from elsewhere and found few friends, if any. Yvonne, who does not work, expressed her loneliness in the community in terms of her lack of connections to family; she had married into Playa Tranquila and did not get along well with her husband's family. Likewise, Lupita, who also married into the community, started a restaurant but then left after finding few people she could work with in the area. Although there is not a definitive causal link, I found it interesting that social isolation had such a concrete connection to business success in the community. Talking with Lupita and Yvonne, they never connected their failure to start or maintain a business to their lack of community connections. However, in other conversations about the community, they felt isolated through a lack of visits from other women, an absence of involvement in community events and opportunities, and a general hesitancy to arrange visits or opportunities themselves. Every other woman I interviewed, and most I knew through my general work in the community, had family in the community that they relied on, either through blood or marriage ties, for business needs as well as personal support.

Connections to the community are thus important for labor and resources needed by the women's enterprises. In addition, providing goods and services to the wider community can be seen as a value added by each of these women's enterprises. Although few discussed this topic in any detail, most were proud of their ability to provide for the community and enjoyed doing so. Family connections appear to be crucial for the women and their businesses, supporting a tendency to base the business in or next to the home.

Working in Domestic Spaces

Adela's restaurant was a simple affair. Several plastic tables and chairs emblazoned with beer logos sat underneath a palm-thatched roof. During lunch and dinner, Adela served many of the workers from the local hotel construction project, feeding them fresh fish, tacos, and other Mexican dishes. Adela's mother and sister helped her prepare and serve the food, while Adela coordinated beer and tortilla deliveries, menus, and purchasing. Even Adela's ten-year-old daughter helped a little in the restaurant, at least when she wasn't watching TV in the air-conditioned bedroom next to the kitchen.

Adela was a very bright young woman who had supported herself and her young daughter ever since her husband left her. She worked for a while at a tourist restaurant in another community but eventually left to start her own restaurant. Adela collaborated with the MPA staff on an economic development program that led to some start-up money and supplies. After a year, she finally opened her restaurant in the heart of the community.

Like many of the small businesses in Playa Tranquila, Adela's restaurant was a family affair, involving her mother, sister, and even her daughter in the daily tasks. While Adela seemed to be the central force behind the business, she admitted that it would have been impossible without help from the others. Adela remembers her mother's work in the small boutique hotel and her father's unfailing support as Adela sold clams or other goods before the restaurant project.

Many of these businesses thus operated out of the physical space of the home or created a labor space next to it. Paulina's husband, for example, built her an oven in her yard when it was too difficult to negotiate regular use of the community's oven. She credits the success of her baking

FIGURE 9 Bread oven in Playa Tranquila in front of an older home around 2002.

business to her husband, who does much of the work heating the oven and helping with other aspects of the baking. He even built a shelter near the oven to protect Lupita from the hot sun.

In these cases, we see an overlap between domestic and extra household work, with spaces and labor shared across several activities, which often blend formal and informal activities (see Arizpe 1977; Moser 1978). Understanding the women and their microenterprise projects requires a more flexible idea of work and workplace, echoing Wilk's (1989) argument that households should be understood as sets of activities and relationships rather than as a structure. This also resonates with literature on multiple livelihoods, as women with household responsibilities and small businesses have always had, and how their movements in and through activities support their efforts (see also Trouillot 1992).

What struck me about the family orientation in these businesses was the overlap and contradiction between how family and community were valued in these enterprises, and the ways that family became a resource or strategy for these women. The strength of connection, when integrated into the work, became a valuable resource for these businesses. Whether it was selling goods to community members, hiring friends and family to work on the projects, or collaborating closely with family, the women were able to accomplish more than they could on their own. Suprahousehold dynamics and cooperation became a strategy for households and their members (see also Wilk 1989). The women do not see a contradiction in valuing family and using them strategically; like nonmarket values entering the market, and market items gaining noneconomic values, it encourages us to see how these values move and flow and even how people can resist a focus on economic values (Zelizer 2011; Okura Gagné 2020). The values and strategies adopted by the women reflected some of their experiences and expectations as women, particularly the use of the household space and skillset. The next section discusses strategies in the community more broadly and then the value of multiple activities or livelihoods, investments, and external social networks for women in particular.

Strategies

Driving away from one of Baja California's many fishing communities one afternoon in 2002, I was waved down by a woman and her son on the side of the road. I vaguely recognized the pair, and since people often asked me to get them things from town, I slowed to a stop to ask what they needed. In this case, the son wanted to know if I could take his mother to a doctor's appointment in Loreto since she had been suffering from health problems and needed some tests. I agreed, still trying to place the family in my ever-expanding mental map of family relations and community frictions. We had a pleasant drive into town, a half hour of chatting about her health, her family, and my work. I left doña Rosa at the medical clinic after she assured me that she had a ride back to the community.

Doña Rosa had made an appointment, and I arrived in time to get her there. If I had not been going to town that day or had not stopped, would she have missed the appointment? Asked someone else for a ride? Called to reschedule? From what people said and what I saw in other cases, doña Rosa would simply have waited for another ride and gotten there on time or not. As the saying "with God's favor" (*con el favor de Dios*) suggests, people were often content to leave things up to God, or fate, or chance, trusting that things would be taken care of. Like doña Rosa, most people in the community approached problems with seemingly simple, if not risky, techniques of awaiting a ride, anticipating government programs, making requests of wealthy tourists or government offices, or pooling community resources through raffles, *compadrazgo* relationships, or explicit requests for donations. These techniques worked, or if they didn't, people tried something else. Lest this seem entirely fatalistic, individuals in the fishing communities knew a great deal about their surroundings and exploited that knowledge to make these strategies work. An American middle-class suburbanite might find doña Rosa's strategy for finding her way to medical care entirely perplexing, but she certainly understood the comings and goings of trucks on the road to Loreto well enough to depend on them as a solution to her problem. The residents of Playa Tranquila and similar fishing communities solve resource problems by deciding among available options that emerge from the interaction of social connections, cultural ideas, and immediate needs. These strategies helped people cover unexpected expenses, such as doctors' visits or surgeries, but also often were an attempt to supplement the household income.

I have discussed these strategies in the context of the women's cooperative (Peterson 2014b), but they are also shared across the community and most strongly conveyed by the women's microenterprises. The women relied on many of the same strategies for developing and maintaining their businesses. Cooperation, family connections, multiple projects, prior work, external social networks, and a work ethic were crucial for them, as described above. For the men in the community, cooperation was a key value and strategy in fishing and other livelihood strategies, while some also created a set of livelihood options (particularly those who ranched or worked in tourism), and the household as a whole often had multiple options at the same time, including contributions from adults and older children who worked in stores.

Women and others varied widely in their use of these strategies, and my analyses suggest that those women who employ a combination of these are more likely to have a successful (longer lasting) business than those who rely on just one. For example, the women I interviewed about their businesses emphasized these strategies in our discussions, focusing on their motivations, desire to learn, prior experience, and support from family and others. Learning new skills and support seem crucial for the women who continued their businesses over time; I noted similar patterns for other women as well.

I used to think the Hijas del Mar cooperative was unique and that no one else in the community and possibly Mexico had been able to do what they had done. I've written about how the combination of being women and a cooperative made them unique and got them attention and funding they needed (Peterson 2014b). Yet after talking with other women in the community with their own microenterprises, there are two important commonalities that may actually matter more than the differences. As discussed above, these women seemed to earn very little, if anything, from their efforts, yet some had been working in these businesses for decades. Second, the women relied on many of the same strategies for developing and maintaining their businesses: a specific kind of work ethic, family connections, prior work experiences, and working on multiple projects at the same time or over time seemed crucial for them. Even though one business might work for a while, most of the women talked about what they had done in the past as well as planned for an unknown future. For example, many women I interviewed emphasized the need to adapt to changes in the community in order to survive: "We have to adapt or leave. So we look for other opportunities, a shoe store, bakery, ice-cream shop, soda shop."

Multiple Projects and Investments

Adela's restaurant depended on several of the strategies I observed in the community. She, like many other women, had a positive attitude toward work, almost tirelessly continuing to build her business. She also drew on family connections to create a cooperative work environment, relied on external networks to secure resources and funding, and had a history of work that prepared her, in terms of skills and experience, for running her own restaurant. Many other women had a history of running small businesses that they opened with their parents or as teenagers. Several worked for the boutique hotel in the community until it closed. Like Adela's mother, they received bonuses when the hotel closed, which many invested in their own businesses. Developing Adela's restaurant meant building on these previous experiences, her variety of work experiences, and investing some of the money from them into the new endeavor.

Other women had a wider range of work experiences, some of which they continued to pursue. Maria's tortillas were only one reason people came to visit her. She and her daughters had sewn for years, making school uniforms, party dresses, and other outfits for those in the community. Before electricity, they invested in a generator to run the sewing machines. But before that, they attached modern sewing machines to the old sewing machine pedal stands. Maria also did laundry, embroidered, and helped take care of the children in the area. Clearly a very busy woman, she did not rely on any one business. Like the Hijas, the combination of different efforts allowed her to invest in generators, washing machines, and kitchen upgrades that supported not only her business but also her domestic needs.

Being based in household activities, the women's work drew on previous, usually gendered, activities and skills like cooking, sewing, and laundry. But I would argue that the household-based activities also encouraged easy movement between these, allowing the women to go from one activity to another without having to travel somewhere else or reconfigure the workspace, similar to how Trouillot (1992) discusses how movement works with multiple livelihoods in the Caribbean.

The ability to create a set of activities and skills helped the women hedge against fluctuations in demand and supplies, allowing them to remain busy.

Yet these activities also created the opportunity to invest earnings from one activity into future plans, building restaurants and other businesses slowly and incrementally. In some cases, earlier activities allowed the women to create connections to those beyond the community, some of which could provide resources or other support for their efforts.

External Support through Relationships or Embeddedness

Just as work in fisheries and tourism involved nonlocal, even global, connections, the women's businesses also often reached out beyond the boundaries of the community for resources and help. The women's cooperative, for example, worked closely with the LBNP (an MPA) and a U.S. resident biologist to develop aquaculture and also worked with another U.S. citizen to develop their tropical fish exporting business. Other organizations also supported their efforts over time, including Mexican-based NGOs and scientific organizations, as well as their eventual buyers in Los Angeles (see Peterson 2014b for more detail).

Other women found some support in NGOs that provided courses, such as for sewing, painting, or other skills, and one learned nail art through a DVD she ordered. For a while, the Loreto MPA also supported a few women's efforts to open restaurants or bread businesses as part of their economic development work, to some extent reframing their relationships with them as reciprocal obligations (Peterson 2014b; see also Hirsch 2020). Most women had few professional supports from outside of Playa Tranquila, and the Hijas del Mar were unusual in their ability to get attention and resources from national and international organizations. But the connections to tourists were important for many, as well as family relationships that bridged geographical distances.

Before joining a cooperative, one of the members worked for a U.S. couple, earning money she would invest in the cooperative and using their freezer to make Popsicles before the rest of the community had electricity. Several other community members worked in housekeeping for longer-term visitors or permanent residents, while others provided services like food or trash pickup for short-term visitors. A few community members were able to migrate to the United States for periods of time to continue work with those they met through tourism in the community.

FIGURE 10 An embroidered tortilla wrap from Playa Tranquila.

The cooperative was able to mobilize these connections to access resources and new skills, beyond what others usually accomplished. For example, I heard several times from the MPA staff that a fisherman had come by to ask them for help in getting electricity in Playa Tranquila. This request went unfulfilled, while the women's cooperative was able to access grants, equipment, and advice from the same office. The women probably received a bit more attention because a women's cooperative was relatively rare and therefore noteworthy at the time, but they also worked very hard to coordinate and create these networks.

Creating connections to resources did require balancing gender norms with the novelty of women starting businesses, but many of the women also worked to create these connections and then to use them to get what they needed. The strategy of what several women called "pushiness" was useful, if only up to the point where they violated expectations of appropriate behavior. However, more often than not, the women were able to use these networks to get what they need and to declare that their businesses were successful.

Success

Selling mangoes, bread, or clothing to neighbors may seem entrepreneurial and income focused, except that this process was deeply social, and often buyers were extended family members. Similarly, washing clothes might also seem like a profitable small business, but it was similarly steeped in social connections and values of hard work and family. The income earned from selling mangoes joined that from innumerable Popsicles, tamales, and other goods to create an international tropical fish exporting project, which in turn contributed very little to the incomes of the owners. These and other women used different microenterprises to build new business and opportunities, continuing cycles of investment and innovation that indicated success. In part, this success came from the deeply social aspects of the business, including meeting the needs of family and friends in the community, keeping themselves occupied, and enriching the local social networks. For others outside of the community, success reflected other values, including environmental sustainability and women's advancement. Profit is only one aspect of an ethical economy and often not the most important. While the women themselves lacked any substantial income from the cooperative project, they had managed to create an international business from nothing and to provide income for many of their family and friends in the community. Success in this project is not defined by personal profit but by the ability to create new opportunities in the community.

When I visited in 2023, I saw that success was also about being able to continue despite challenges, even if it meant pausing during global pandemics. The women's cooperative was just starting to plan for activities again after a hiatus for COVID-19, though many of the members and others had continued to do some work on their own around baking, sewing, or other services.

Conclusions

Usually translated as "getting ahead," *salir adelante* is used by many in the community to explain their longer-term goals for their business or household. I find that although there is some interest in improving their lives through education or home improvement, the overall tenor of the discussions surrounding *salir adelante* is one of doing OK rather than excelling or leaving others behind. Examining the values of livelihoods and household management reveals that values of social interaction, support, and morality dominate the decisions of individuals and households to *salir adelante.*

This chapter has focused on women and their microenterprises and how these businesses are valued beyond economic profits. Managing multiple livelihoods, the women navigate gender expectations and roles by attaching a variety of values to their work, highlighting the importance of the work for their families and selves, and providing tangible value to the community through goods, services, and employment opportunities. While as entrepreneurs, the women might be focused on self-management (Okura-Gagné 2020; Pfeilstetter, 2021), their moral economies are more geared toward family and community rather than individual profits (Shever 2008; Cruz-Torres 2023; Beresford 2020). Valuing and using family are not a contradiction here because of this. However, ideas around neoliberal entrepreneurship, like gig economies, also blur the boundaries between productive and nonproductive time, home and work spaces, and public and private spaces, as we see here, but can introduce precarities as well (Stead 2021).

Clearly, the women in Playa Tranquila are becoming a certain type of entrepreneur but one that seems to evade the neoliberal economic models of entrepreneurship. In this way, perhaps new identities, subjectivities, and forms of agency are emerging from the relationships between gender, markets, and family (see also Cruz-Torres 2023; Radel 2012), as the next chapter continues to explore.

CHAPTER 4

BEING GOOD CHILDREN OF THE SEA

The Loreto Bay National Marine Park (later, the Loreto Bay National Park) was created by Mexican presidential decree on July 17, 1996. The creation was the result of years of letters, meetings, and speeches about the need for the MPA by a group of Loretano environmentalists, and President Ernesto Zedillo Ponce de León's response to their petition was clearly a victory for those who had campaigned for the MPA. The story of this campaign has become legend in Loreto, complete with the ambiguities, inconsistencies, and hero worship that characterize most local legends. These stories and their differences are key for understanding the place the new MPA was to have in the communities of Loreto.

There were as many versions of the story of the MPA's creation (or reasons for supporting the MPA) as there were people to tell them, though with some important throughlines. Usually, the stories followed the lines of different interest groups: environmentalists told one version, while tourism entrepreneurs voiced another, and the fishers articulated something very different from either of these.[1] However, the

---

1. The major players in MPA discussions were local residents, including Loreto-area fishers, tourism entrepreneurs, and environmentalists, alongside the MPA and other government agency staff. Some environmentalists and scientists were from the United States and other Mexican states.

reasons for supporting the MPA varied widely within these groups as well, such as when individuals' identities as fisher, tourism entrepreneur, and environmentalist overlapped or when fishers disagreed about the best way to support fishing and the environment. Unsurprisingly, the different justifications for the MPA and the corresponding interests had a continuing impact on the functioning of the MPA, as we'll see in the next chapter.

Three main threats dominated stories about resource use and the MPA: nonlocal industrial trawlers, some kinds of artisanal fishing, and non-Loreto-area fishers.[2]

Trawlers

Ann and Don O'Neil were married retirees from the United States who lived in Loreto together for many years. They loved living in the area so much that they researched and wrote a book about Loreto, their last home together. Ann became involved with creating the MPA through her work with a local NGO and committee about the bay starting in the 1980s. In their 2001 book, the O'Neils describe why they worked to protect the Loreto environment:

> When we first came to Loreto in 1973, the fish were so plentiful that no one imagined that this could ever change. Yellowtail swarmed and boiled so close to shore we could sometimes catch them from the beach in front of our house. . . . But all night long we could hear the chugging motors of shrimp boats passing back and forth between our beach and Carmen Island. Occasionally, the lights of a Japanese factory ship would light up the sky beyond the peaks of Carmen Island. Tuna boats came in with helicopters and nets to spot and round up huge schools of tuna and other fish. Gradually, the fish were no longer plentiful. (O'Neil and O'Neil 2001, 263–64)

---

2. Trawlers were largely viewed as external to Loreto, though this was complicated as several workers on trawlers were from Loreto.

Like many other residents of Loreto, they saw the industrial fishing as detrimental to the area and to their own lives.[3] Ann was the only non-Mexican in the Loreto conservation group, which included several Mexicans who had worked in government, natural resource extraction, tourism, science, and NGOs. They met once a week to plan the effort, which led to the letter to the Mexican president Zedillo requesting the MPA.

Luis, who owned a sportfishing business and collaborated with Ann to request the MPA, explained its creation:

> We pressured [President Zedillo] directly and I think we finally just bored him. We wrote a letter through the local government, the municipality, every week for six months. And because the president had a personal interest in the gulf, because he enjoys diving, and the people he had working in the Department of Fisheries and whatnot were truly in love with the gulf, had done thesis work on the gulf, we finally convinced all the authorities to declare this a national protected area or a national park, whereas many, many people had tried to do that in the past with no success. . . . We had hoped for a larger area, but we had to settle for a measly 500,000 acres [laughter]. (Interview, January 2002, in English)

Concern about the large trawlers' effects on the local marine life was one of few issues that united different groups behind creating the MPA. Many creation stories suggest that the MPA was intended to halt the shrimp trawlers from fishing in the area near Loreto, either because they were a nuisance due to noise or were destroying the environment, including practices that "killed all the species, mainly the little animals," as one fisherman explained.

"Taxi drivers, housewives, and many other residents" all shared these concerns, according to an environmentalist. The trawlers were also easily expelled from the area just through the act of designating the LBNP since trawlers cannot work in these areas under Mexican law.

---

3. Industrial fishing refers here to trawlers and other massive boats in the area. This can also be connected to a history of foreign exploitation of fishing areas by Japanese, Korean, and other foreign interests (described in chapter 1).

Nets, Spears, and Purse Seines

One day early in my research, I met with a sportfishing business owner with a very successful business in Loreto and many ideas about how to improve the area. Luis gave me an overview of the area, recounting that around thirty years ago, people started to use nets on the bay. In the seven miles between Loreto and Isla Coronado, he remembered counting twenty-five one-mile-long nets and wondered how people thought fish would get through. In this time, he estimated that there has been a 70 percent decrease in "natural resources," including fish, clams, scallop, and lobster: "overexploitation of these by people from Loreto and other places has led to lower population levels." He kept coming back to the refrain of using resources wisely, "rather than overstuffing oneself on tacos, one has to find a balance." His solution was "no nets, no exceptions."

The connection between equipment and overfishing was made multiple times by different tourism entrepreneurs, NGO representatives, and environmentalists. Luis also claimed that local artisanal fishers were at fault,

> And then on the opposite end—people who just don't care—fishermen kill everything they can. Unfortunate. They complain all day about things getting smaller, and less but won't admit that it's their obstinance that's causing the problem. [They] carry a gun in the boat and kill sea lions. (Interview, 2002, in English)

These ideas were echoed by other environmentalists and those working in tourism. Both groups focused on the activities of the local artisanal fishers, whom they felt were not going to change their practices. For example, although he thought that local people were becoming more educated about the marine resources and their depletion, Luis argued that "old fishers [are] dead set in their ways." He continued,

> The level of education, the fact that more information is not readily available to them, causes them to continue in the traditional part of fisheries or hunting instead of—they fall back on tradition or the only thing they have to do for subsistence. . . . It's hard to explain to some of them the reasons why [not to fish], the dos and don'ts.

Another wanted "to teach [fishers] how to use the resource respectfully, in a sensible way. . . . We have plans to educate the women, to teach them what they lack, including information about MPA regulations and its importance." Education was viewed as the solution to resource use issues, particularly when the problem was seen as ignorance and greed. Other environmentalists claimed that fishers showed neither the initiative to change nor guilt over their illegal overuse of resources, nor even the kind of unity needed to address the depletion: "They choose to overfish."

Almost every sportfishing business owner and environmentalist I interviewed from 2001 to 2003 mentioned the problem of the artisanal fishing nets, which they blamed for environmental degradation through overfishing. While long stretches of nets were a primary concern for many who supported the MPA, including sportfishers and environmentalists, other threats included equipment like spears, pistols, purse seine nets or nets with smaller-gauge holes, and fishing without a permit; the MPA became a way to eliminate these "unhealthy" fishing practices. Another sportfishing owner and environmentalist described artisanal fishing nets as "chiquitos," referring to the small holes in which smaller and younger fish become trapped, and blamed them for the disappearance of sharks in the area.

Spearfishing was a focus of regulation while I was there from 2001 to 2003. The MPA director at the time, who had been a fisherman in other parts of BCS before earning a degree in biology, discussed the development of the MPA as a multistage approach that started with removing the large shrimp trawlers and finalizing the management plan, and continued with removing the illegal artisanal spearfishing. Although recreational sportfishers could legally spearfish, many in tourism criticized the illegal artisanal spearfishing for its "barbaric" means of killing fish while they slept, which ensures a larger take. In addition, artisanal fishers who did not use spears or pistols to fish criticized those who did.

In Playa Tranquila, don Antonio fished with lines and without a permit but still considered himself an environmentalist who supported the MPA as a way to limit fishing with small gauge nets, spears, or purse nets, and to protect species. However, unusual among fishers and others, don Antonio also criticized his own use of the resource, lamenting the damage he had done as a fisherman over the decades with nets. Other fishers also saw nets as an issue, and several other local fishing communities prided themselves on using lines rather than nets as a more environmentally sustainable practice. Overall, fishers blamed other kinds of artisanal fishing, industrial trawlers, and nonlocal fishers for resource depletion. Although the fishers were glad to see the trawlers restricted, they also saw the potential effects of an MPA on their own livelihoods, particularly as the focus of MPA management shifted to their own uses of nets, spears, and guns.

External Nonlocal Fishing

Many fishers believed that the sportfishers and tourism entrepreneurs initiated the process of MPA formation to completely halt the commercial fishing in the area, including both the industrial boats everyone saw as a problem and the small artisanal fishing that locals depended on for their livelihoods. In one instance, one fisherman lamented that "they [the tourism interests] want us to disappear." The two groups competed for the same species of fish, and local artisanal fishers claimed the sportfishing enterprises blamed them for smaller catches and therefore declining business:

> From the growth of the two [tourism and artisanal fishing] industries, the idea to protect the species was born, concurrent with the idea that artisanal fishing was exploiting the fish. Tourism, as a source of income, was the main impetus, later the shrimp industry was named at fault. The park became the legal way to protect species. The agreement coincided with a Mexican promise to care for its resources, and the MPA was born. The fishers did not ask for this, and only later found out about the decree. (Interview with fisherman, August 2002)

Many fishers were unaware of the MPA until 1999, when they received a copy of the MPA's second management plan. Some refused to sign the plan without reviewing it, believing the document would have dire consequences for their livelihoods. Because there were long-standing conflicts between artisanal fishing and sportfishing over the species and areas that both fished, it was easy for the local artisanal fishers to see malicious intent in sportfishing's support of the MPA.

Once the artisanal fishers became aware of the MPA, they tried to help shape its management and activities. Because Mexican fishing law does not restrict permits to certain areas of Mexican coastline or fishing grounds, many fishers fish in nonlocal areas. The decline in fish throughout the Gulf of California has exacerbated this problem, as fishers who have exhausted local fishing in one area then move on to richer fishing grounds. Local fishers in the Loreto area were therefore very interested in limiting access to local fishing areas, which they felt were being destroyed by outsiders (see also Armenta-Cisneros et al. 2021). In creating an MPA, they saw the potential for local permits to allow only Loretanos to fish Loreto waters.

Several fishing community leaders mentioned the control that permit holders, often from outside of Playa Tranquila, have over prices and costs, sometimes describing them as a "mafia" that has encouraged poaching and centralized the profits. Fishers thus also wanted to reduce or eliminate the power of the permit holders who now run much of the local fishery. Organized by one of their own, a group of fishers proposed to protect certain areas at certain times (April to July) and to eliminate fishing for jurel (yellowtail) near one of the islands while scientists completed a study of the population and an assessment of the potential resource use there. But when they met with authorities to discuss changes to the plan, their proposed modifications were rejected time after time, according to one fisherman. Many critiqued the rules that affected artisanal fishing and the lack of legal permits for fishers: "The park won't let us work, and there are fewer permits," according to one spearfisherman. While some fishers never admitted to supporting the MPA in any way, many came to recognize benefits of the MPA for them, particularly the promise of local control of resources.

Planning Processes: Exclusion by Design

The MPA thus arose from diverse and contradictory motives. For almost all involved, the MPA was expected to solve the problems caused by the decline of local resources and the resulting uncertainties over livelihoods. How people understood the reasons for the decline reflects long histories among different groups, in-group divisions, and shifting alliances. The perception of what and who was responsible for local resource decline and uncertainties played a large role in decisions made about the MPA's purpose and activities in terms of what behaviors should be controlled. Control was a central concern of those involved with the planning process for the MPA—and underlying this was blame laid on certain groups whose behaviors they sought to control. And unfortunately, decades of conflicts over resources were also linked to these ideas about blame and control. Ultimately, the MPA became a strategy for not just creating sustainable use but for controlling those whose uses were deemed detrimental to the long-term sustainability of the MPA.

All of the MPA creation myths focused on restricting or excluding some kinds of users or behaviors, like trawlers, outsiders, nets, or spears. Many of those who talked about excluding others were also identified as users to exclude by other individuals or kinds of resource users; thus, another important kind of narrative about the MPA creation involved explaining how and why one's own uses of the MPA were supposed to be exempt from regulations. For artisanal fishers, the MPA is another attempt to exclude, extricate, and exterminate artisanal fishers and their families who should have a right to fish in its waters due to their long-term residency in the area. Sportfishers also felt excluded by the scientists and environmentalists who wanted to limit their use of the resources and felt they should be exempt from the MPA's policies since they brought important economic resources to the region and saw their consumption of fish as more sustainable than that of local fishers.

The narratives of blame and control were only the beginning of an institution that soon constructed its own contradictory relationships to local histories, conflicts, and alliances, complicating the situation even more. As we see below, the different perceptions of the motives for the MPA had serious ramifications for how the MPA was conceptualized and functioned.

Why an MPA Became the Solution

MPAs, as well as other kinds of protected areas, have become a standard way to address resource decline or the potential for resource decline as they provide a way to gain control over marine areas and to restrict access to marine resources. As we see in the accounts of the Loreto area, blame for resource decline has led to efforts to exclude certain users, including trawlers, certain artisanal fishing equipment, and non-Loretano fishers. At the root of resource overuse, under Hardin's tragedy of the commons model, is individual greed. And in this model, greed was a "choice" since local fishers "choose to overfish" or don't take "responsibility" for the local environment; and similarly, those from other states "look to maximize their earnings in as little time as possible," according to one LBNP management plan that applies key ideas from Hardin (CONANP 2000, 40). The references to "responsibility" and general care for resources echo neoliberal ideas around entrepreneurship, which can further exclude users through blame and regulating against what are understood to be irresponsible or illogical uses of limited resources (see also Skidelsky 2020; Elyachar 2019; Viatori and Bombiella Medina 2019). By the logic of tragedy of the commons model, those who do not behave rationally are ultimately to blame for their own exclusions (Martínez-Reyes 2016).

These ideas about exclusion draw on Hardin's tragedy of the commons and are also connected to the core set of individualistic assumptions underlying neoliberal economics (Mansfield 2004). The focus is on individuals driven by self-interest to exploit natural resources, and the strategies to counter this are government or private control, restrictions, fines, and prosecution, which have become a dominant approach for conservation efforts like MPAs (Brondo and Bown 2011; Carrier 2001; Mansfield 2007; West, Igoe, and Brockington 2006). For example, Mexican law prohibits the capture of certain species, and the LBNP forbids certain kinds of fishing in certain areas. In MPAs like the LBNP, breaking laws or marine park regulations could lead to fines, equipment confiscation, or even jail. Policing (*vigilancia*) was strongly supported by environmentalists and those in the tourism sector, who expected that restrictions would control inevitable resource overuse by artisanal or outside fishers and improve environmental quality in the area. One environmentalist argued that policing was the key for controlling this problem of overfishing: "For the MPA to function, it needs policing. . . . Vigilance of the park is like having the police on the streets to prevent robberies; if there are no police, then there will be crimes" (interview, Loreto-area environmentalist, April 2002).

However, there are several assumptions in Hardin's tragedy of the commons that aren't quite met in Loreto or other places. As we saw in chapter 1, the artisanal fishers are not motivated by greed but by a need to take care of their families. They were not maximizing profits but trying to "get by" and to care for their communities and environments. The challenge, as the fishers described it, was to meet their needs in a context that undervalued their labor and product, particularly given the costs of gasoline and other equipment needed to fish. Individual greed was not capturing the complex economic, political, and social interactions that led to poorly paid fishers. The MPA efforts neglected the variety of values associated with the marine area as well as the larger context of marine resource use, as described in earlier chapters, like the value of work, family, community, relationships, and environment (see also Stern 2010; Tallis et al. 2008; Song, Chuenpagdee, and Jentoft 2013). The efforts also neglected the rich knowledge that fishers and their families had about the local marine area. A more democratized means of knowledge sharing and management processes could be accomplished with greater recognition of the value of fishers' knowledge (García-Quijano and Valdes Pizzini 2015). Moving the focus away from individual greed and the fishers as uneducated changes the dynamic of the model of the commons, shifting our focus to the embeddedness of the resources in webs of local and global interactions (see also Ostrom 1990) and to the social contexts where decisions about resources are made (Uphoff and Langholz 1998; Agrawal 2001).

In contrast to Hardin, Elinor Ostrom and others have shown that government control or other forms of privatization are not the only solution and emphasize that communities can and do develop enforceable rules to limit use and to exclude certain uses or users (Ostrom 1990; Vollan and Ostrom 2010; Cox, Arnold, and Villamayor Tomás 2010; Acheson 1988), which has also led to a focus on community participation in planning and management (Dietz, Ostrom, and Stern 2003), as in Loreto.

The Loreto MPA was born from assumptions embedded in the narratives above that emphasize blame for resource degradation and that then promote restricting individual access as a solution. While the Loreto case has begun to show the limitations of individual greed as a motivation, the assumptions of blame and restriction have important implications for how the MPA was designed and managed, even as more users, including the fishers, became involved in what turned into a more participatory process of planning. But as we see, disagreements about who was to

Creating a Management Plan: 1998–2001

The presidential decree of the MPA in 1996 delimited the area of the LBNP (see map 1 in the introduction) and suggested that a future management plan address conservation and restoration of resources, restrictions on construction and use of structures, limitations on artisanal and sportfishing activities, and "only will permit activities related to the perseveration of aquatic ecosystems and their elements . . . approved by competent authorities" (CONANP 1996, 3; my translation). The process of planning for the MPA occurred in several stages after the decree, beginning with the hiring of a park director and his staff (see table 1). The development of each of these three management plans differed widely and from 1998 to 2003 became more inclusive and participatory over time as the park director and his staff learned more about local stakeholders and their needs and concerns. The seemingly repetitive process of management planning improved on itself during this period, though unfortunately, the 2019 version did not appear participatory to many.

Yet the process of creating the management plans also reveals the values and ideas about the marine area, its users, and their role in degrading the area's natural resources. This happens, as I show below, in assumptions about who and what should be controlled and why, and who should be involved in making decisions about that control. As we saw above, ideas about the tragedy of the commons were important for understanding why resources were being depleted, and ideas about participatory processes were beginning to become important for protected area management in general. How these two sets of ideas interacted in Loreto also reveals some of the assumptions about decision-making. These values, assumptions, and models matter as they become inscribed, implicitly or explicitly, into planning decisions and activities, including participatory processes of planning themselves, as we see below and in the next chapter.

TABLE 2 Timeline of Loreto Bay National Park

Date	Event
1980s	Local environmentalists and others begin thinking about ways to protect local resources
1992	Loreto becomes a municipality
1995	Local environmental NGO founded
1996	July: Parque Nacional Bahia de Loreto decreed
	September: Director of park arrives
1997	Efforts to organize fishers about park issues
1998	The Nature Conservancy becomes involved
	Universidad Autónoma de Baja California Sur management plan published and rejected
1999	MPA staff begins second management plan draft
2000	Second plan is sent to Mexico City and published
2001	July and October meetings about third plan
2003	January publication of third plan
2019	April publication of fourth plan

• • •

The management planning process began in 1998 with a plan solicited from biologists at a local state university, la Universidad Autónoma de Baja California Sur. Carlos, one of the MPA staff members, told me that the three large volumes of the plan were "nice and detailed, as a scientific document. But it lacked something. It had a scientific focus but was a document without the consensus of the community" (interview, 2002).

Almost everyone involved with creating the MPA was opposed to this management plan because it prohibited all uses of the area, including tourism and boating. Carlos suggested that the management plan just didn't incorporate the context of the MPA and the local needs. "We realized it was unworkable," he conceded, "and decided to start over. That's when we started holding meetings with everyone." Carlos and other staff members suggested that the primary problem was with the map of specific use zones for the park, which restricted all uses in a few areas, causing everyone to unite against the plan. Initial outcries over the 1998 plan thus led to a more participatory planning process that included workshops with tourism owners, fishers, and others. Carlos admitted, "The first meeting with the fishers was very difficult, as they thought the park shared the blame for the plan. The fishers did not differentiate between the park and the university that had written the plan."

Following this first plan, the hope in Loreto was that a more participatory process of MPA planning would yield a more acceptable and workable management plan. Throughout 1999, the MPA staff met with different people and groups: "Daily, the employees would talk with people, asking them what they needed and wanted. In addition, we talked with scientists about special sites which should be protected," according to one employee. Over six months of informal meetings with different groups, the MPA staff asked what they wanted in the MPA and its management plan and believed they were able to build trust through these meetings.

The MPA staff worked hard to present themselves as allies to the fishers. Some of the staff, including the director, had been fishers before receiving degrees in biology and realized that this perspective was valuable in talking with artisanal fishers. They tried to approach the fishers as equals, not as employees of the government or NGOs, highlighting common personal backgrounds as fishermen of the same gulf or as Baja Californianos (depending on the person). During presentations about the MPA, the staff also worked to provide advice to fishers, mainly about how to form the cooperatives which would then allow fishers to secure fishing permits when they were available again. The staff wanted the fishers to understand why cooperatives (or permits) were necessary after so many years of fishing without these. The MPA staff worked to cultivate a sense of empathy and friendship with the fishers by using slang, local accents, and calling the fishers *compa* as a way of drawing on the close relationships that formal *compadrazgo* ties entail.

The MPA staff's willingness to help the fishers form cooperatives, their support for local Loreto-specific fishing permits, and their general willingness to meet repeatedly with fishers during the management plan discussions led many in the fishing communities to see the value of the MPA. In addition, the MPA staff worked with several groups in the communities to develop economic alternatives to fishing, like aquaculture or tropical fish export businesses, such as the one the Hijas del Mar started. This was a response to the fishers coming to the MPA office for help with everything from getting electricity to using the phone, and also to the director's interest in providing some kind of "reparations" for regulating fishing in the area, for "taking away their resources." The staff members also talked about the value of alternatives to fishing as a way to lessen the impact of fishing on the environment through lower-resource-intensive uses.

After talking with many of those affected by the MPA, the park staff wrote a new management plan. While more people were satisfied with this version, a series of three workshops was planned for the summer of 2001 to get final feedback on the plan. The MPA management planning exercises attempted to include a variety of local voices through the many discussions and workshops with artisanal and sportfishers and the large group meetings in 2001. I attended the second of these, held in July 2001, as I'd coincidentally managed to plan a visit to the area at that time to assess it as a potential field site for my dissertation work.

• • •

I entered the large meeting room at Loreto's Hotel La Pinta in July 2001 unsure of what would happen—I had not met anyone besides the one staff member, Carlos, and this was my crash course in the issues surrounding the MPA and Loreto more generally. Carlos introduced me to a few people and helped me differentiate fishers from tourism owners and environmentalists. At the tables spread around the room, I could see one central table of fishers, from a family I would get to know well later on, flipping through the 2001 MPA plan. Another older fisherman stood against the wall, nodding at me when introduced but otherwise uninvolved in the hubbub. Other tables were filled with tourism entrepreneurs I would later interview, including several who were also environmentalists, as well as government representatives from agencies like Conapesca, Profepa, and the municipal government.[4] There were few artisanal fishers from the area, and no fishers from other places in Mexico.

---

4. La Comisión Nacional de Acuacultura y Pesca (Conapesca) is the National Aquaculture and Fisheries Commission of Mexico (created in 2001; previously referred to as Pesca; Celaya Tentori and Almaraz Alvarado 2018) and La Procuraduría Federal de Protección al Ambiente (Profepa) is Mexico's Federal Attorney General's Office for Environmental Protection.

The focus of the planning meeting, and the plan in general, was the rules and regulations for using the waters and islands within the MPA. The meetings tried to establish allowable and unallowable uses of the waters, with a primary emphasis on artisanal fishing. Those who attended had to receive an invitation and hopefully the current management plan draft, limiting involvement in the process to those recognized by the MPA staff as stakeholders in the process. The discussion at the meeting focused on regulating artisanal fishing and how to exclude those that are most blamed for the declining marine environment (see Peterson 2011 for more detail).

The meeting was well-attended by NGOs, sportfishers, biologists, government representatives, and a few artisanal fishers. All told, about seventy-five people attended each day. Conducted by the MPA and the Secretariat of Environment and Natural Resources (SEMARNAT, formerly SEMARNAP), the meetings included an introduction to the MPA by the MPA staff, presentations by each group on their management recommendations, and discussions of these recommendations.

• • •

The majority of the meeting involved an overhead projector showing pages from the 2001 plan, and attendees would suggest certain changes to the specific rules on the page. Over several hours, many changes were added to the pages—slashed-out lines and scribbled-in words cluttered once pristine pages. At one point, the focus shifted to large, black-lined maps displayed on the wall, which became overlaid with blue, red, and green lines that showed what activities were allowed around islands and sea mounds (see figure 11). Another important resource for the participants was a large, table-size map of the MPA area, which participants used to delineate recommended protected and restricted areas.

It became clear to me throughout the meeting that the fishers had not read the plan ahead of time; I would later learn that they did not receive a copy in advance like the other groups. In addition, the language of the plan tended toward technical or scientific writing, which was difficult to parse for fishers who had received only an elementary school education. However, this was only one way that the fishers and their perspectives were excluded from the planning process. The meetings often happened at times when they would be fishing, and attendance at the meetings

FIGURE 11 Workshop map in use while drafting the management plan, July 2001.

required both the ability to go without income for a day and transportation into town. Many fishers were also unaware that the meeting was taking place at all. In addition, during the meeting, several topics important to the fishers were dismissed as "tangential" to the main business, including concerns about government corruption.

While the goal was to have a participatory planning process, these kinds of limitations meant that some participants were not as able to contribute to the process as others (for more detail, see Peterson 2011; see also Young 2001). As we see in Loreto, there are challenges to incorporating local participants, like the artisanal fishers, into MPA planning processes. Under these conditions, the ideals of participatory planning were difficult or perhaps impossible to meet. The Loreto case even suggests that these processes can mask inequalities and biases under a veneer of open governance. Opening up the planning processes did little to counter the dominating discourses of blame and exclusion, particularly given the initial motive of limiting artisanal fishing. In addition, it became easy for those in charge to ignore the limitations facing fishers who wanted to participate, in terms of cost, literacy, and even access to the plan ahead of time. All of this meant that a presumably open process began with its own exclusions that were reinforced over time.

After recommendations were made, the MPA staff distributed a printed list of them, and also projected the list onto the wall. Discussions were heated at points, and several recommendations were altered significantly. After two days of meetings, only half of the recommendations had been discussed, but a meeting for the next week was scheduled. Interestingly, no one was sure how many of these changes would be included in the final plan; the version under discussion at this meeting had been already accepted by the Mexican government, and several people on the MPA staff indicated that only small changes would be made to the official management plan. Yet ignoring the sweeping changes suggested by almost every group (with the exception of the scientists who only suggested changes in wording), including MPA boundaries and the use of illegal nets, could potentially alienate the MPA from the local resource users. In addition, involving local users through participatory processes still failed to capture local use patterns and resource management strategies and associated values because the planning processes primarily focused on restrictions for individual users.

Interestingly, the meetings also revealed a large amount of confusion about the MPA and its purpose, and many people saw the MPA as a way to ensure their control over resources rather than as a reserve to conserve them. Tellingly, two days before the meetings, the MPA threw a poorly attended fifth-anniversary party for itself.

After the meetings ended, the unedited and contradictory recommendations were sent to Mexico City, where SEMARNAT would use them to create a new management plan. I planned to be back in Loreto in the fall and hoped to see how the plan was introduced to the communities. However, it was to be another year and a half before the plan was finally published in January 2003 (CONANP 2003).

• • •

The involvement of fishers and other community members in the process of management planning was important to the MPA staff and given by the director of the MPA as an example of the progressiveness of the MPA. Community-based conservation or community-based natural resource management developed in response to the failure of highly centralized conservation projects and is based on the central premises of the coexistence of nature and humans and identifying the locus of action, rights, responsibilities, and capabilities within communities (Western and Wright 1994). As a way to include local issues in conservation projects, community-based efforts have been heralded as the best approach to resolving differences between the needs of local individuals and other demands on natural resources (Peterson et al. 2010; Western, Wright, and Strum 1994), and many critiques of protected areas focus on the lack of involvement of local people in their design and management (Walley 2004; Simonian 1995; Brosius, Tsing, and Zerner 2005; Pellowe and Leslie 2021).

Yet community participation, as we see above, is not so straightforward as just extending an invitation to attend a meeting. Research indicates that participants often contest the meanings of important terms, including definitions of community, conservation, ethical land use, tradition, and participation (Peterson 1997; West 2006, 2016; Viatori and Bombiella Medina 2019), which can then lead to conflicts or misunderstandings (Cleaver 1999; Cooke and Kothari 2001; Peterson et al. 2010). Problems for conservation efforts can arise from superficial treatment of community in terms of structure and heterogeneity, needs, and perspectives, leading to conflicts with cultural conceptions of land use and power relations in a region (Kaus 1992; Haenn 2005; Little 1994). These efforts must also overcome problems of trust and poor communication endemic to conservation efforts (Strum 1994; Peterson 1997; Haenn 2005; Weisgrau 1997; Dawson et al. 2021). However, inclusion requires more than a seat at the table since barriers to participation include things like scheduling, access to materials, language, and opportunities to contribute in a meaningful way. Parkins and Mitchell (2005) describe a typology of exclusions, including internal exclusions around culture, language, and norms of presentation such as the format of knowledge sharing like slideshows (see also García-Quijano and Valdes Pizzini 2015), and procedural exclusions like access to information and how ideas were documented, discussed, or excluded from discussion, as also happened in the meeting above.

In addition, Kaus (1992) suggests that conservationists have often falsely focused on internal challenges rather than social externalities, including land use patterns, regional or global economic relationships, and political representation, including existing relationships between the state and individuals (Ferguson 1994). As we see above, there is a lack of awareness of the economic and social contexts that constrain fishers that can prevent them from attending or engaging in discussions (see also Peterson 2010). Corbera et al. (2011) emphasize that lack of tenure over resources is the biggest obstacle to successful environmental programs, and other studies focus on this as well (Young 2001), though power differentials play an important role in exclusions (Apostolopoulou et al. 2021). In addition, many protected areas in Mexico and other areas of the world are essentially "paper parks" that have little reality beyond their official decrees because they lack funding, clear goals, and local involvement and do little to protect the resources of the area (Simonian 1995; Beddington, Agnew, and Park 2007; Talavera Martínez and Massieu Trigo 2021; Maxwell et al. 2020; Réyez 2016). The illusion of participation in this process unfortunately sets the stage for the next few years or even decades, as "participants" continue to feel excluded and marginalized, even despite efforts by the MPA staff to work with them.

· · ·

The management plans after 2001, including the 2003 and 2019 versions, remained largely unchanged from the 2000 version in part because of a lack of impact of the participatory processes on the official regulations. While the process did open up discussions among different groups and allowed for some collaboration, the changes were negligible (see Peterson 2015 for a more complete analysis of the 2003 plan). Media around the development and publication of the 2019 plan suggests that it developed from the 2003 discussions as well as some additional conversations in 2009 that led to a consensus (Eco Alianza de Loreto 2019). Government notices suggest that the new plan was needed to address "new socioeconomic realities of the area" (*fue necesaria de acuerdo a las nuevas realidades socioeconómicas de la zona*) (CONANP 2019).

What remained the same was that the bulk of the regulations concerned artisanal fishing. Sportfishing and tourism were largely left unregulated by the new management plans, and they were asked primarily to inform their clients of the rules of the area. This was in contrast to the larger number of rules about equipment and catch numbers the plan had for artisanal fishing. The later 2019 plan introduced subzones that increased the restrictions on more areas of the MPA (108–6,219 hectares), as well as increased restrictions on the size and kind of motor vehicles allowed, with tourism and sportfishing only prohibited in some of the new subzones (CONANP 2019). In fact, in 2003, tourism uses of the park were praised as "low impact and economically beneficial to the area" (CONANP 2003, 12, 13, 19). Industrial fishing was also left out of the 2003 plan. As I argue elsewhere (Peterson 2015), the emphasis on artisanal fishing reflects a general trend in protected area management to target the behaviors of the poorer stakeholders (see, e.g., West, Igoe, and Brockington 2006), despite more recent work that suggests inequality matters more than poverty as a factor (Travers et al. 2019; Apostolopoulou et al. 2021; Kuymulu 2011; Maestre-Andrés, Calvet-Mir, and Apostolopoulou 2018), or at least urges us to consider a more complex view of poverty (Raycraft 2019; Dowie 2011). There is growing evidence that sustainability efforts like protected areas can increase poverty, as access to resources is further restricted or removed from those who most need them to survive (Travers 2019; Quadri-Barba, Sims, and Millard-Ball 2021; Ortega Santos 2021; Ángeles Villa and López Vergara, 2022), even in areas where the tourist industry is strong (Sims and Alix-Garcia 2017; Talavera Martínez and Massieu Trigo 2021). As a result, sustainability is experienced unevenly by people in places like Loreto.

Notably different from the 2003 plan, there was an absence in the 2019 plan about promoting local social development in communities (*desarrollo social de las comunidades*), though the focus on conservation and education remained central, leading to a focus on sustainable projects (*proyectos sustentables*) instead. Unlike the 2003 plan, there is no language in the 2019 plan about identifying new sustainable uses, nor involving users in developing sustainable uses (CONANP 2019).

Conversations in 2023 suggest that the new plan may not have much of an impact on the area. The MPA still lacks jurisdiction over the area, and fishing permits are still difficult to get. Fishers were accused of underreporting their catch, but fishers also felt no confidence in the government agencies involved in fisheries. Interestingly, new rules about tourism required fishers to use different boats for artisanal fishing and tourism outings, increasing barriers around tourism for fishers. The fishers were feeling very constrained by the regulations they had no role in creating. In other parts of the state, protected area rules have not helped the species they intend to protect, benefiting only the tourism sector (Gómez-Pech, García Silberman, and Barrasa García 2022).

A longtime environmentalist in Loreto remains pessimistic due to what he calls the social problem—an inherent conflict between fisheries and conservation that is impossible politically to resolve without impoverishing the fishers or destroying the environment. The next chapter examines this issue with a focus on how the MPA staff were able to manage the area.

Conclusion

The Loreto MPA developed in a context of conflicting desires and expectations of what it would do, including removing industrial trawlers, getting rid of problematic equipment, and increasing local control over marine resources. Yet each of these desires contained assumptions, values, and ideas that affected the planning processes and, as we see in the next chapter, activities of the MPA staff. At the heart of all of these motives was an idea of exclusion, and assumptions that valued resources were being degraded or destroyed by a specific set of actors associated with technologies like trawlers, spears, or nets. This idea of exclusion comes directly from Hardin's concept of the tragedy of the commons—tourism owners and conservationists were interested in getting control over the area away from the fishers and were using the tragedy of the commons model to justify exclusion.

While both artisanal and tourism fishing could be understood as active (over)exploitation of the local resources, only one seemed to be morally questionable, being labeled greedy or selfish. The solution to others' selfish behaviors was regulation, while tourism uses were to be protected because they were believed to be morally in line with conservation ethics despite a similar capacity for overfishing.

Yet the tragedy of the commons or common pool resources model does not have much of a role for culture or livelihood strategies in an economic, political, and social context rather than simple greed. The fishers we met in the earlier chapters viewed fishing as part of their heritage and social lives, as well as one strategy among many for handling uncertainties of climate and society (see also Acheson 1988; Salas et al. 2018; Kadfak 2019). Chapter 3 also showed the value of cooperation and multiple livelihoods for the community; while little infrastructure for communal regulation had developed in Playa Tranquila, Hardin's model neglects this possibility, which other cases show can be very effective for managing the commons (Ostrom 1990; Quintana and Basurto 2021).

In part, the fishers of Playa Tranquila found themselves ill-equipped to develop community-level management strategies because of the influence of outside fishers, markets, politicians, and global consumers on prices and demand reflected in their model, which explains why many of them looked to the park to help minimize this influence. Despite the importance of cooperation, managing resources requires that models consider more about how the surrounding context affects resource use (Agrawal 2001). While these values did not appear to be shared during the management planning process, the next chapter shows how the MPA staff began to appreciate these after the plan was submitted, having learned a lot about the fishers during the pre-meeting discussions with them. In addition, the tragedy of the commons literature and the subsequent community-based management strategies are still largely focused on individual actions and motivations (Peterson 2014a). The attention to individual behaviors comes from a reading of economics and profits that treats the individual as if they live to maximize profits, without regard for other values or goals. Even for many of those continuing to refine common pool resource management strategies, the idea that it is individual greed that causes problems and should be controlled through community norms seems to remain unquestioned. Ideas of agency that depend on selfishness or choice ignore a range of other potential ways for fishers to act on their surroundings and how context affects action, and lead to solutions that assume mitigating or curtailing individual actions will resolve resource overuse.

Aside from the tragedy of the commons, few other models for managing fisheries exist, and the challenge is to identify an alternative model for understanding the intersection of fisheries, economies, and markets, with attention to the larger contexts and other ways resources are valued. One potential alternative comes out of political ecology, which examines the extralocal influences on resource use and management, including international trade, national and international politics, and historical relations of wealth and inequalities. For Loreto, this approach would emphasize the influence of pricing, markets, inequalities, and politics on the fisheries, incorporating the issues raised above. One limitation of this approach is the difficulty of identifying specific causal relationships because of the overlapping influence of these factors. While overfishing is clearly more than just an individual behavior, the exact contributions of gas prices, market fish prices, and permitting practices to overfishing are unclear.

The growing literature on livelihoods points to another possibility of moving past primarily economic evaluations of livelihood success. As discussed in chapter 1, livelihoods frameworks stress the importance of noneconomic values in people's lives. In addition, the attention to the effects of specific contexts on well-being also brings in some of the concerns above about social and political factors (e.g., Coulthard, Johnson, and McGregor 2011; Agarwala et al. 2014). The attention to autonomy and agency also addresses issues of political participation in processes like the development of the MPA management plan (e.g., Peterson 2011). The challenges of indicators, measurement, and comparison remain, but these frameworks provide an opportunity to consider the variety of values, motives, and aspirations involved in making a living from fishing or other means.

This chapter reveals how challenging it was to agree on management ideas, as ideas about blame, control, and responsibility depended on perspectives and histories, which then affected planning processes in unexpected ways. The unsettled completion of the 2001 and even 2019 plans unfortunately set the stage for management challenges related to these ideas that limit the ability to implement regulations, as the next chapter explores.

CHAPTER 5

"QUE HACE EL PARQUE?"
What's the MPA Doing?

Don Javier was very proud of the letter he and some of his neighbors had written, and he showed it to me with a graveness that I had never seen before, his eyes bright under his white cowboy hat. "This," he said, "is our response. This will show them our reality and tell them what we know as fishermen." Used to the joking and smiles he almost always flashed once he got his bright new dentures, I was unsure how to respond except to ask what had happened. "Those others," he said, gesticulating toward the part of the community where another family lived, "wrote a letter denouncing Pedro." Don Javier did not need to use a last name because everyone knew Pedro, the local Conapesca official in charge of fisheries. He practically spit, "Pedro! Can you imagine? They said he is corrupt and not doing his job and that he should be fired. But he is the only one protecting us, who lets us fish. He is on our side. And this letter will go to the governor and tell him what a good job Pedro is doing." Don Javier had taken the letter house to house to get signatures, despite not being able to read the letter himself. He planned to hand it to the governor at an upcoming meeting and hoped that by pleading his case as an impoverished old fisherman, the governor would help him get his boat back from Profepa, which had seized it a few weeks before for illegal fishing.

Don Javier signed the letter because he knew that almost all fishers fished illegally in one way or another. They used photocopies of fishing permits, dived for clams, dumped trash from boats, spearfished, or engaged in other activities they felt were necessary to make a living but that were not necessarily legal. Everyone was outside of the law. Don Javier knew that to live, he had to bend the rules and that a good official looked the other way on these kinds of infractions and let them fish to feed their families. The other fishermen, the ones who wrote the letter, were not all full-time fishermen, he claimed, and several were working with the local MPA as observers who would inform the MPA of any infractions they saw. While don Javier blamed the other families in the community for writing the first letter, the truth was that some of his relatives and closest friends had written and signed it.

Don Antonio is another older fisherman and close friend of don Javier's who signed this first letter denouncing Pedro. Don Antonio believed that fishermen are "children of the sea" because the sea supports their lives, and this brings a responsibility to care for it. He felt there was a need for something like the MPA, which could limit the human impact on the sea and could also reign in destructive fishing practices, which Pedro allowed to continue. Don Javier missed the earlier times when there were fewer rules, which for him meant less livelihood uncertainty. But don Antonio wanted greater certainty, too, and knew that the current system was unsustainable. Eloquent despite having only a few years of formal education, don Antonio explained, "Poaching is a very big problem that requires policing, and this is why the MPA is the solution for the fishermen. This will lead to better yields, with stability. The MPA will secure the future of the family." However, don Antonio lamented that the MPA was largely ineffective, "without a single result" because of a lack of support from other government agencies, particularly Pedro's, who he claimed dealt in bribes rather than permits. "In five years, there will be nothing left. The MPA talks of a future that will never happen." This despair led don Antonio and others to write a letter denouncing Pedro in hopes that this would create a more supportive environment for the MPA's efforts. While the signers of that letter thought that the MPA could improve the local environment and fishing livelihoods, they also saw the barriers to this. As another fisherman lamented, "Things aren't going to improve. There is too much corruption in the policing of the MPA, and we need a strong government."

Don Javier and don Antonio's perspectives represent two of the diverse perspectives about fishing and the marine area that were common in Playa Tranquila by the time I arrived in 2002. The two letters were one of the few times that these differences manifested in an organized conflict; usually, disagreements over the MPA were fodder for gossip in the community, especially if one of the local fishers lost his catch and his boat for breaking the rules, which happened once a year or so. However, the debates over the MPA, both before and after its founding, were inevitably linked to livelihoods for the fishers and others. The two perspectives above argue that the sea is a source of life for the region, but they differ in how to protect this life-giving ability and how to be good children of the sea.

• • •

This chapter attempts to answer the question in its title, one that fishers and other community members asked—what is the MPA doing? The letters described above are an example of the tension and contradictions in this question: the MPA is both a threat to livelihoods for don Javier but is also not doing enough to protect the fragile marine resources from don Antonio's perspective. In addition, after the management plan was submitted to officials in Mexico City in 2001, the MPA stopped spending as much time in the fishing communities in contrast to their frequent presence to discuss the last plan; community members noted and puzzled over their absence, and many began speculating about what the staff could be doing and why they were not coming to talk with them about permits or cooperatives. Many fishers asked me, knowing I went to the office occasionally, "What's the MPA doing?" (*¿Que hace el parque?*). If the last chapter examined ideas during the planning phase about what the MPA should do, the period after 2001 showed what the MPA could actually do in terms of its limitations and possibilities for action. As I show below, the values from the last chapter still frame both constraints and options on MPA activities through expectations of what the MPA would do. I also argue that what the MPA could do, in terms of decision-making, was further inhibited by the contexts of local, national, and even international economies, politics, and cultures.

As I noted in the previous chapter, between July 2001 and January 2003, which coincided with my initial fieldwork period, the MPA staff and fishers were waiting for the plan to be published, and MPA activities shifted to reflect what the MPA staff could do without a management plan, while also anticipating what the final management plan might eventually look like.[1] First of all, the MPA could enforce Mexican fishing law in the area. Second, it could initiate and continue monitoring projects and environmental education efforts with different resource users. Finally, the MPA could promote and support economic alternatives to fishing in response to both concerns about environmental impact and the low incomes of the fishers. The MPA attempted to do all of these, with varying degrees of success. The options around and constraints on these activities depend on the values driving the MPA and its context, including ideas from the tragedy of the commons model, interactions of the MPA with other agencies and organizations, and relationships with the artisanal fishers.

In addition, the views about these (in)abilities reveal how actors understand their own and others' capabilities to act, and how this affects certain policy decisions. Under the uncertainties of resource scarcity and management, this chapter argues that to fully understand policies and their impacts, we need to examine ideas about agency and action as well. Given that the MPA staff and fishers come to similar conclusions about these ideas, at least in some contexts, this chapter concludes with the idea that rather than a focus on individual greed or action, relationships to people, institutions, and contexts are critical elements of access and action.

Meetings and Planning

Reading through my fieldnotes, I was reminded of how many meetings I attended or heard about as part of my research. I have 273 mentions of meetings in 286 typed pages of notes; meetings were definitely a key activity and concern of the community and the MPA. MPA staff

---

1. A large part of this chapter focuses on the period 2001–2003 when I was living in Loreto. After 2003, a new director was hired, and I lost contact with the MPA staff, especially since I could no long stop by to see what they were doing. Conversations in occasional visits suggested that few things changed over the next twenty years. I include some updates throughout.

repeatedly told me that meetings were key to successful management. Meetings included informal chats with community members to identify issues and potential solutions, more formal affairs with explicit agendas and goals such as registering fishers, and discussions with potential funders, NGOs, and government agencies to find support for the MPA work. While many fishers, tourism entrepreneurs, and others worried that the MPA's work consisted of paperwork, or felt that it should include more patrolling, it was clear that a lot of the staff time was taken up with meetings. While many of these meetings were perceived by community members as "useless" in terms of outcomes, the MPA staff found them valuable ways to connect and build relationships. Other organizations and agencies used meetings to "find out what the people need" (interview, community member, April 2002), though I often heard from participants that they see these meetings as useless and that they would not attend if money were not a possible outcome. As one fisherman stated in a July 2002 interview, "I'm cynical of things happening, there will be ten more meetings before anything changes with the permit situation." Some meetings did have concrete outcomes, and that potential seemed to keep people coming to them.

The MPA staff often met with fishers or other community members who stopped by their marina office, either as part of ongoing projects, for updates about the management plan, or issues, which ranged from the whether the squid fishery would open again, to land conflicts, to utility bills. Other meetings happened in the fishing communities themselves, organized as a part of the expectations laid out by the current 2001 management plan draft, to review the regulations of the MPA, to talk about the fishing permit process, or discuss education, capacity building, monitoring, and even patrolling matters. The MPA director felt that these face-to-face interactions were valuable for building and maintaining relationships. He also thought that community members bringing issues to the MPA signaled deeper relationships, especially when these were around nonmarine topics.

As part of planning, the MPA staff attended workshops offered by nonprofits, collaborating scientific institutions, and some of the funders of the MPA about how to improve environmental education, monitoring, or other efforts. For example, in one three-day workshop I attended, MPA staff, scientists, environmentalists, and one fisherman discussed the "sources of pressure" on the MPA. I was disappointed that the topics and examples were not specific to the Loreto area, nor did the facilitators ask for these as part of the session. Instead, small group discussions focused on a lack of education in the fishing communities as a key pressure on the resources, with a few disparaging remarks about fishers' language and perceived ignorance. One MPA staff member, who seemed agitated by the direction of the conversation, bluntly asserted that local corruption by a government official was a central issue for the MPA, but his comment was ignored, and the conversation immediately returned to talking about how to improve education about regulations. A local environmentalist at the meeting told me that he found the whole workshop useless because the wrong people were in the room, so it lacked the local relevance that involving community members could add. Another workshop was driven by the facilitator to focus on trash as a key issue, with an emphasis on the need to change behaviors and little attention given to specific plans about how to accomplish this and none to any infrastructural issues that some saw as the root of the problem.

In terms of what the MPA could do, meetings were low cost and high visibility, building connections with organizations and individuals. Meetings were also a way to prepare for the publication of the forthcoming management plan, and the need to more actively manage the area with the new rules. However, the criticism that meetings often lacked concrete outcomes showed the limitations of this strategy. Other activities showed more promise in leading to action.

Educational Activities and Monitoring

In late November 2001, shortly after I arrived in Loreto, the MPA hosted the Week of Conservation, as decreed by Mexico's president at that time, Vicente Fox Quesada. Excited to learn how the staff interacted with the community around one of their major goals, I eagerly attended the events, which I'd also heard advertised by one of the cars with mounted loudspeakers that roamed the city letting people know about upcoming events or political campaigns. Sitting outside of the marina office, older students learned what a marine park is and how it cares for species of reptiles, trees, and mammals, and each student received a booklet about keeping nonnative species off the islands. A younger group got a presentation around animals, trash, and diving, peppered with quizzes about the names of local species, sea turtle life cycles, environmental impacts of boats versus kayaks, and key terms like endemics. The next day, the youngest group learned how to lower their impact on the environment by using latrines or covering their "pee-pee" and "poo-poo" as well as the importance of leaving shells and animals on the islands instead of taking them home.

Most of the educational efforts I knew about from 2001 to 2003 were directed at schoolchildren, including lectures and activities around caring for the marine area and its species. These events were often done in collaboration with a local environmental organization. The environmentalist running the local marine museum suggested that in the past nine years every child in town had been through the museum. Yet the MPA staff also tried to engage everyone "from the mayor to the fishers" according to the director, and they printed materials and posters, as well as held workshops and other events, including courses and materials for tourism guides and others to help them learn about the area.

Educational efforts highlighted a key concern for some community members about fishing communities. Those involved in tourism or environmental conservation often claimed the *falta de educación*—"lack of education" but really a code word for ignorance—of the fishers was the main cause of their overfishing. One MPA employee suggested that

> The fishermen are the most difficult to convince because they work directly with the sea . . . and they may not understand because of their educational levels, so the MPA is here to educate them.

Another wanted "to teach [fishers] how to use the resource respectfully, in a sensible way. . . . We have plans to educate the women, to teach them what they lack, including information about MPA regulations and its importance." One central effort of the MPA was to improve communication about what was permitted in the area, since they felt that more clarity would improve compliance.

However, despite this interest, there was also a concern that "the old fishers are dead set in their ways," as one key environmentalist claimed. Others, including environmentalists and an MPA employee, also commented that they were optimistic in being able to work with the kids but somewhat resigned to not being able to change their parents' behaviors. Several MPA staff members were hopeful that what children learned would affect their parents, and I did observe several instances in which children's conservation ideas affected parents' responses. For example, one environmentalist commented that he has heard kids telling their parents what is not allowed and that they're not going to eat something because it's wrong (see Peterson 2017 for another narrative around this).

Monitoring was also a primary activity for the MPA staff, in collaboration with other organizations and scientists. There was an interest in how species and areas were faring under the MPA's efforts and the impacts of different activities, including the levels of invasive species on the islands, like rats and cats, which can damage local ecosystems. Through my MPA connections, I met scientists interested in mollusks and sharks, as well as other species and areas like the islands in the gulf. One effort of the MPA from 2001 to 2003 was creating a map of the sea mounds (*bajos*) in the area, given the fishers' deep knowledge of these. This monitoring was seen as critical for management and conservation, according to one environmentalist, who would like to see the entire Gulf of California monitored as part of a region-wide protection effort since both fish and fishers migrate within it.

Both education and monitoring were relatively easy for the MPA staff to accomplish, given both staff expertise and NGO support. Education also fit with the goal to reduce resource degradation through awareness of the impacts of behaviors, such as those debated in the previous chapter.

Vigilancia: Enforcing Mexican Laws in the MPA

Even though the area-specific management plan would not be approved until 2003, the MPA was subject to a variety of laws that could be enforced without it, including Mexican laws that made fishing for certain species and artisanal spearfishing illegal. The decree of the MPA also added additional restrictions against industrial fishing, as described in the last chapter. Given the focus on vigilance during the management plan discussions, particularly by tourism and environmentalist interests, *vigilancia* was a priority for the MPA staff. Vigilance included several activities of the MPA or others: patrolling, enlisting fishers to patrol, working on getting permits for local fishers, and controlling tourism access through fees and permits. Each of these differed in the ability of the MPA staff to accomplish them as well as related critiques and successes.

Patrolling

Patrolling the area meant identifying and reporting infractions, including illegal activities like trawling, taking illegal species, and fishing without a permit. The MPA staff had the boats and staff to do this and assistance from others like environmentalists to develop strategies, including circuits of the marine area and stations in the north and south. Even the fishers encouraged vigilance of spearfishers, nonlocal fishers, or others as a way to protect their fishing areas. Many people viewed vigilance as a preventative policing activity, as with the environmentalist's quote from the previous chapter, "if there are no police, then there will be crimes."

The focus on patrolling links to the ideas of blame from the previous chapter and draws on the tragedy of the commons model to presuppose that identifying and sanctioning certain behaviors would prevent resource degradation. First of all, who and what should be policed depends on the perspective of the speaker, as discussed in the previous chapter. In general, environmentalists and tourism entrepreneurs wanted all artisanal fishing more regulated, while artisanal fishers wanted to see more limits on certain kinds of artisanal fishing, including spearfishing, net fishing, fishing by nonlocal Mexican residents, and industrial fishing like shrimp and sardine boats (with the exception that fishers almost never talked about regulating their own fishing techniques). For example, several fishers viewed poaching (*guaterismo*) at night as a very big problem that needed policing and that the park could thus help improve production and stability, while spearfishers and others disagreed. Artisanal fishers were also likely to complain that tourism-based sportfishing was poorly regulated. In essence, debates about vigilance replicated arguments about the purpose of the MPA, as described in the previous chapter. Given these contradictions, the MPA staff found vigilance almost impossible to get right for the communities (see also Stamieskin, Wielgus, and Gerber 2009).

Some patrolling activities were universally supported by community members, particularly against outsiders. According to the MPA director, even before the management plan process started, the fishers were successful in asking shrimp trawlers from Sinaloa and Sonora to leave. The MPA continued, with support from Conapesca and Profepa, to ask trawlers to leave, and a few violators were tried and convicted once the park was established, according to one environmentalist. Many environmentalists, tourism operators, and fishers also lauded some of the results of vigilance efforts, which they felt had led to greater numbers of fish and other species in the marine area. Residents mentioned the return of pelicans, sardines, shrimp, turtles, giant squid, and yellowtail tuna. Ann O'Neil, the long-term resident and author mentioned in chapter 2, noted that "the return of pelicans is a sign of good things—it means there are nutrients in the water and smaller fish come for this" (interview, November 2001). At meetings with fishers from other areas, Loreto-area fishers praised the value of the protected area for marine populations near Loreto, though they noted that areas farther from town were not seeing as much change.

Residents and MPA staff pointed to the virtual elimination of trawlers and the reduced numbers of nets and fishing boats as key means for achieving these perceived increases:

> Without doubt, one of the biggest successes of the creation of the Loreto Bay National Park has been the reduction in the presence of the shrimp boats in the area due to the constant actions of inspection and vigilance that was done with the help if the competent authorities like PROFEPA, CONAPESCA, the Mexican army, the city's public safety officers, and the vigilance committees of fishers. (Gutiérrez Barreras 2001, 39)

A figure accompanying this statement shows that starting from six prosecutions for illegal fishing in 1997, a year after the MPA was decreed, there were eleven actions in 1999, twenty-two in 2000, and eighteen in 2001. In terms of spearfishing, MPA staff explained that they had "almost totally eliminated night diving" in 2002 in part by encouraging free diving without an oxygen source as a compromise that would reduce pressure on the species being fished. In more recent accounts, Castillo Velasco Martínez noted that illegal activities increased from 2007 to 2017, with a lower point in 2015; vigilance activities also increased during this time (2021). Collaborating with environmental NGO Pronatura Noroeste, the MPA implemented a long-range camera in 2017 and a drone surveillance system in 2022 (Pronatura Noroeste 2022). The camera, according to Pronatura Noroeste, increased detection of illegal activities in artisanal fishing by 300 percent and in tourism by 1,200 percent (2018). While BCS has one of the highest rates of prosecution for illegal fishing, there is a lack of systematic study of this in the country (Alfaro, Carpio Domínguez, and Castro Salazar 2023).

Although almost everyone agreed that more vigilance had helped improve the fisheries and the marine area in general, they also universally believed that the MPA staff were not doing enough and that many illegal activities were still happening. "Vigilance is not happening," claimed a fisherman who thought that prosecuting illegal spearfishing would improve the fisheries production for fishers (July 2002). Another claimed that "the marine park doesn't work [*no sirve*] because there is no vigilance" and that any calls to the MPA office are useless because authorities never arrive (August 2002). Other fishers discussed the unrest (*disequilibrio*) or dissent (*inconformidad*) around fishing regulations, feeling that there was no one in control of the fishing: "we need the security of the MPA. Without this, there will be problems tomorrow, and no development [*desarrollo*]." As of 2023, concerns around vigilance continued to plague the MPA in part due to the lack of resources for this activity (Lauterio Martínez et al. 2022).

Artisanal fishers also critiqued the MPA for the uneven and seemingly targeted prosecution of artisanal fishing over the duration of my research. Several fishers had their boats seized by authorities while I was in the area, including don Javier as mentioned at the start of the chapter. These events were widely discussed in the fishing communities, even implicating neighbors in the prosecutions. "Why choose these people to prosecute? We don't want problems, but other fishers are bribing authorities, while the authorities choose to attack fishers" (interview, July 2002).

Stories about lost boats, cars, or fees circulated through the fishing communities, but these were also discussed in terms of inconsistencies in how each case was treated due to connections or other variables. These accounts also often included the motives for illegal fishing—illness, family finances, or other reasons why they knowingly broke the law. From a community member who collaborated with the MPA on other projects:

> The MPA has helped us a lot, but it has gone bad [*ha ido mal*] with [a staff member] for taking the boats from our relative. Raul [the director] is better. Before, there was a lot of trust. But because he needed to go to the doctor for heart issues, [the fisher] needed 8,000 pesos and worked illegally. (Interview, July 2002)

In another case, an older fisherman's boat was seized, but he was unable to "pay them off to get his boat back, unlike another fisherman" who was able to quickly recuperate his *panga* (interview, April 2002). Prosecuting illegal fishing by local fishers led to a loss of trust with the MPA staff since fishing community members largely saw illegal fishing as an economic need. However, despite popular perception, it was not the MPA prosecuting illegal fishing but Conapesca and the military, as I explain below.

Tourism business owners and environmentalists were also critical of the vigilance activities. One tourism owner said, "They [motioning toward the MPA] hate to see me show up since I tell them they're not doing their jobs" (interview, 2001). According to another tourism entrepreneur, their relationship with the park was "up and down," especially given the leniency with artisanal fishers, "who seem to be able to break the rules while the MPA staff turn their heads." In contrast, those in tourism complained that the sportfishers were expected to meticulously follow rules, which seemed to change often. For example, in 1999, the businesses were expected to submit reports of their outings, but there was never any cooperation from businesses, so this ceased. In addition, one tourism business owner felt unable to report any infractions by artisanal or sportfishing, as they felt that this led to harassment by other businesses and government agencies (interview in English, February 2002). New permits for tourists' use of the MPA were also implemented in 2002 and continued to be required into 2023, with fewer issues over time.

• • •

A primary barrier to patrolling was jurisdictional. In actuality, the MPA staff assisted other agencies with vigilance because it technically lacked the jurisdiction to prosecute illegal fishing, according to the MPA staff.

As one staff member commented, "We have no ability to inspect, give permits, or control the number of fish caught." The MPA staff worked with other organizations, including Conapesca and the military, to directly prosecute illegal fishing. They also collected reports and evidence about illegal fishing, but enforcement was not under their purview.

Some residents were aware of this limitation. For example, a fisherman commented that the MPA "can't prosecute [*levantar una acta*] because it doesn't have the ability. They need a plan to reach higher authorities, but it's not the director's fault" (interview, July 2002). Another fisherman criticized the impossibility of getting fishing permits but with the understanding that the MPA had its hands tied there:

> The MPA staff tried to speed up the permit process but lacked the support of the city. The current problem of fishing permits is that [Cona]pesca takes the boats and product [as part of prosecuting illegal fishing] and this then involves bribes. There is a lack of trust in the authorities. (Interview, July 2002)

The limits on prosecution were understood largely in terms of corruption in partner organizations. While corruption is often accepted by local residents as part of the politics of Mexico, these accusations also helped them explain some of the challenges facing the MPA (for more on corruption as political bureaucracy in Mexico, see Klooster 2000; Lomnitz-Adler 2000; Vásquez-León 1994; Young 2001). Many residents, MPA staff, and others leveled corruption charges against Conapesca and Profepa, both key partners in vigilance activities. Many in the communities claimed that the inspectors were corrupt, taking bribes to look the other way on spearfishing or even more serious infractions.

In response to these issues, the MPA began to work on an "Observer" program in 2002 with funding from NGOs. The program asked local fishers to take MPA staff out in their boats to document and report any illegal activities in exchange for some compensation. The goal was to send documentation of illegal activities to government offices in the state capital or even to Mexico City so as to bypass corrupt officials in Loreto. While this program was not universally admired in the fishing communities, given its potential to prosecute local fishers, several fishers or their family members became Observers, who also helped with some of the monitoring projects described above (see also Fernández-Rivera Melo et al. 2012 on continuing efforts).

Talking with two fishers in June 2002, an MPA staff member suggested that the Observer program would provide video or pictures to send to La Paz or Mexico City because "there is less corruption there. . . . There is currently no structure for vigilance in Loreto." Several of the MPA staff explained optimistically that they felt their approach was a move away from corruption and toward a new culture of politics in Mexico, expecting their example to influence residents and politicians alike. The MPA felt that they could do little more than videotape infractions because relations with the other agencies did not encourage joint efforts. MPA staff told me that they sent these videotapes to the state or national offices, over the heads of the local authority, but that unfortunately, this also ended up being ineffective. In 2023, the MPA still lacked jurisdiction to prosecute illegal activities, continuing to complicate vigilance activities.

Local Permit Efforts

Given the increased vigilance over their activities due to the MPA and its efforts, the local fishers were particularly interested in getting the permits that would allow them to fish legally. Most had been fishing under the permit of a *permisionario* (permit holder) who acted as a middleman for sales and also provided loans for boats and other equipment. Fishers believed that getting their own permits would help them to reduce their dependence on *permisionarios*. However, the MPA in 2002 estimated there were just three permits for three hundred fishers through this *permisionario* system. Several fishers still remembered when "it was possible to fish freely, without permits," and most associated the need for permits with the arrival of the MPA (though fishers worked with *permisionarios* for a long time before the MPA came into existence). As one fisherman suggested, "The problem is [Cona]pesca. They don't let us work—they deny us permits. They would rather take a bribe than give us a permit, which would lead to better pay and less *guaterismo* [poaching]" (interview, April 2002), an issue raised in the letter at the start of the chapter. Another fisher claimed that there weren't permits because "there isn't pressure from the people or buyers." Most fishers were also interested in area-specific permits that would prevent nonlocals from fishing in the area, as mentioned in the previous chapter. Several tourism operators and environmentalists similarly expressed an interest in "regionalizing the fishing" (interview, April 2002).

Although they generally supported the idea of permits, local fishers also distrusted the permitting process. One fisherman shared with me that "I'm fishing legally, but I can't really afford the permits so maybe I'll need to sell my house to buy a permit, but then why would I need to fish? It is easier to fish illegally, and impossible to fish legally" (interview, fisher, January 2002). Others were skeptical of whether permits would actually restrict nonlocal people from fishing since, as Mexican citizens, they were eligible to get permits. Others knew that permits could take a long time to get, given that the federal government was not giving permits at the time. While they waited, they would continue to fish without permits, risking prosecution for illegal fishing. This kind of moral economy, where illegal activities were necessary to survive, conflicts with the state's expectations as expressed through laws (Peluso 1992; Edelman 2012), though it also resonates with the perception that corruption is an integral part of Mexican bureaucracies. Overall, these conflicts reveal how local fisheries were pressured toward illegal fishing and overexploitation by the economic and political contexts that provided them few other options for how to survive.

The MPA staff also lamented the slow permitting process for artisanal fishing. The compromise, according to the MPA staff, was to have informal agreements with fishers to not prosecute them for not having permits. From 2001 to 2003, park management was thus largely accomplished by informal agreements with the local population. The informal agreements also included restricted times of the year and places in the MPA for fishing, but these were largely ignored from 2001 to 2003. For example, beginning in April and lasting until September, fishers are not to use nets. However, the park did not expect to enforce this until the management plan was published.

• • •

A few fishers were also aware of this informal agreement, as one fishing community representative explained,

The law says that we've reached maximum exploitation, and doesn't allow more permits. So, fishers had to fish illegally. This led to corruption because [Cona]pesca was accepting fish for sale as if it had a permit behind it. In part, this was out of necessity. . . . We're missing an agreement about how many permits to give for each area, and the registration effort will help with this, with a number of requests, fishers, permit holders, cooperatives, etc. (Interview, July 2002)

A lack of trust connects to the informal agreements as well as to corruption of MPA partner organizations, which meant uneven enforcement and a perceived lack of agreement:

They should let them fish and give permits, rather than [Conapesca] saying one thing one day, [and] another [day] something else. They would like to see an agreement about when and where fishing can happen. There is no agreement now. (Interview, fisher, April 2002)

As a result of these perceived inconsistencies, some fishers wrote a letter to the officials in the state capital and Mexico City denouncing the local enforcement agencies, while another group wrote a counter letter, as described at the start of this chapter. Some fishers believed the letters actually led to more prosecutions for illegal fishing, and one story circulating in the community was that divers turned in one fisherman in retaliation for the letter.

• • •

MPA staff worked with local fishers to form cooperatives, which could then get permits to fish, hoping to see an increase in the number of permits in the area. They collected information from fishers at meetings in the fishing communities, asking about where and how they fished and what they caught and emphasizing that all fishers needed to be registered to better regulate fishing. This registration, according to the director, would prevent nonfishers from getting permits. However, the staff lacked the ability to give permits, which was under Profepa (see Peterson 2010 for more detail), and as one staff member explained to me, the Carta Nacional Pesquera was "closed"—no more permits could be given as of August 2000, though there was hope that this could be changed (interview,

March 2002). In the face of this challenge, the MPA tried to maintain the same number of fishers in the area and to "guarantee the security of the [local] fishers." MPA staff found that in many cases, confronting nonlocal fishers about the need for permits encouraged them to leave (interview, staff member, April 2002).

However, fishers were highly skeptical of forming cooperatives to get permits, given the experiences of their relatives on the Pacific side of the Baja peninsula with cooperatives. Several fishers said that the cooperative president alone benefits as he can funnel dues, proceeds, and other funds toward himself. Others were doubtful that cooperatives would do well on the gulf side, given the lack of high-value species like lobster and abalone that they believed were necessary to see financial benefits from cooperatives. One fisherman described cooperatives as an "association without anything" (*asocio sin nada*) in that it had no benefits for them. However, many became part of cooperatives at the MPA staff's urging, even if these were largely on paper. In any case, fishers continued to fish in small groups. Cooperatives did become a useful form for nonfishing efforts, though, as the case of the Hijas del Mar discussed in the previous chapter shows.

Tourism Permits

The MPA also started a permit process for tourism in which tourists or their guides would need to pay for a permit to fish or boat in the area. Originally, the fee for the permit was MXN\$57, but this was decreased to MXN\$20 in early 2002 due to both complaints about the complexity of the process and confusion about the fees. I talked with one local tourism owner in 2001 who said that the local ministry of the environment (now SEMARNAT) would make him fill out a form, go to the bank, and return with a receipt to get the permit stamped. "And if the office is closed, you're out of luck." He was also required to buy a whole book of permits whether he used them for clients or not (interview in English, December 2001). In April 2002, U.S. residents and tourists were talking with each other about the fees and discussing on the shortwave radio and at meetings about the confusion surrounding who needed to pay them and how much they were. One U.S. resident mentioned that the week before Easter in 2002, MPA, Profepa, and FONATUR (government tourism agency) officials went to the beaches and asked people for their permits. When she went to town to buy the permit, she had to make multiple phone calls to determine what it would cost, and the quoted fee of MXN$120 seemed to depend on the size of her camper:

> Americans [U.S. tourists or residents] would not mind paying a small amount to stay there, but rules and policies have been uneven in the past, and people have never returned to make good on their threats of checking that people have paid or left. This seems to have been an attempt to clear the beaches, despite that Americans take better care of the beaches, and leave less trash. (Interview, April 2002)

In May 2002, a short article in the local newspaper highlighted the value of the fees for supporting the MPA's work protecting the area but noted that the cruise ships were refusing to pay it (*Sudcaliforniano*, May 10, 2002, Loreto edition). A local U.S. resident discussed this fee in the context of an earlier attempt to charge charter flights fees in order to promote Mexican airlines, which backfired, ultimately decreasing tourism, according to him. One fisherman, in April 2002, suggested that "there is going to be some kind of revolt soon [against the MPA], with the damage it's done to tourism, with fees on top of fees."

Others wondered where the money from the fees was going to go. "The people of the MPA say it's going to equipment and vigilance, but I don't know. We'll see if there are more fish. The tourists pay it, not me, but they sometimes ask where the money will go. I don't worry if they don't pay it, it's not my fault" (interview, tourism operator, December 2001). However, these fees continued through 2023, requiring each person on a boat in the MPA to wear a paper bracelet indicating that the MXN$90 fee had been paid; most businesses included them with the cost of the outing.

$$\bullet \quad \bullet \quad \bullet$$

While limitations due to jurisdiction and partner corruption were the most frequent explanations for the lack of MPA success, residents also saw the MPA staff as ineffective for other reasons. For example, some local people complained that the MPA staff spent more time writing reports than actually managing the MPA: "They are nice and wonderful people, but their jobs are in effect to send reports to Mexico City, rather than to manage the park" (interview, environmentalist and tourism operator, December 2001). While at least one environmentalist faulted the MPA for lacking "urgency" around their conservation efforts, the overwhelming perception was that the MPA's efforts and reports "went nowhere." "It reports, but there are not results," said one fisherman. "It lacks what it needs to be an MPA [*falta que es un parque*]" (interview, April 2002).

In addition, there were complaints that the MPA staff missed meetings or were generally disrespectful to people or that the meetings were poorly timed at peak tourism outings in the late afternoon or for artisanal fishing opportunities. There were also concerns that the MPA's staff often failed to respond to calls or requests. In addition, some fishers believed that the MPA staff "don't know the area" and compared some of their efforts to "tourists with video cameras" when they recorded meetings with fishers (interview, March 2002).[2] One tourism operator agreed that the "authorities aren't around and cannot care for the bay because they don't know it. It's so simple, to learn about the water and what is there, and how to care for it. But the government has no interest in this public resource" (interview, December 2001).

In addition, some residents believed that the MPA staff were corrupt. One reported that the director buys illegally caught local lobster, while another said that the staff spend time "playing in boats with women," and a third that they were accepting bribes to ignore reports of illegal behaviors. In general, tourism owners felt that the MPA was corrupt because it didn't prosecute more fishers. One tourism entrepreneur and environmentalist claimed, "The [MPA] director could do something about the turtle poaching but chooses not to, mainly in fear of a community outrage" (interview, January 2002). In contrast, fishing communities saw the close ties between the MPA and tourism business owners as evidence that "the law is corrupt" and that tourism supported *vigilancia* because of a conflict with artisanal fishing (interview, April 2002). I spoke to a few

---

2. The MPA staff recorded several meetings with the fishers when discussing the MPA planning process described in the previous chapter. I was never able to view these.

people who claimed the MPA was being audited for corruption in 2002 but was unable to confirm this. In any case, the presumption seemed to be that the institution was corrupt, and it is possible these concerns were tied to a change in personnel in 2003.

Overall, the MPA was viewed externally and internally as largely ineffective in its vigilance activities despite some important successes. The major issue was contextual: the MPA lacked jurisdiction and partners were unable to support patrolling efforts to the extent desired, whether that was due to corruption or other limitations. The need to complete reports and the unavailability of permits similarly constrained options for the MPA staff.

What the MPA staff could do was also limited by the conflicting ideas around blame and control, which led to the pointed critiques above about ineffectiveness. Yet the MPA was also attempting to manage the MPA without costing the fishing communities their livelihoods, which was considered the social problem (*problematica social*) that led to informal agreements and the capacity-building activities discussed in the next section. This approach developed from the MPA's changing views of the fishers and their awareness of root causes of resource degradation, gained through the years of discussions and building relationships.

Yet the contextual constraints and conflicting demands on the MPA strained relationships with fishers, environmentalists, and tourism, eroding trust and agreements built during the management planning processes. Understanding the reasons for the ineffectiveness of the MPA also differed in important ways, as tourism owners and environmentalists tended to blame internal corruption, laziness, or other MPA staff characteristics, while fishers tended to see the limitations posed by the context external to the MPA. We'll return to this difference after we examine how the MPA staff fared in the capacity-building efforts in fishing communities.

Capacity Building

In 2002, the director of the LBNP, Raul, spoke about the members of the local fishing communities: "While the economy influences them to live this way, we want them to live better." The MPA director and staff identified one of the underlying problems of resource degradation as the lack of opportunities available for the fishers and "realiz[ed] the role we need to play" in helping the communities, despite the fact that this was beyond the scope of their work. Raul said that he fears that people in Loreto without opportunities will put more stress on the fishing; in addition, he said the MPA staff felt some guilt in "taking away the resources" and enforcing rules that they knew made it harder for fishers to make a living: "fishers are as endangered as some of the animals because of the rules." As a result, MPA staff began working on economic development projects (*capacitacion*), including supporting the development of aquaculture, aquarium fish exporting, bread making, and restaurants in the fishing communities, some of which I described in chapter 3. Aquaculture and tropical fish export projects were thought to be less-intensive uses of the area, especially given the potentially higher market prices for these products.

Raul told me in 2002 that he didn't know of other Mexican protected areas that have used this approach to local communities, especially marine areas. He also talked about other ways to bring opportunities the fishing communities, from teaching administration of businesses, studying, building latrines, and fixing houses and mentioned programs by other NGOs and businesses intended to foster alternatives to fishing or lower-impact fishing, like certified sustainable fishing products.

In the same interview, Raul suggested that local projects would give people greater roots to the area, replacing a nomadic fishing existence with a more family-focused life. He himself had worked for many years as a migratory fisherman, he explained, wandering and hopping (*brincando*) from place to place. His goal is to give them a place to stay—despite economic pressures to fish this way, he wants them to "live better." Raul also acknowledged that he and fishers may have different ideas and goals and while it was easy to find work opportunities, unfortunately these never seemed to coincide with the needs or desires of the people (interview, February 2002).

In June 2002, Raul discussed the MPA's role in development through the Program for Regional Sustainable Development (Programa de Desarrollo Regional Sustentable), which came to the relatively wealthy state of BCS because of a new focus on coastal areas. According to the director, the program would provide money for development projects, as in other protected areas, and that he had the "green light" to propose projects for funding, which might include beach cleanups or marina development.

However, despite believing that the communities were starting to respond to the MPA positively, such as by asking for help, he questioned the role of protected areas in development, since "managing money leads to managing [*manejar*] problems. . . . As biologists, we lack the background needed to study communities." He hoped to develop partnerships so that the city or other organizations could distribute money fairly (interview, June 2002). In protected areas, capacity building is now widely viewed as a way to reduce stress on natural resources, encouraging entrepreneurship as one approach to improve resource use, as in Loreto and other areas of BCS (Monteforte-Sánchez 2020).

The MPA staff supported a variety of projects from 2001 to 2003 and beyond, including aquaculture, bread making, tourism, and restaurants, as part of the capacity-building efforts. The relative success of these contrasts with the vigilance activities described above, showing how slight changes in context around jurisdiction or ability to act lead to very different results both in activities and relationships with community members.

Capacity Building via Aquaculture

In 2001, there were three active aquaculture projects in the Loreto area collaborating with the MPA, all working with mollusks (mano de leon scallops or "catarina" clams): (1) a small-scale project developed between Lupe, a fisherman living in the town of Loreto, and one of the park staff members, (2) the women's cooperative project that was described in chapter 3, and (3) Paloma, which was the largest and oldest and which involved an *Americano* biologist, international investors, MPA staff, and four Playa Tranquila residents to cultivate the clams. Here, I focus on the role of the MPA in the first two efforts; I had less knowledge about Paloma's collaboration with the MPA.

The MPA's role in each project varied widely, depending on a variety of factors. For example, Lupe's and the women's cooperative interacted very frequently with the MPA, as they were less experienced than the Paloma team with aquaculture and (for the women) cooperatives in general. MPA staff worked with both to teach them aquaculture techniques and theories and also helped them with paperwork for permits and other administrative needs of the project. In the Paloma project, the lead biologist took care of much of the coordination and technical needs of the project, requiring less support from the MPA, which generally helped to coordinate meetings, acquire permits, and look for contracts. The key staff member working on the aquaculture projects, Carlos, had an advanced degree in biology and experience on aquaculture projects, and thus was well situated to assist with various needs. The MPA staff could also provide links to other projects, courses, and resources through their networks to nonprofits and universities.

Lupe's work in aquaculture started in 1990 when he worked on a project farther north in Baja California, but he was unable to keep that going after the permits stalled out. He and the MPA director started collaborating on aquaculture when it seemed possible to get a permit for the Loreto area around 2001. The MPA staff helped him get this permit and the initial supplies he needed. Despite setbacks due to limited supplies, space, and funding, Lupe persisted, building his own baskets (*jaulas*) for the clams, which he was finally able to harvest after a year. He estimated that the first year of the project was not economically viable, given that he spent MXN$20,000 on supplies and transportation and that clam prices were low (scallops were selling at higher prices). The MPA provided materials like baskets and fabric that were essential to continuing the project. Lupe appreciated their support and mainly felt that the permit process was a major barrier to success and something the MPA and other government agencies could help with: "The problem is with the authorities and getting permits—there are interests at work [that impede these processes]" (interview, January 2003).

The women's cooperative started working on aquaculture, eventually joining with Paloma later on. They credit their efforts to the support of the MPA and other organizations: "We obtained all of this through work and government support. If we need something now, we are prepared and don't need help like before" (interview, February 2003). The women often stopped by the MPA offices to get help with paperwork or to arrange for workdays in which MPA staff and others would help them with the aquaculture maintenance or tropical fish exporting (another collaboration with the MPA). The women felt like they learned from the MPA and others and were able to be more independent—the cooperative president showed me some PowerPoint slides about their growing independence in 2011, documenting how their relationships shifted over a decade. These relationships started with the MPA, and the women were able to make their own connections through some of these networks (see also Peterson 2014b). I spoke with Carlos in March 2002 about the cooperatives and their efforts, and he was quick to admire the strong organization of the women's cooperative, which he said was more likely to follow up and get things done than the men's cooperatives he'd worked with despite having less experience with permits and formal paperwork associated with cooperatives and the aquaculture project. MPA staff said that women in other fishing communities in the Loreto area were also interested in working with them, like the Hijas del Mar cooperative had.

Successes and Challenges of Capacity Building

Capacity-building efforts were successful in several ways. First, they connected the fishing communities and MPA staff in opportunities to interact and learn from each other through regular positive interactions, which were unlike those they had around rule enforcement. The emphasis on bringing opportunities to the communities was, according to community members and MPA staff, good for building trust. This activity also met a need of the fishing communities; as one fisherman said, "People don't want to fish, but they have no options" (interview, January 2002). Fishers continued to have ideas for development, which they often shared with the MPA staff, including how to build tourism businesses with resources from the government for initial purchases and maintenance. Many looked to the MPA for solutions like this, perhaps seeing this as an extension of the older patronage system where a relationship, particularly that with a weaker tie (Granovetter 1985), could connect them to needed resources.

Second, the projects provided concrete evidence to community members that the MPA staff understood their lives and needs; forming cooperatives meant getting closer to legal fishing permits and possibly higher incomes, and alternative economic opportunities became important sources of money, even while these were on a smaller scale. These activities were also relatively successful, especially when compared with vigilance efforts. In part, it is because these did not require going through specific agencies (which could be unsupportive of their activities) but allowed for multiple possible solutions and therefore more flexibility around obstacles or constraints like budgets and interagency collaboration (Cleaver 2002; Acheson 2002; see also Peterson 2010 for more detail). It was more possible to support alternative economic activities in the given context of the MPA than to prosecute illegal fishing or provide area-specific permits.

However, capacity building also faced some challenges. Working on projects with select groups or individuals was often viewed as favoritism, and those who weren't involved with these still wondered what the MPA was doing. Some community members felt they had tried to interest the MPA in working with them on projects like aquaculture, tourism, or trash pickup but had felt that the MPA was unable to get past the politics of some of these projects, including complex permit processes for ornamental fish or aquaculture. In addition, several community members were distressed by a later decision to restrict capacity-building efforts to marine-focused activities, leaving the bread ovens and other efforts unsupported after the ovens had been built.

Community members also critiqued the expertise of the staff, including concerns that they do not know the people, particularly the fishers. One fisherman said that his neighbors didn't know the staff people well enough to tell them apart. Another fisherman commented that the staff were biologists rather than administrators, so they were not good at working to help with alternatives to fishing. There were also some concerns that there was a lack of follow-through or there were misunderstandings that were never cleared up; in one case, a fisherman felt misunderstandings directly led to the failure of his economic development project and that meetings and more frequent responses to his requests would have prevented this.

Capacity-building efforts are also problematic in how they frame people as needing help rather than as experts in their livelihoods (Walker et al. 2008; Ramachandran 2021; Li 2007). Reviewing examples from around the world, Paige West finds that capacity building, like entrepreneurialism and other ideas discussed above, brings in neoliberal values that often conflict with local processes and understandings, which are often focused on social relationships. Describing one case in Papua New Guinea, she explains,

What they failed to understand was that by producing the idea of un-derdevelopment and by telling Gimi that they were poor and needed de-velopment in order to value and conserve their forests—they were both discounting Kabe's way of seeing and being in the world (by not attempting to understand it and by assuming that forest use was only contributing to the loss of biological diversity) and working to create the notion of "lack" among Gimi. This notion, that old ways and tradition had to be changed so that people could access cash and development, inadvertently contrib-uted to the devaluation of Kabe's kinds of knowledge, an epistemology and ontology that has unintended conservation benefits. (West 2016, 130)

These are dispossessions of knowledge and sovereignty over the future as well, according to West. As with prior efforts at development, capac-ity building can degrade traditional values, weaken social institutions, and undermine social mechanisms, leading also to deep dissatisfaction with government programs that don't address the actual needs of fishers (Ramachandran 2021). "Othering" people both includes them through assisting them and excludes them by portraying them as threats (An-dreucci and Zografos 2022).

Efforts in Playa Tranquila by fishers and others have continued to rely on NGOs, government agencies, and others to move forward. As of 2023, there was a dissatisfaction with capacity building, particularly workshops, that brought in one-time support without recognizing the long-term resource needs for sustainability. In one case, community members received chickens to raise and sell but didn't know what to do once they were sold, as they were nonreproductive. Developing relation-ships can better support longer-term resource needs for sustainability, as opposed to one-time workshops. Few community members felt that they were able to convert their skills and interests to longer-term and larger-scale efforts without more supportive relationships to help build new livelihoods, as they had seen with the MPA staff.

The Perception of Agency in MPA Management

An important question for many was why the MPA staff were ineffective—was it due to laziness, corruption, or institutional design? Members of the fishing communities talked about the MPA and its staff very differently than did the tourism owners and environmentalists, and this was often tied to how fishers saw themselves and how others viewed them as well.

As we saw in previous chapters, people in the fishing communities viewed themselves as caught up in relational links that posed barriers or provided opportunities, while tourism owners and environmentalists saw fishers as greedy and selfish in their actions. These differences reflect at least two different models of agency and hence construed the fishers' ability to act very differently. Ideas about agency coming from neoliberal economics rely on specific moral readings of behavior in line with assumptions around responsibility and rational maximization of value. This leads those talking about artisanal fishers to connect ideas of self-interest and irrationality with illegal behaviors (like spearfishing) and to attribute rationality to similar behaviors by those practicing other kinds of fishing. In contrast, using another model of agency, relationships become both obstacles that encourage illegal behavior like corruption and openings for legal opportunities like capacity building. The contradictions around agency, environmental values, and individual rationality are difficult to understand without recognizing how more powerful people can impose their moral readings on the actions of some, like the fishers, that they do not hold for others, like sportfishers. Environmentalists, for example, rarely impugned or questioned the moral character of sportfishers, construing them as "good actors" who were maximizing profit with minimal impact on the environment, in contrast to artisanal fishers who selfishly maximized their impact on the environment despite earning minimal profits from it. Similarly, the moral values around the environment behaviors led to an inconsistency around neoliberal ideas—maximizing individual benefit through illegal activities was illogical rather than rational economic individualism.

Multiple ideas about agency also affect how different groups perceive the MPA and its ability to act. As we see above, those in the fishing communities largely saw the MPA as constrained by its relationships to other agencies and reporting responsibilities and that its ability to act in vigilance was severely limited as a result. In contrast, tourism interests and environmentalists tended to see the MPA staff as incompetent, ignorant, or corrupt—they believed that the MPA lacked the capacity to police because of internal characteristics, rather than external influences.

Dispossession, power, and agency are intimately connected in how some perceptions become truth and then influence policy.

This chapter has highlighted how the MPA staff viewed other groups as well. Just as the various groups had ideas about the MPA's agency, the MPA staff's ideas about these groups affected their activities, particularly the fishers, as we see above. The MPA staff's ideas about fishers' agency changed over time, diverging from those of tourism and NGO interests and bringing them in greater alignment with the ideas of many in the fishing communities. The early capacity-building activities were seen as an opportunity to educate the fishers about their overfishing and destructive behaviors. Yet after working with the fishers to address complaints about the early management plans and drawing on some experiences as fishers themselves, the MPA staff began to see overfishing as a result of constraints the fishers face in making ends meet rather than their greed. Capacity building became a way to lessen these constraints and the dependency on fishing. These are important perspective shifts around agency for fishers and had significant implications for the MPA efforts and the success of these, as they have the potential to do in many economic development or capacity-building contexts, particularly given inequalities and class differences in play (Gomberg-Muñoz 2010; Green 2000; Seckinelgin 2006).

Yet MPA staff views of fishers and others around agency and the marine resources still largely focus on the individual as the fulcrum for change and knowledge as the solution—to evade corrupt local authorities, staff encouraged residents to take evidence up the chain of command, and to reduce overfishing, fishers are trained for other industries like tourism. Yet in many cases, those being educated were already experts. For example, women starting a bakery were given training in baking despite years of experience, and others were taught to sew when they already knew how to (see chapter 3). In focusing on knowledge as the route to action, the MPA staff assumed people were not succeeding because of a lack of expertise, which the MPA staff could then provide to them through capacity building (see also Green 2000; Mathews 2005). Research on traditional ecological knowledge shows that assuming people lack knowledge erases or dispossesses them of their actual expertise, as we saw in chapter 4 (see also Lauer 2023). Yet in many cases, as with ignoring traditional ecological knowledge, it was not the expertise that was absent but rather the resources needed to enact it. The women and fishers had plenty of knowledge about the local environment and its resources but not the economic and social resources needed to enact the knowledge effectively to get ahead. In misrecognizing the barriers for the fishing communities, the MPA staff also misattributed agency for the fishers and their families, blaming individual ignorance for structural barriers that prevented enacting skills and expertise. In these ways, ideas around agency are strongly tied to neoliberal economic expectations around individual rationality (Ganti 2014; Pfeilstetter 2021), overlaid with unrecognized inequalities in access to options (Chen 2013).

The fishing communities' ideas around agency for themselves and the MPA highlights important differences with the MPA staff ideas as well. The fishing communities' members' focus on relationships as means for influence, resources, and thus effort is critical here. Individual effort is not the focus; rather, how people can use social networks becomes critical for success. And when those social networks fail, as in the case of vigilance or getting a tourism-oriented boat, people expect to shift to other networks. The MPA staff became an important resource for many community efforts outside of fishing, including issues around electricity and other concerns very far from the water because the MPA was a new option for addressing older issues. However, when the MPA staff were no longer able to justify nonmarine projects like bread ovens, fishing communities were less able to access resources. Policies and regulations set far from the communities and MPA determined the shape of relationships and support. In this sense, some aspects of agency could be understood to emerge from social contexts of interaction and to be co-constructed with other people (Bunn and Lamb 2019; Sewell 1992) rather than be solely an individual quality (Barad 2003). But overall, understanding agency both of MPA staff and fishers requires considering this wider context of relationships and access to resources and how various relationships, institutions, and actions, as well as the views of oneself and of others, can create obstacles to action and success. Ideas about agency are thus an important means for dispossession, as well as the potential to combat this, particularly when noneconomic values can disrupt neoliberal economic processes.

Conclusion

It seems clear that ideas of agency shape interpretations of behaviors like fishing and resource management and lead to different policies and practices, like those around vigilance and capacity building. The design of the MPA, and vigilance activities in particular, depends on a model of individual rationality in terms of both maximizing (interpreted as greed in fishers) and responsibility (in caring for or managing the resource). Yet this model misses the importance of contexts like market prices and bureaucratic corruption that can set up constraints for behavior. Capacity building also shows how a context can better support action, and the importance of flexibility in options for success. Behind both of these examples are ideas about agency that intersect with neoliberal individualism, in the case of tourism or environmentalist perspectives, or, in the case of the MPA staff and fishers, ideas about agency are interwoven in the context of relationships and ideas might even emerge from this through coproduction. As a result, the policy recommendations coming from tourism owners, fishers, and the MPA staff differ significantly from each other, producing the tensions between these models.

. . .

Acknowledging agency as multiple discourses becomes an important step toward developing more successful natural resource management strategies and toward understanding the variety of ways that people experience and understand agency. This means that we might be able to reenvision motives, goals, and strategies so that we can find alternatives to current models of resource management that privilege ideas of individual agency over culture and social interactions and systems, as we see in the concluding chapter.

CONCLUSION

My visit to Playa Tranquila in 2023 was my first visit in a long time, and the excitement of catching up with old friends was weighed down by the losses of those years. Don Javier would never greet me again from a plastic chair in front of his house wearing his iconic white cowboy hat. I will miss the stories of the community's past that doña Carmen would tell me over fresh-roasted coffee. I won't be able to catch up with Isabel to hear about her many past jobs and what she was doing now, nor see doña Ana make a difficult project happen through sheer force of will. Don Antonio won't be able to tell me more about how fishers can care for the sea. Other community members whom I knew less well have also died, several during the COVID-19 pandemic despite the efforts the community took to block off the main road into Playa Tranquila during the early stages of the pandemic. Each home I visited had losses to acknowledge and mourn, and they wanted to share my own losses as well; death, health, and fishing were heavy but necessary conversations.

We had to also talk about how much the children had grown and how some of them were now parents, making my friends *abuelos* and *bisabuelos* (great-grandparents). New houses, shiny cars, freshly painted tourism boats, and new ideas about businesses and educational opportunities refreshed familiar conversations about memories we shared, trips we took, and changes we observed over the past two decades. Some friends were busy for weeks at a time, preparing for a business expo or traveling, while I ran into others at the now-expanded grocery store who pressed me into joining them for a second lunch.

Despite these changes, I was most struck by what had not changed. I had already written a draft of this book when I arrived in Loreto in June 2023, and the visit revealed how much the underlying issues I wrote about were unchanged, for the fishers and their families, for environmentalists, and for Loretanos generally. Everyone lamented that the marine environment was still severely degraded, with species continuing to disappear, including the chocolate clams Loreto is known for. Just as in 2001 and other years, it is difficult to talk about the marine area with any hope, especially since it seems the same management problems continue to plague the area.

At the end of this visit, I finally took a snorkeling trip, unsure why I'd never done this before in Loreto. I was amazed by the sea life and seascapes, enjoying the cool water as I swam through schools of brightly colored sergeants major (*petaca rayada*) and shimmering triggerfish (*cochi*), which I knew were also delicious. From the boat, we also saw an olive ridley sea turtle and a cowhead mobulus ray. I couldn't help wondering what this might have been like twenty years ago, and I was somewhat glad I wasn't spending the day lamenting more changes in the environment.

As always, I left my friends and the Loreto area wanting to return again soon but also aware that life often gets in the way. I was more determined to complete this book as well, given what appear to be intractable problems for managing natural resources like these. After twenty years, I knew the rhythms and patterns in this book were repeating themselves, much like those of previous boom-and-bust cycles. But I also saw glimmers of hope and change, such as the high school students who wanted to study marine biology so they could come back and be part of the solution to issues facing their families and the environment. The youngest children of the sea, like Mario, were even more determined to be heard (Peterson 2017).

* * *

Don Javier's relocation from the beach to the center of the community introduced the challenges around seeing this sale and similar actions as "choices" in the traditional decision-making sense, given political, social, economic, and even historical contexts that made the sale seemingly more inevitable than optional. Throughout the chapters, we have seen other choices that similarly depend on the context, presenting themselves more as inevitabilities than as options one might choose between. Fishing, starting new businesses, patrolling the MPA, and other decisions emerge from the entanglement of contexts, a variety of values, and what has worked in the past, rather than as rational individuals maximizing economic value. Yet the expectations that people behave as rational economic actors also influenced options and constraints around action.

When we try to understand those in Playa Tranquila, the MPA, and others as motivated only by economic values, we ignore their connections to the environment, each other, and other aspects of their lives. This separation from context, including nature, becomes dispossession and commoditization, as people, places, and resources are perceived as only their economic value or ability to produce or affect economic values. Tourism, conservation, and capacity building often bring in neoliberal models about rational individuals through their plans and accounting, also erasing the multiple values that motivate fishers and others to care for their families.

In contrast, understanding tourism, small businesses, and environmental stewardship through the values in Playa Tranquila shows how relationships can lead to innovations that fit community needs as well as the social and political contexts. Instead of separating people from contexts, seeing them as entangled leads to an appreciation for the ways people use their contexts, respond to them, and fight for sovereignty over these assemblages. These values are not without contradictions, like relying on family as a strategy while it is also an important value, seeing fishing as work and play and a way to care for the sea. Saavedra Gallo and colleagues (2021, 164; my translation) suggest that "the sea is not a source of resources to satisfy the calculating selfishness of individuals who move in the market, the sea is the space where artisanal fishing life takes place. They constitute part of the same place, the one that gives meaning to life, the one where life happens." This encourages a moral approach to the sea as well, around stewardship, but these hybrid configurations are, at the end, dominated by cultural and historical values that are not easy to connect to neoliberal logics (Saavedra Gallo et al.

2021). In considering how to center noneconomic values and their links to relationships and ideas about agency as foundational to connections to the environment, we must look at alternatives to current neoliberal markets and value systems. Greco and Apostolopoulou (2020) suggest that we can build on existing ideas about social needs and social wealth. How might this change our view of fishing, tourism, and natural resource management?

To consider the first question from the introduction, why the fishers continued to fish despite fishing's economic precarity, we can look at the political economy, ecology, and moral economy of the community which, like Thompson (1971) suggests for Britain in the eighteenth century, allows us to see the political, economic, and social processes that lead to the emergence of class inequalities. Through these lenses, we can better visualize and address the roots of differential access to resources, including how national fishing policies in Mexico have largely ignored fishers and their well-being, leaving them open to dispossessions through tourism and conservation, while large producers and investors continue to benefit (García 2020; see also Alcalá 2003):

> The society and the Mexican State has [*sic*] a historic debt with small-scale fishermen, because by act or omission, they have been turned into a silenced, excluded, cornered and deprived "sector." ... It is time for justice to be done in this "sector" and their families, emphasizing on [*sic*] indigenous people, women and young people, who in spite of the adversities, still see work at sea as a dignified horizon in life. (García 2020, 102)

Thompson (1971), Scott (1976), Peluso (1992), West (2016), Córdoba Azcárte (2020), and others highlight both how powerful interests can lead to livelihood "choices" but also how noneconomic values are important points for resistance and innovation, including the determination to maintain values apart from those introduced by industrialization or neoliberal economic ideas. Fishing in Playa Tranquila is a compromise between a very challenging context for livelihoods and a moral economy that values fishing. Community values also contribute to innovations; with more resources, connections, and opportunities, fishers and their families are building new futures for the community through education, small businesses, and care for the environment.

In answer to the second question, we have seen how the MPA and tourism deeply affected fishing and other livelihoods through dispossessions. For example, access to waters suitable for fishing has been limited by both land privatization and marine conservation efforts. A focus on economic rationality in terms of incentives and wage work has ignored and even undermined the noneconomic values and strategies community members use to adapt to change. In ignoring the needs and expertise of community members in marine resource management and tourism development, these efforts continued to dispossess residents of their sovereignty. A focus on economic rationality easily combines with discourses around nature, culture, and responsibility to make exclusions seem like the only reasonable thing to do (Viatori and Bombiella Medina 2019), as the environment becomes "intelligible and governable through insertion into financialized logics" (Sullivan 2013, 211–12). What might seem like neutral terms, including *resilience* and *vulnerability*, are loaded with assumptions that can marginalize communities with less power and control, as we saw with limitations around capacity building. Scientists and academics are not necessarily neutral either. As Córdoba Azcárte (2020, 190) warns about tourism studies, academic approaches that ignore relationships of power can only contribute to the cycles of exploitation: "Reducing tourism to discussions about its benefits and disadvantages loses sight of both the predation that makes these benefits possible and the forms of entrapment that they in turn create."

Finally, the last question from the introduction asks why the environmental management strategies of fishers, MPA employees, and tourism initiatives largely failed to change what they had hoped in the area. Like with the fishers, this book has shown how environmental management has also been stuck between conflicting values around humans and nature in a context that is at best unsupportive and at worst hostile to caring for the environment. It is critical to recognize that these conflicts come from a focus on economic incentives, motives, and rationality, rather than thinking that humans and nature are inherently opposed to each other. In writing about management, tourism, or other ways forward, Arturo Escobar argues that design can be dangerous and destructive, eliminating possible futures rather than imagining them alongside communities. Design involves separation, control, and appropriation, which come alongside capitalist modernity and its assumptions around rationality and ways of being (Escobar 2018), and as we see in Loreto, this does not always lead to the best result. In some ways, participatory processes in conservation efforts are an attempt to avoid designs that separate, control, and appropriate; but as we saw in chapter 4, these processes are difficult to do well due to both power differentials among participants and the overarching focus on economic values that tends to dominate the discourse. Newer conversations around common pool resource governance (building from the tragedy of the commons) are hopeful in identifying important ways to prevent separation from context and dispossessions, including polycentric governance (Andersson and Ostrom 2008), integrating ideas about social capital (Brondizio, Ostrom, and Young 2009), and focusing more on well-being and social sustainability rather than economic utility (Cashore and Bernstein 2023).

● ● ●

We are left with an important question: What can we do to improve marine resource conservation given all of this? A more contextually informed understanding of marine resource decision-making looks beyond individual greed or knowledge to recognize how the surrounding economy, politics, and culture can shape the options available as well as perceptions about these options. In other words, answering why the fishers fish or what the MPA is doing means examining their ability to act, the options they perceive, and the different values that matter for them, including environmental, relational, and cultural.

In focusing on the strategies used by the communities, we see how they are potentially polyvalent and useful for actors. However, those same strategies can also foreclose other kinds of values or alternatives, such as when women's microenterprises or artisanal fishing are understood as purely economic activities rather than as part of a large complex of activities motivated by a panoply of values (see also Escobar 2008; Gibson-Graham 2006). It is hard to escape from the economic framing that dominates discussions of livelihoods and choices. However, approaching values, strategies, and events through economization, as suggested by Çalışkan and Callon (2009, 2010), allows us to see how discourses of economics shape our lives and futures. Moving our focus to grounded strategies allows us to think more about who engages in them and to what ends. It allows us to see as well how these strategies intersect with values, institutions, and relationships, rather than glossing neoliberalism as an intractable, hegemonic system that governs all human activity.

This book has examined several contexts of decision-making, including day-to-day household and organizational decisions and longer-term planning and policymaking, to see how similar the underlying processes and issues are. How we think about decisions, choices, and agency matter for developing programs and policies that improve environmental conservation and economic well-being. In twenty years, nothing much has really changed in how Loreto tries to address these problems, and as I argue here, this is due in large part to a flaw in how decisions, choices, and agency are understood by people in power. Without appreciating how the context affects decisions and the constraints it introduces, we will likely struggle against the same challenges to successful resource management in Loreto and elsewhere for another twenty years.

REFERENCES

Abrams, Lynn. 2012. "'There Is Many a Thing that Can Be Done with Money': Women, Barter, and Autonomy in a Scottish Fishing Community in the Nineteenth and Twentieth Centuries." *Signs: Journal of Women in Culture and Society* 37 (3): 602–9. https://doi.org/10.1086/662700.

Abu-Lughod, Lila. 1990. "The Romance of Resistance: Tracing Transformations of Power through Bedouin Women." *American Ethnologist* 17 (1): 41–55. https://doi.org/10.1525/ae.1990.17.1.02a00030.

Acheson, James M. 1988. *The Lobster Gangs of Maine.* Hanover, N.H.: University Press of New England.

Acheson, James M. 2002. "Transaction Costs Economics: Accomplishments, Problems, and Possibilities." In *Theory in Economic Anthropology*, edited by Jean Ensminger, 27–58. Walnut Creek, Calif.: Altamira.

Agarwala, Matthew, Giles Atkinson, Benjamin Palmer Fry, Katherine Homewood, Susana Mourato, J. Marcus Rowcliffe, Graham Wallace, and E. J. Milner-Gulland. 2014. "Assessing the Relationship between Human Well-Being and Ecosystem Services: A Review of Frameworks." *Conservation and Society* 12 (4): 437–49. https://doi.org/10.4103/0972-4923.155592.

Agrawal, Arun. 2001. "Common Property Institutions and Sustainable Governance of Resources." *World Development* 29 (10): 1649–72. https://doi.org/10.1016/S0305-750X(01)00063-8.

Agrawal, Arun. 2005. *Environmentality: Technologies of Government and the Making of Subjects.* New Ecologies for the Twenty-First Century. Durham, N.C.: Duke University Press.

Ahearn, Laura M. 2001. "Language and Agency." *Annual Review of Anthropology* 30:109–37. https://doi.org/10.1146/annurev.anthro.30.1.109.

Alcalá, Graciela. 2003. *Políticas pesqueras en México (1946–2000): Contradicciones y aciertos en la planificación de la pesca nacional.* Mexico City: El Colegio de México.

Alfaro, Dinorah del Carmen Torres, José Luis Carpio Domínguez, and Jesús Ignacio Castro Salazar. 2023. "Pesca ilegal en México durante el periodo 2010–2022. Una exploración desde la criminología verde." *Revista mexicana de ciencias penales* 7 (21): 119–44. https://doi.org/10.57042/rmcp.v7i21.665.

Anderson, Joan B., and Denise Dimon. 1998. "Married Women's Labor Force Participation in Developing Countries: The Case of Mexico." *Estudios económicos* 13 (1): 3–34.

Andersson, Krister P., and Elinor Ostrom. 2008. "Analyzing Decentralized Resource Regimes from a Polycentric Perspective." *Policy Sciences* 41 (1): 71–93. https://doi.org/10.1007/s11077-007-9055-6.

Andreucci, Diego, and Christos Zografos. 2022. "Between Improvement and Sacrifice: Othering and the (Bio)political Ecology of Climate Change." *Political Geography* 92:102512. https://doi.org/10.1016/j.polgeo.2021.102512.

Ángeles Villa, Manuel, Alba E. Gámez Vázquez, and Ricardo Bórquez Reyes. 2017. "Neoliberalización, turismo y socioeconomía en Baja California Sur, México." *Estudios regionales en economía, población y desarrollo: Cuadernos de trabajo de la Universidad Autónoma de Ciudad Juárez* 7 (41): 3–27.

Ángeles Villa, Manuel, Alba E. Gámez Vázquez, and Antonina Ivanova. 2009. "On the Impact of Tourism on the Economy of Baja California Sur, Mexico: A SAM Approach." In *Sustainable Development and Planning IV*, 2:783–90. Southampton, UK: WIT Press. https://doi.org/10.2495/SDP090722.

Ángeles Villa, Manuel, and Andrea Carolina López Vergara. 2022. "La teoría crítica en el estudio del turismo en Baja California Sur: Una mirada preliminar." In *Abordajes críticos del turismo: Conceptualizaciones y estudios de caso*, 59–80. Mexico City: Ediciones Navarra.

Apostolopoulou, Elia. 2020. *Nature Swapped and Nature Lost: Biodiversity Offsetting, Urbanization and Social Justice*. Cham: Springer Nature.

Apostolopoulou, Elia, Anastasia Chatzimentor, Sara Maestre-Andrés, Marina Requena-i-Mora, Alejandra Pizarro, and Dimitrios Bormpoudakis. 2021. "Reviewing 15 Years of Research on Neoliberal Conservation: Towards a Decolonial, Interdisciplinary, Intersectional and Community-Engaged Research Agenda." *Geoforum* 124:236–56. https://doi.org/10.1016/j.geoforum.2021.05.006.

Appadurai, Arjun, ed. 1986. *The Social Life of Things: Commodities in Cultural Perspective*. New York: Cambridge University Press.

Arellanes-Cancino, Yaaye, Dante Ayala-Ortiz, and Martina Nava. 2022. "Current Gender Perspective of Artisanal Fishing in Three Michoacan Lakes." *Ciencia pesquera* 30 (1–2): 217–36.

Arizpe, C. O., and M. Verdugo Partida. 2020. "Bahía de Loreto National Park." In *Loreto: Challenges for a Sustainable Future*, edited by Paul Ganster, Oscar Arizpe Covarrubias, and Vinod Sasidharan, 35–56. San Diego: San Diego State University Press.

Arizpe, Lourdes. 1977. "Women in the Informal Labor Sector: The Case of Mexico City." *Signs: Journal of Women in Culture and Society* 3 (1): 25–37. https://doi.org/10.1086/493437.

REFERENCES

Armenta-Cisneros, Miguel, Miguel Angel Ojeda-Ruiz, Elvia Aida Marín-Monroy, and Alfredo Flores-Irigoyen. 2021. "Opportunities to Improve Sustainability of a Marine Protected Area: Small-Scale Fishing in Loreto, Baja California Sur, México." *Regional Studies in Marine Science* 45:101852. https://doi.org/10.1016/j.rsma.2021.101852.

Asad, Talal. 2000. "Agency and Pain: An Exploration." *Culture and Religion* 1 (1): 29–60. https://doi.org/10.1080/01438300008567139.

Barad, Karen. 2003. "Posthumanist Performativity: Toward an Understanding of How Matter Comes to Matter." *Signs: Journal of Women in Culture and Society* 28 (3): 801–31. https://doi.org/10.1086/345321.

Barco, Miguel del. 1980. *The Natural History of Baja California*. Translated by Froylan Tiscareno. Los Angeles: Dawson's Book Shop.

Beddington, J. R., D. J. Agnew, and C. W. Clark. 2007. "Current Problems in the Management of Marine Fisheries." *Science* 316 (5832): 1713–16. https://doi.org/10.1126/science.1137362.

Benería, Lourdes. 1992. "Mexican Debt Crisis: Restructuring the Economy and the Household." In *Unequal Burden: Economic Crisis, Persistent Poverty, and Women's Work*, edited by Lourdes Benería and Shelley Feldman, 83–105. Boulder: Westview.

Benería, Lourdes, and Martha Roldán. 1987. *The Crossroads of Class & Gender: Industrial Homework, Subcontracting, and Household Dynamics in Mexico City*. Chicago: University of Chicago Press.

Beresford, Melissa. 2020. "Entrepreneurship as Legacy Building: Reimagining the Economy in Post-Apartheid South Africa." *Economic Anthropology* 7 (1): 65–79. https://doi.org/10.1002/sea2.12170.

Bestor, Theodore C. 2004. *Tsukiji: The Fish Market at the Center of the World*. California Studies in Food and Culture 11. Berkeley: University of California Press.

Boholm, Åsa, Annette Henning, and Amanda Krzyworzeka. 2013. "Anthropology and Decision Making: An Introduction." *Focaal* 2013 (65): 97–113. https://doi.org/10.3167/fcl.2013.650109.

Bojorquez Luque, Jesus. 2022. "Turismo, despojo y conflictor social en Todos Santos, Baja California Sur (México): El caso de playa Punto Lobos." In *Abordajes críticos del turismo: Conceptualizaciones y estudios de caso*, edited by Escalera Briceño, 81–112. Mexico City: Ediciones Navarra. http://192.100.164.85/bitstream/handle/20.500.12249/3137/Abordajes%20cri%CC%81ticos%20del%20turismo.pdf?sequence=3&isAllowed=y#page=82.

Bordonaro, Lorenzo I. 2012. "Agency Does Not Mean Freedom. Cape Verdean Street Children and the Politics of Children's Agency." *Children's Geographies* 10 (4): 413–26. https://doi.org/10.1080/14733285.2012.726068.

Bordonaro, Lorenzo I., and Ruth Payne. 2012. "Ambiguous Agency: Critical Perspectives on Social Interventions with Children and Youth in Africa." *Children's Geographies* 10 (4): 365–72. https://doi.org/10.1080/14733285.2012.726065.

Brondizio, Eduardo S., Elinor Ostrom, and Oran R. Young. 2009. "Connectivity and the Governance of Multilevel Social-Ecological Systems: The Role of Social Capital." *Annual Review of Environment and Resources* 34:253–78. https://doi.org/10.1146/annurev.environ.020708.100707.

Brondo, Keri Vacanti. 2017. *Land Grab: Green Neoliberalism, Gender, and Garifuna Resistance in Honduras.* Tucson: University of Arizona Press.

Brondo, Keri Vacanti, and Natalie Bown. 2011. "Neoliberal Conservation, Garifuna Territorial Rights and Resource Management in the Cayos Cochinos Marine Protected Area." *Conservation and Society* 9 (2): 91–105.

Brosius, Peter J., Anna Lowenhaupt Tsing, and Charles Zerner, eds. 2005. *Communities and Conservation: Histories and Politics of Community-Based Natural Resource Management.* Lanham: AltaMira.

Brown, Katrina, and Elizabeth Westaway. 2011. "Agency, Capacity, and Resilience to Environmental Change: Lessons from Human Development, Well-Being, and Disasters." *Annual Review of Environment and Resources* 36:321–42. https://doi.org/10.1146/annurev-environ-052610-092905.

Bryant, Rebecca, and Madeleine Reeves. 2021. "Introduction: Toward an Anthropology of Sovereign Agency." In *The Everyday Lives of Sovereignty: Political Imagination beyond the State*, edited by Rebecca Bryant and Madeleine Reeves, 1–18. Ithaca: Cornell University Press.

Bunn, Matthew, and Matt Lumb. 2019. "Education as Agency: Challenging Educational Individualisation through Alternative Accounts of the Agentic." *International Education Journal: Comparative Perspectives* 18 (1): 7–19.

Burton, Valerie. 2012. "Fish/Wives: An Introduction." *Signs: Journal of Women in Culture and Society* 37 (3): 527–36. https://doi.org/10.1086/662686.

Calestani, Melania. 2009. "An Anthropology of 'the Good Life' in the Bolivian Plateau." *Social Indicators Research* 90:141–53.

Çalışkan, Koray, and Michel Callon. 2009. "Economization, Part 1: Shifting Attention from the Economy towards Processes of Economization." *Economy and Society* 38 (3): 369–98. https://doi.org/10.1080/03085140903020580.

Çalışkan, Koray, and Michel Callon. 2010. "Economization, Part 2: A Research Programme for the Study of Markets." *Economy and Society* 39 (1): 1–32. https://doi.org/10.1080/03085140903424519.

Cariño, M. Micheline, and Adelina Alameda. 1998. "Historia de las relaciones hombre-espacio, 1500–1940." In *Diagnóstico ambiental de Baja California Sur*, edited by Susana Mahieux, 3–54. La Paz, Mexico: Fundación Mexicana para la Educación Ambiental, Sociedad de Historia Natural Niparajá.

Cariño, Martha Micheline, and Mario Monteforte. 1999. *El primer emporio perlero del mundo: La compañia criadora de concha y perla de Baja California SA y perspectivas para Baja California Sur.* Baja California: Universidad Autonoma de Baja California.

Carpenter, Carol. 2020. *Power in Conservation: Environmental Anthropology beyond Political Ecology.* London: Routledge.

Carrier, James G. 2001. "Limits of Environmental Understanding: Action and Constraint." *Journal of Political Ecology* 8 (1): 25–44. https://doi.org/10.2458/v8i1.21578.

REFERENCES

Cashore, Benjamin, and Steven Bernstein. 2023. "Bringing the Environment Back In: Overcoming the Tragedy of the Diffusion of the Commons Metaphor." *Perspectives on Politics* 21 (2): 478–501. https://doi.org/10.1017/S1537592721002553.

Castillo Velasco Martínez, Iris Aurora del. 2021. "Evaluación de la sustentabilidad del turismo de naturaleza en el Parque Nacional Bahía de Loreto y sus áreas de influencia: Recomendaciones para su manejo sustentable." PhD diss., Centro de Investigaciones Biológicas del Noroeste, S.C. http://dspace.cibnor.mx:8080/handle/123456789/3080.

Celaya Tentori, Minerva, and Araceli Almaraz Alvarado. 2018. "Recuento histórico de la normatividad pesquera en México: Un largo proceso de auge y crisis." *Entreciencias: Diálogos en la Sociedad del conocimiento* 6 (16): 33–48.

Certeau, Michel de. 2011. *The Practice of Everyday Life. 1.* 3rd ed. Translated by Steven Rendell. Berkeley: University of California Press.

Chant, Sylvia. 1994. "Women, Work and Household Survival Strategies in Mexico, 1982–1992: Past Trends, Current Tendencies and Future Research." *Bulletin of Latin American Research* 13 (2): 203–33. https://doi.org/10.2307/3338275.

Chant, Sylvia H. 1991. *Women and Survival in Mexican Cities: Perspectives on Gender, Labour Markets, and Low-Income Households.* Manchester: Manchester University Press.

Chen, Eva. 2013. "Neoliberalism and Popular Women's Culture: Rethinking Choice, Freedom and Agency." *European Journal of Cultural Studies* 16 (4): 440–52. https://doi.org/10.1177/1367549413484297.

Chibnik, Michael. 2011. *Anthropology, Economics, and Choice.* Austin: University of Texas Press.

Cisneros-Montemayor, Andrés M., and Miguel A. Cisneros-Mata. 2018. "A medio siglo de manejo pesquero en el noroeste de México, el futuro de la pesca como sistema socioecológico." *Relaciones. Estudios de historia y sociedad* 39 (153): 99–127. https://doi.org/10.24901/rehs.v39i153.392.

Cleaver, Frances. 1999. "Paradoxes of Participation: Questioning Participatory Approaches to Development." *Journal of International Development* 11 (4): 597–612. https://doi.org/10.1002/(SICI)1099-1328(199906)11:4<597::AID-JID610>3.0.CO;2-Q.

Cleaver, Frances. 2002. "Reinventing Institutions: Bricolage and the Social Embeddedness of Natural Resource Management." *European Journal of Development Research* 14 (2): 11–30. https://www.tandfonline.com/doi/abs/10.1080/714000425.

Cohen, Scott A., and Erik Cohen. 2019. "New Directions in the Sociology of Tourism." *Current Issues in Tourism* 22 (2): 153–72. https://doi.org/10.1080/13683500.2017.1347151.

Cole, Michael. 1998. *Cultural Psychology: A Once and Future Discipline.* Cambridge, Mass.: Harvard University Press.

Cole, Sally Cooper. 1991. *Women of the Praia: Work and Lives in a Portuguese Coastal Community.* Princeton: Princeton University Press.

Comaroff, John L., and Jean Comaroff. 1997. *Of Revelation and Revolution, Volume 2: The Dialectics of Modernity on a South African Frontier.* Chicago: University of Chicago Press.

Comitas, Lambros. 1964. "Occupational Multiplicity in Rural Jamaica." In *Proceedings of the American Ethnological Society 1963*, edited by Garfield Friedl and Ernestine Friedl, 41–50. Seattle: University of Washington Press.

CONANP (Comisión Nacional de Áreas Naturales Protegidas). 1996. *Decreto por el que se declara área natural protegida, con el carácter de Parque Marino Nacional.* Mexico City: Gobierno de Mexico. https://dof.gob.mx/nota_detalle.php?codigo= 4892805andfecha=19/07/1996#gsc.tab=0.

CONANP. 2000. *Programa de manejo Parque Nacional Bahía de Loreto, México.* Mexico City: Comisión Nacional de Áreas Naturales Protegidas.

CONANP. 2003. *Plan de manejo Parque Nacional Bahia de Loreto, Baja California Sur.* Mexico City: Comisión Nacional de Áreas Naturales Protegidas. https://dof .gob.mx/nota_detalle.php?codigo=705458andfecha=06/01/2003#gsc.tab=0.

CONANP. 2019. *Programa del manejo del Parque Nacional Bahía de Loreto.* Mexico City: Gobierno de Mexico. https://www.conanp.gob.mx/programademanejo/ resumenes/ResumenBahiaDeLoreto.pdf.

Cooke, Bill, and Uma Kothari, eds. 2001. *Participation: The New Tyranny?* New York: Zed Books.

Corbera, Esteve, Manuel Estrada, Peter May, Guillermo Navarro, and Pablo Pacheco. 2011. "Rights to Land, Forests and Carbon in REDD+: Insights from Mexico, Brazil and Costa Rica." *Forests* 2 (1): 301–42. https://doi.org/10.3390/f2010301.

Córdoba Azcárate, Matilde. 2020. *Stuck with Tourism: Space, Power, and Labor in Contemporary Yucatan.* Berkeley: University of California Press.

Coulthard, Sarah, Derek Johnson, and J. Allister McGregor. 2011. "Poverty, Sustainability and Human Wellbeing: A Social Wellbeing Approach to the Global Fisheries Crisis." *Global Environmental Change* 21 (2): 453–63. https://doi.org/10.1016/ j.gloenvcha.2011.01.003.

Cox, Michael, Gwen Arnold, and Sergio Villamayor Tomás. 2010. "A Review of Design Principles for Community-Based Natural Resource Management." *Ecology and Society* 15 (4): 38. https://www.jstor.org/stable/26268233.

Crespo Guerrero, José Manuel, and Joaquín Daniel Nava Martínez. 2020. "Configuración territorial de la pesca comercial ribereña en la Reserva de la Biosfera Los Petenes, Estado de Campeche (México)." *Estudios geográficos* 81 (288): e040. https://doi.org/10.3989/estgeogr.202055.055.

Cruz-Torres, María L. 2001. "Local-Level Responses to Environmental Degradation in Northwestern Mexico." *Journal of Anthropological Research* 57 (2): 111–36. https://doi.org/10.1086/jar.57.2.3631563.

Cruz-Torres, María L. 2023. *Pink Gold: Women, Shrimp, and Work in Mexico.* Austin: University of Texas Press.

Cruz-Torres, María Luz. 2012. "Contested Livelihoods: Gender, Fisheries, and Resistance in Northwestern Mexico." In *Gender and Sustainability: Lessons from Asia and Latin America*, edited by María L. Cruz-Torres and Pamela McElwee, 207–28. Tucson: University of Arizona Press.

REFERENCES

Cruz-Torres, María Luz, and Pamela McElwee. 2017. *Gender, Livelihoods, and Sustainability: Anthropological Research*. New York: Routledge.

Dash, Nicole, and Hugh Gladwin. 2007. "Evacuation Decision Making and Behavioral Responses: Individual and Household." *Natural Hazards Review* 8 (3): 69–77. https://doi.org/10.1061/(ASCE)1527-6988(2007)8:3(69).

Dawson, Neil M., Brendan Coolsaet, Eleanor J. Sterling, Robin Loveridge, Nicole D. Gross-Camp, Supin Wongbusarakum, Kamaljit K. Sangha, et al. 2021. "The Role of Indigenous Peoples and Local Communities in Effective and Equitable Conservation." *Ecology and Society* 26 (3): Art. 19. https://doi.org/10.5751/ES-12625-260319.

Delgado Ramírez, Claudia Elizabeth. 2021. "Entre jaiba, camarón, sardina y erizo: Mujeres en la producción pesquera y la reproducción social en el noroeste de México." *Revista Latinoamericana de antropología del trabajo* 5 (12): 235–58.

Dietz, Thomas, Elinor Ostrom, and Paul C. Stern. 2003. "The Struggle to Govern the Commons." *Science* 302 (5652): 1907–12. https://doi.org/10.1126/science.1091015.

Doane, Molly. 2012. *Stealing Shining Rivers: Agrarian Conflict, Market Logic, and Conservation in a Mexican Forest*. Tucson: University of Arizona Press.

Dove, Michael R., Andrew Salvador Mathews, Keely Maxwell, Jonathan Padwe, and Anne Rademacher. 2008. "The Concept of Human Agency in Contemporary Conservation and Development." In *Against the Grain: The Vayda Tradition in Human Ecology and Ecological Anthropology*, edited by Bradley B. Walters, Bonnie J. McCay, Paige West, and Susan Lees, 225–54. Lanham: AltaMira.

Dowie, Mark. 2011. *Conservation Refugees: The Hundred-Year Conflict between Global Conservation and Native Peoples*. Cambridge, Mass.: MIT Press.

Durand, Leticia. 2014. "¿Todos ganan? Neoliberalismo, naturaleza y conservación en México." *Sociológica (México)* 29 (82): 183–223.

Durrenberger, E. Paul. 2011. Introduction to *The Anthropological Study of Class and Consciousness*, edited by E. Paul Durrenberger, 1–27. Boulder: University Press of Colorado.

Eber, Christine. 2000. "'That They Be in the Middle, Lord': Women, Weaving, and Cultural Survival in Highland Chiapas, Mexico." In *Artisans and Cooperatives: Developing Alternative Trade for the Global Economy*, edited by Kimberly M. Grimes and B. Lynne Milgrim, 45–64. Tucson: University of Arizona Press.

Eco Alianza de Loreto. 2019. "Soundings May 2019." *Eco Alianza de Loreto | Loreto, B.C.S.* (blog), May 14, 2019. https://ecoalianzaloreto.org/soundings-may-2019/.

Edelman, Marc. 2012. "E. P. Thompson and Moral Economies." In *A Companion to Moral Anthropology*, edited by Didier Fassin, 49–66. New York: Wiley.

Elyachar, Julia. 2019. "Neoliberalism, Rationality, and the Savage Slot." In *Mutant Neoliberalism*, edited by William Callison and Zachary Manfredi, 177–95. New York: Fordham University Press.

Escobar, Arturo. 1995. *Encountering Development: The Making and Unmaking of the Third World*. Princeton: Princeton University Press.

Escobar, Arturo. 2008. *Territories of Difference: Place, Movements, Life, Redes*. Durham, N.C.: Duke University Press.

Escobar, Arturo. 2018. *Designs for the Pluriverse: Radical Interdependence, Autonomy, and the Making of Worlds*. New Ecologies for the Twenty-First Century. Durham, N.C.: Duke University Press.

Esteva, José María. 1865. *Memoria sobre la pesca de la perla en la Baja California: Informe hecho para el gobierno por el Visitador General de Rentas José María Esteva, en 1857*. Mexico City: A. Boix, a cargo de M. Zornoza. https://library.ucsd.edu/dc/object/bb6555640z.

Everett, Margaret. 1997. "The Ghost in the Machine: Agency in 'Poststructural' Critiques of Development." *Anthropological Quarterly* 70 (3): 137–51. https://doi.org/10.2307/3317673.

Ferguson, James. 1994. *The Anti-politics Machine: "Development," Depoliticization, and Bureaucratic Power in Lesotho*. Minneapolis: University of Minnesota Press.

Fernández-Rivera Melo, F. J., A. Hernández-Velasco, M. Luna, A. Lejbowicz, and A. Sáenz-Arroyo. 2012. *Protocolo de monitoreo del Parque Nacional Bahía de Loreto y Parque Nacional Cabo Pulmo, Baja California Sur*. La Paz, Mexico: Comunidad y Biodiversidad A. C. Programa Península de Baja California. https://cobi.org.mx/protocolo-de-monitoreo-del-parque-nacional-bahia-de-loreto-y-parque-nacional-cabo-pulmo-baja-california-sur/.

Fischer, Edward F. 2014. *The Good Life: Aspiration, Dignity, and the Anthropology of Wellbeing*. Stanford: Stanford University Press.

Fischer, Edward F., and Peter Benson. 2006. *Broccoli and Desire: Global Connections and Maya Struggles in Postwar Guatemala*. Stanford: Stanford University Press.

Fletcher, Robert. 2020. "Neoliberal Conservation." In *Oxford Research Encyclopedia of Anthropology*. https://doi.org/10.1093/acrefore/9780190854584.013.300.

FONATUR (Fondo Nacional de Fomento de Turismo [National fund for tourism development]). 2003. *Loreto: Principales indicadores turisticos 1996–2001*. Loreto, Mexico: Loreto FONATUR office.

Ganster, Paul, Oscar Arizpe-Covarrubias, and Vinod Sasidharan. 2020. *Loreto, Mexico. Challenges for a Sustainable Future*. San Diego: San Diego State University Press.

Ganster, Paul, Oscar Arizpe Covarrubias, and Antonina Ivanova Boncheva. 2007. *Loreto*. San Diego: San Diego State University Press.

Ganti, Tejaswini. 2014. "Neoliberalism." *Annual Review of Anthropology* 43:89–104. https://doi.org/10.1146/annurev-anthro-092412-155528.

García, Milton Gabriel Hernández. 2020. "Propuestas para la revitalización de la pesca ribereña y la conservación de los ecosistemas costeros en México." *Revista de geografía agrícola* 64:81–103. https://doi.org/10.5154/r.rga.2019.64.04.

García, Nuria Jiménez. 2021. "Mujeres del manglar. Transgresión de los espacios masculinos y lucha por la visibilidad y aceptación de mujeres pescadoras en Oaxaca, México." *Tekoporá. Revista Latinoamericana de humanidades ambientales y estudios territoriales* 3 (2): 24–48. https://doi.org/10.36225/tekopora.v3i2.135.

García-Quijano, C. G., and M. Valdes Pizzini. 2015. "Ecosystem-Based Knowledge and Reasoning in Tropical, Multispecies, Small-Scale Fishers' LEK: What Can Fishers LEK Contribute to Coastal Ecological Science and Management?" In *Fishers' Knowledge and the Ecosystem Approach to Fisheries, Experiences and Lessons in Latin America*, edited by J. Fischer, 19–40. Rome: FAO.

Garro, Linda C. 1998. "On the Rationality of Decision-Making Studies: Part 2: Divergent Rationalities." *Medical Anthropology Quarterly* 12 (3): 341–55. https://doi.org/10.1525/maq.1998.12.3.341.

Gavaldón, Ana, and Julia Fraga. 2011. "Rompiendo esquemas tradicionales en la pesca artesanal: Las mujeres trabajadoras del mar en San Felipe, Yucatán, México." In *Pescadores en America Latina y El Caribe: Espacio, población, producción y política*, edited by Graciela Alcalá, 15–47. Mexico City: Universidad Nacional Autónoma de México.

Gerhard, Peter. 1956. "Pearl Diving in Lower California, 1533–1830." *Pacific Historical Review* 25 (3): 239–49. https://doi.org/10.2307/3637014.

Gershon, Ilana. 2011. "Neoliberal Agency." *Current Anthropology* 52 (4): 537–55. https://doi.org/10.1086/660866.

Gibson-Graham, J. K. 2006. *A Postcapitalist Politics*. Minneapolis: University of Minnesota Press.

Gigerenzer, Gerd, Peter M. Todd, and ABC Research Group. 2000. *Simple Heuristics that Make Us Smart*. New York: Oxford University Press.

Gobierno del Estado de Baja California Sur. Secretaría de Promoción y Desarrollo Económico. Centro Estatal de Información. 2005. *Compendio estadístico 1998–2004. Municipios de Baja California Sur. Cuaderno de datos básicos 2005, tomo I y II*. La Paz, Mexico: Publicaciones CEI. https://biblioteca.setuesbcs.gob.mx/administrador/biblioteca/publicaciones/pdf/Compendio1998-2004_red.pdf.

Gobierno del Estado de Baja California Sur. Secretaría de Turismo y Economía, Dirección de Informática y Estadística. 2024. "Loreto. Información estratégica 2024." https://biblioteca.setuesbcs.gob.mx/ficha/.

Gomberg-Muñoz, Ruth. 2010. "Willing to Work: Agency and Vulnerability in an Undocumented Immigrant Network." *American Anthropologist* 112 (2): 295–307. https://doi.org/10.1111/j.1548-1433.2010.01227.x.

Gómez Pech, Enrique Humberto, Ana García Silberman, and Sara Barrasa García. 2022. "Conflictos socioambientales en torno al turismo del tiburón ballena en la Bahía de la Paz, Baja California Sur, México." *Scripta Nova* 26 (2): 125–45.

González de la Rocha, Mercedes, and Agustín Escobar Latapí, eds. 1991. *Social Responses to Mexico's Economic Crisis of the 1980s*. La Jolla: Center for U.S.-Mexican Studies.

Grandia, Liza. 2012. *Enclosed: Conservation, Cattle, and Commerce among the Q'eqchi' Maya Lowlanders*. Culture, Place, and Nature: Studies in Anthropology and Environment. Seattle: University of Washington Press.

Granovetter, Mark. 1985. "The Problem of Embeddedness." *American Journal of Sociology* 91 (3): 481–510.

Greco, Elisa, and Elia Apostolopoulou. 2020. "Value, Rent, and Nature: The Centrality of Class." *Dialogues in Human Geography* 10 (1): 46–51. https://doi.org/10.1177/2043820619876386.

Green, Maia. 2000. "Participatory Development and the Appropriation of Agency in Southern Tanzania." *Critique of Anthropology* 20 (1): 67–89. https://doi.org/10.1177/0308275X0002000105.

Gudeman, Stephen. 2016. *Anthropology and Economy*. New York: Cambridge University Press.

Guest, Greg. 2003. "Fishing Behavior and Decision-Making in an Ecuadorian Community: A Scaled Approach." *Human Ecology* 31 (4): 611–44. https://doi.org/10.1023/B:HUEC.0000005516.70903.18.

Gutiérrez Barreras, J. A. 2001. *Reporte marino y costero del municipio de Loreto, B.C.S., México: GEA y PNBL*. Loreto, Mexico: GEA and PNBL.

Haenn, Nora. 2005. *Fields of Power, Forests of Discontent: Culture, Conservation, and the State in Mexico*. Tucson: University of Arizona Press.

Hardin, Garrett. 1968. "The Tragedy of the Commons." *Science* 162 (3859): 1243–48.

Harvey, David. 2005. *A Brief History of Neoliberalism*. New York: Oxford University Press.

Harvey, David. 2012. "The 'New' Imperialism: Accumulation by Dispossession." In *Karl Marx*, edited by Bertell Ollman and Kevin B. Anderson. London: Routledge.

Hastie, R. 2001. "Problems for Judgment and Decision Making." *Annual Review of Psychology* 52:653–83. https://doi.org/10.1146/annurev.psych.52.1.653.

Hernández, Luis César Almendarez. 2023. "Perfil del pescador deportivo que visita Isla Cerralvo y localidades contiguas, Baja California Sur, México." *El periplo sustentable* 44:212–28. https://doi.org/10.36677/elperiplo.v0i44.17072.

Hirsch, Eric. 2020. "Hidden Treasures: Marca Perú (PeruTM) and the Recoding of Neoliberal Indigeneity in the Andes." *Latin American and Caribbean Ethnic Studies* 15 (3): 245–69. https://doi.org/10.1080/17442222.2020.1798077.

Hirsch, Jennifer S. 1999. "En El Norte La Mujer Manda: Gender, Generation, and Geography in a Mexican Transnational Community." *American Behavioral Scientist* 42 (9): 1332–49. https://doi.org/10.1177/00027649921954930.

Hodgson, Dorothy Louise. 2001. *Once Intrepid Warriors: Gender, Ethnicity, and the Cultural Politics of Maasai Development*. Bloomington: Indiana University Press.

Holmes, George, and Connor J. Cavanagh. 2016. "A Review of the Social Impacts of Neoliberal Conservation: Formations, Inequalities, Contestations." *Geoforum* 75:199–209. https://doi.org/10.1016/j.geoforum.2016.07.014.

Hutchins, Edwin. 1995. *Cognition in the Wild*. Cambridge, Mass.: MIT Press.

Irigoyen, Ulises. 1943. "Carretera transpeninsular de la Baja California." *Investigación económica* 3 (2): 139–54.

Ivanova, Antonina, Martha Micheline Cariño Olvera, Mario Monteforte-Sánchez, Ekaterine A. Ramírez Ivanova, Wendi Domínguez, Antonina Ivanova, Martha Micheline Cariño Olvera, et al. 2017. "La economía azul como modelo de sustentabilidad para estados costeros: El caso de Baja California Sur." *Sociedad y ambiente* 14:75–98.

Jaeger, Carlo C., Thomas Webler, Eugene A. Rosa, and Ortwin Renn. 2013. *Risk, Uncertainty and Rational Action*. New York: Routledge.

Janssen, Marco A., Skaidra Smith-Heisters, Rimjhim Aggarwal, and Michael L. Schoon. 2019. "'Tragedy of the Commons' as Conventional Wisdom in Sustainability Education." *Environmental Education Research* 25 (11): 1587–604. https://doi.org/10.1080/13504622.2019.1632266.

Jordán, Fernando. 1995. *Mar Roxo de Cortés: Biografía de un golfo*. Mexicali, Mexico: UABC.

Juárez Mancilla, Judith, Plácido Roberto Cruz Chávez, Alberto Francisco Torres García, and Adilene Sarahí Castillo Espinoza. 2020. "Traditional and Alternative Tourism in Loreto, BCS." In *Loreto: Challenges for a Sustainable Future*, edited by Paul Ganster, Oscar Arizpe Covarrubias, and Vinod Sasidharan, 141–59. San Diego: San Diego State University Press.

Jungermann, Helmut. 2000. "The Two Camps on Rationality." In *Judgment and Decision Making: An Interdisciplinary Reader*, 2nd ed., edited by Terry Connolly, Hal R. Arkes, and Kenneth R. Hammond, 575–91. Cambridge: Cambridge University Press.

Kaaristo, Maarja. 2018. "Engaging with the Hosts and Guests: Some Methodological Reflections on the Anthropology of Tourism." In *Anthropology of Tourism in Central and Eastern Europe: Bridging Worlds*, edited by Sabina Owsianowska and Magdalena Banaszkiewicz, 71–88. Lanham: Lexington Books.

Kacou, Kablan P., Lavagnon A. Ika, and Lauchlan T. Munro. 2022. "Fifty Years of Capacity Building: Taking Stock and Moving Research Forward." *Public Administration and Development* 42 (4): 215–32. https://doi.org/10.1002/pad.1993.

Kadfak, Alin. 2019. "More than Just Fishing: The Formation of Livelihood Strategies in an Urban Fishing Community in Mangaluru, India." *Journal of Development Studies* 56 (11): 2030–44. https://doi.org/10.1080/00220388.2019.1650168.

Kaus, Andrea. 1992. "Common Ground: Ranchers and Researchers in the Mapimí Biosphere Reserve." PhD diss., University of California, Riverside.

Keane, Webb. 1997. "Religious Language." *Annual Review of Anthropology* 26:47–71. https://doi.org/10.1146/annurev.anthro.26.1.47.

Kim, Do Own (Donna). 2023. "'Pay for Your Choices': Deconstructing Neoliberal Choice through Free-to-Play Mobile Interactive Fiction Games." *New Media & Society* 25 (5): 943–62. https://doi.org/10.1177/14614448211018177.

Kincaid, Jamaica. 1988. *A Small Place*. New York: Farrar, Straus and Giroux.

Klooster, Daniel. 2000. "Institutional Choice, Community, and Struggle: A Case Study of Forest Co-management in Mexico." *World Development* 28 (1): 1–20. https://doi.org/10.1016/S0305-750X(99)00108-4.

Kraak, Sarah B. M. 2011. "Exploring the 'Public Goods Game' Model to Overcome the Tragedy of the Commons in Fisheries Management." *Fish and Fisheries* 12 (1): 18–33. https://doi.org/10.1111/j.1467-2979.2010.00372.x.

Krzyworzeka, Amanda. 2013. "Decision-Making in Farming Households in Eastern Poland." *Focaal* 2013 (65): 129–44. https://doi.org/10.3167/fcl.2013.650111.

Kuymulu, Mehmet Barış. 2011. "From US with Love: Community Participation, Stakeholder Partnership, and the Exacerbation of Inequality in Rural Jamaica." *New Proposals: Journal of Marxism and Interdisciplinary Inquiry* 4 (2): 45–58.

Lauer, Matthew. 2023. *Sensing Disaster: Local Knowledge and Vulnerability in Oceania*. Oakland, California: University of California Press.

Lauterio Martínez, Claudia Lorena, Reyna María Ibáñez Pérez, Víctor Hernández Trejo, and Mariana Bobadilla. 2022. "Instrumentos de política económica ambiental para la conservación de servicios ecosistémicos en el Parque Nacional Bahía de Loreto, Baja California Sur." In *Leyendo el territorio: Homenaje a Miguel Ángel Troitiño*, edited by Rojelio Martínez Cárdenas, Luis Felipe Cabrales Barajas, Manuel de la Calle Vaquero, María García Hernández, María del Carmen Mínguez García, Libertad Troitiño Torralba, and Miguel Ángel Troitiño Vinuesa, 304–21. Guadalajara: Universidad de Guadalajara.

Li, Tania. 2007. *The Will to Improve: Governmentality, Development, and the Practice of Politics*. Durham, N.C.: Duke University Press.

Little, Peter D. 1994. "The Link between Local Participation and Improved Conservation: A Review of Issues and Experiences." In *Natural Connections: Perspectives in Community-Based Conservation*, edited by David Western, Michael Wright, and Shirley Carol Strum, 347–72. Washington, D.C.: Island Press.

Lomnitz-Adler, Claudio, ed. 2000. *Vicios públicos, virtudes privadas: La corrupción en México*. Mexico City: CIESAS.

López Vergara, Andrea. 2022. "Turismo, conflictos ambientales en Baja California Sur y la sociedad civil como resistencia. Una revisión desde la teoría crítica." *Revista pensamiento y acción interdisciplinaria* 8 (1): 114–23. https://doi.org/10.29035/pai.8.1.114.

Maaravi, Yossi, Aharon Levy, Tamar Gur, Dan Confino, and Sandra Segal. 2021. "'The Tragedy of the Commons': How Individualism and Collectivism Affected the Spread of the COVID-19 Pandemic." *Frontiers in Public Health* 9. https://www.frontiersin.org/articles/10.3389/fpubh.2021.627559.

Maestre-Andrés, Sara, Laura Calvet-Mir, and Evangelia Apostolopoulou. 2018. "Unravelling Stakeholder Participation under Conditions of Neoliberal Biodiversity Governance in Catalonia, Spain." *Environment and Planning C: Politics and Space* 36 (7): 1299–318. https://doi.org/10.1177/2399654417753624.

Mahmood, Saba. 2009. "Agency, Performativity, and the Feminist Subject." In *Pieties and Gender*, edited by Lene Sjørup and Hilda Rømer Christensen, 11–45. Leiden: Brill.

Mansfield, Becky. 2004. "Neoliberalism in the Oceans: 'Rationalization,' Property Rights, and the Commons Question." *Geoforum* 35 (3): 313–26. https://doi.org/10.1016/j.geoforum.2003.05.002.

Mansfield, Becky. 2007. "Articulation between Neoliberal and State-Oriented Environmental Regulation: Fisheries Privatization and Endangered Species Protection." *Environment and Planning A: Economy and Space* 39 (8): 1926–42. https://doi.org/10.1068/a38176.

Marin-Monroy, Elvia Aida, and Miguel Ángel Ojeda-Ruíz. 2023. "Economic Diversification and Vulnerability in Fishing Communities of the Baja California Peninsula, Mexico." *Latin American Journal of Aquatic Research* 51 (5): 734–46. https://doi.org/10.3856/%x.

Martínez de la Torre, Juan Antonio. 1998a. "La explotación de los recursos naturales renovables, 1940–1993." In *Diagnóstico ambiental de Baja California Sur*, edited by Susana Mahieux, 55–98. La Paz, Mexico: Fundación Mexicana para la Educación Ambiental, Sociedad de Historia Natural Niparajá.

Martínez de la Torre, Juan Antonio. 1998b. "Población y problemas urbanoambientales." In *Diagnóstico ambiental de Baja California Sur*, edited by Susana Mahieux, 55–98. La Paz, Mexico: Fundación Mexicana para la Educación Ambiental, Sociedad de Historia Natural Niparajá.

Martínez-Reyes, José Eduardo. 2016. *Moral Ecology of a Forest: The Nature Industry and Maya Post-Conservation*. Critical Green Engagements: Investigating the Green Economy and Its Alternatives. Tucson: University of Arizona Press.

Mathews, Andrew S. 2005. "Power/Knowledge, Power/Ignorance: Forest Fires and the State in Mexico." *Human Ecology* 33 (6): 795–820. https://doi.org/10.1007/s10745-005-8211-x.

Mattingly, Cheryl. 2012. "Two Virtue Ethics and the Anthropology of Morality." *Anthropological Theory* 12 (2): 161–84. https://doi.org/10.1177/1463499612455284.

Maurstad, Anita. 2007. "To Fish or Not to Fish: Small-Scale Fishing and Changing Regulations of the Cod Fishery in Northern Norway." *Human Organization* 59 (1): 37–47. https://doi.org/10.17730/humo.59.1.q0242m112x223862.

Maxwell, Sean L., Victor Cazalis, Nigel Dudley, Michael Hoffmann, Ana S. L. Rodrigues, Sue Stolton, Piero Visconti, et al. 2020. "Area-Based Conservation in the Twenty-First Century." *Nature* 586 (7828): 217–27. https://doi.org/10.1038/s41586-020-2773-z.

Mendoza-Carranza, Manuel, Amelia Paredes-Trujillo, and Elsy Segura-Berttolini. 2024. "La importancia de las mujeres en la cadena de valor de la pesca marina de pequeña escala y en la ciencia fesquera: Un estudio de caso en la costa de Tabasco, México/The Importance of Women in the Small-Scale Marine Fisheries Value Chain and in Fisheries Science: A Case." *Ciencia pesquera* 32:55.

Miller, Daniel. 1994. *Modernity, an Ethnographic Approach: Dualism and Mass Consumption in Trinidad*. Providence, R.I.: Berg.

Miller, Ethan. 2019. *Reimagining Livelihoods: Life beyond Economy, Society, and Environment*. Minneapolis: University of Minnesota Press.

Mills, Mary Beth. 2003. "Gender and Inequality in the Global Labor Force." *Annual Review of Anthropology* 32:41–62. https://doi.org/10.1146/annurev.anthro.32.061002.093107.

Mitchell Fuentes, Catherine M. 2022. "The 'Struggling Good Mother': The Role of Marginalization, Trauma, and Interpersonal Violence in Incarcerated Women's Mothering Experiences and Goals." *Human Organization* 81 (1): 1–11. https://doi.org/10.17730/1938-3525-81.1.1.

Mitchell, Timothy. 2014. "Economentality: How the Future Entered Government." *Critical Inquiry* 40 (4): 479–507. https://doi.org/10.1086/676417.

Montaño Armendáriz, Angélica, Juan Carlos Pérez Concha, and Gilberto Martínez Sidón. 2022. "Economía social y empoderamiento de la mujer a partir del turismo en zonas rurales: El caso de la ribera, Baja California Sur." In *Reconfigurando territorios a partir de la cultura, el empoderamiento de las mujeres y nuevos turismos*, edited by Ma. del Pilar Alejandra Mora Cantellano, Serrano Oswald, Serena Eréndira y Mota Flores, and V. Enrique, 601–14. Mexico City: UNAM.

Monteforte-Sánchez, Mario. 2020. "Integration of Resident Fisherfolk Communities in Marine Protected Areas by Social Micro-Entrepreneurships of Mariculture: A Case Study at La Paz Bay, South Baja California, Mexico." In *Socio-ecological Studies in Natural Protected Areas: Linking Community Development and Conservation in Mexico*, edited by Alfredo Ortega-Rubio, 537–66. Cham: Springer.

Morgan, Tonatiuh. 2023. "Despojo y expulsión del espacio en el manglito, una narrativa más de la turistificación de La Paz, Baja California Sur." *Temas antropológicos* 44 (2): 21–48.

Moser, Caroline O. N. 1978. "Informal Sector or Petty Commodity Production: Dualism or Dependence in Urban Development?" *World Development* 6 (9): 1041–64. https://doi.org/10.1016/0305-750X(78)90062-1.

Moser, Caroline O. N., and Cathy McIlwaine. 2000. *Urban Poor Perceptions of Violence and Exclusion in Colombia*. Conflict Prevention and Post-conflict Reconstruction. Washington, D.C.: World Bank.

Mosse, David. 2004. *Cultivating Development: An Ethnography of Aid Policy and Practice*. London: Pluto Press.

Mullainathan, Sendhil, and Eldar Shafir. 2013. *Scarcity: Why Having Too Little Means So Much*. New York: Times Books, Henry Holt.

Münster, Daniel, and Ludek Broz. 2015. "The Anthropology of Suicide: Ethnography and the Tension of Agency." In *Suicide and Agency: Anthropological Perspectives on Self-Destruction, Personhood, and Power*, edited by Ludek Broz and Daniel Münster, 3–23. Farnham: Ashgate.

Mykhalovskiy, Eric. 2008. "Beyond Decision Making: Class, Community Organizations, and the Healthwork of People Living with HIV/AIDS. Contributions from Institutional Ethnographic Research." *Medical Anthropology* 27 (2): 136–63. https://doi.org/10.1080/01459740802017363.

Nadel-Klein, Jane, and Donna Lee Davis, eds. 1988. *To Work and to Weep: Women in Fishing Economies*. Social and Economic Papers 18. St. John's: Memorial University of Newfoundland.

Neilson, Alison Laurie, Rita São Marcos, Kas Sempere, Laurinda Sousa, and Clarisse Canha. 2019. "A Vision at Sea: Women in Fisheries in the Azores Islands, Portugal." *Maritime Studies* 18 (3): 385–97. https://doi.org/10.1007/s40152-019-00155-0.

Ochs, Elinor, and Sally Jacoby. 1997. "Down to the Wire: The Cultural Clock of Physicists and the Discourse of Consensus." *Language in Society* 26 (4): 479–505. https://doi.org/10.1017/S0047404500021023.

REFERENCES

Okura Gagné, Nana. 2020. "Neoliberalism at Work: Corporate Reforms, Subjectivity, and Post-Toyotist Affect in Japan." *Anthropological Theory* 20 (4): 455–83. https://doi.org/10.1177/1463499618807294.

O'Neil, Ann, and Don O'Neil. 2001. *Loreto, Baja California: First Mission and Capital of Spanish California*. Studio City, Calif.: Tio Press.

Ortega Santos, Antonio. 2021. "Extractivismo marino-colonial. Apropiación asimétrica de recursos marinos en el golfo de California (México) siglos XVI–XXI." *Relaciones internacionales* 46:99–117. https://doi.org/10.15366/relacionesinternacionales2021.46.006.

Ortner, Sherry B. 1984. "Theory in Anthropology since the Sixties." *Comparative Studies in Society and History* 26 (1): 126–66. https://doi.org/10.1017/S0010417500010811.

Ortner, Sherry B. 2006. *Anthropology and Social Theory: Culture, Power, and the Acting Subject*. Durham, N.C.: Duke University Press.

Ostrom, Elinor. 1990. *Governing the Commons: The Evolution of Institutions for Collective Action*. New York: Cambridge University Press.

Parkins, John R., and Ross E. Mitchell. 2005. "Public Participation as Public Debate: A Deliberative Turn in Natural Resource Management." *Society & Natural Resources* 18 (6): 529–40. https://doi.org/10.1080/08941920590947977.

Parrado, Emilio A., and René M. Zenteno. 2001. "Economic Restructuring, Financial Crises, and Women's Work in Mexico." *Social Problems* 48 (4): 456–77. https://doi.org/10.1525/sp.2001.48.4.456.

Peláez González, Carolina. 2015. "Una mirada a los estudios pesqueros desde las ciencias sociales." *Revista Mexicana de ciencias agrícolas* 2:357–65.

Pellowe, Kara E., and Heather M. Leslie. 2021. "Ecosystem Service Lens Reveals Diverse Community Values of Small-Scale Fisheries." *Ambio* 50 (3): 586–600. https://doi.org/10.1007/s13280-020-01405-w.

Peluso, Nancy Lee. 1992. *Rich Forests, Poor People: Resource Control and Resistance in Java*. Berkeley: University of California Press.

Peluso, Nancy Lee. 2012. "What's Nature Got to Do with It? A Situated Historical Perspective on Socio-natural Commodities." *Development and Change* 43 (1): 79–104. https://doi.org/10.1111/j.1467-7660.2012.01755.x.

Peterson, Nicole. 2010. "Choices, Options, and Constraints: Decision Making and Decision Spaces in Natural Resource Management." *Human Organization* 69 (1): 54–64. https://doi.org/10.17730/humo.69.1.82153826v2484743.

Peterson, Nicole D. 2011. "Excluding to Include: (Non)participation in Mexican Natural Resource Management." *Agriculture and Human Values* 28 (1): 99–107. https://doi.org/10.1007/s10460-010-9258-x.

Peterson, Nicole D. 2014a. "Breaking the Bounds of Rationality: Values, Relationships, and Decision-Making in Mexican Fishing Communities." *Conservation and Society* 12 (3): 245. https://doi.org/10.4103/0972-4923.145135.

Peterson, Nicole D. 2014b. "'We Are Daughters of the Sea': Strategies, Gender, and Empowerment in a Mexican Women's Cooperative." *Journal of Latin American and Caribbean Anthropology* 19 (1): 148–67. https://doi.org/10.1111/jlca.12064.

Peterson, Nicole D. 2015. "Unequal Sustainabilities: The Role of Social Inequalities in Conservation and Development Projects." *Economic Anthropology* 2 (2): 264–77. https://doi.org/10.1002/sea2.12030.

Peterson, Nicole D. 2017. "Caguama (Sea Turtle): Anthropology and Humanism." *Anthropology and Humanism* 42 (1): 42–43. https://doi.org/10.1111/anhu.12158.

Peterson, Nicole D., Kenneth Broad, Ben Orlove, Carla Roncoli, Renzo Taddei, and Maria-Alejandra Velez. 2010. "Participatory Processes and Climate Forecast Use: Socio-cultural Context, Discussion, and Consensus." *Climate and Development* 2 (1): 14–29. https://doi.org/10.3763/cdev.2010.0033.

Peterson, Tarla Rai. 1997. *Sharing the Earth: The Rhetoric of Sustainable Development.* Columbia: University of South Carolina Press.

Pfeilstetter, Richard. 2021. *The Anthropology of Entrepreneurship: Cultural History, Global Ethnographies, Theorizing Agency.* London: Routledge.

Phillips, Lynne, and Suzan Ilcan. 2004. "Capacity-Building: The Neoliberal Governance of Development." *Canadian Journal of Development Studies/Revue canadienne d'études du développement* 25 (3): 393–409. https://doi.org/10.1080/02255189.2004.9668985.

Porco, Travis C., Daozhou Gao, James C. Scott, Eunha Shim, Wayne T. Enanoria, Alison P. Galvani, and Thomas M. Lietman. 2012. "When Does Overuse of Antibiotics Become a Tragedy of the Commons?" *PLOS ONE* 7 (12): e46505. https://doi.org/10.1371/journal.pone.0046505.

Pronatura. 2022. "Parque Nacional Bahía de Loreto." *Pronatura Noroeste AC* (blog), August 1, 2022. https://pronatura-noroeste.org/parque-nacional-bahia-loreto/.

Quadri-Barba, Paulo, Katharine R. E. Sims, and Adam Millard-Ball. 2021. "Using Cultural Heritage Sites in Mexico to Understand the Poverty Alleviation Impacts of Protected Areas." *Conservation Science and Practice* 3 (2): e339. https://doi.org/10.1111/csp2.339.

Quinn, Naomi. 1978. "Do Mfantse Fish Sellers Estimate Probabilities in Their Heads?" *American Ethnologist* 5 (2): 206–26. https://doi.org/10.1525/ae.1978.5.2.02a00020.

Quintana, Anastasia C. E., and Xavier Basurto. 2021. "Community-Based Conservation Strategies to End Open Access: The Case of Fish Refuges in Mexico." *Conservation Science and Practice* 3 (1): e283. https://doi.org/10.1111/csp2.283.

Radel, Claudia. 2012. "Gendered Livelihoods and the Politics of Socio-environmental Identity: Women's Participation in Conservation Projects in Calakmul, Mexico." *Gender, Place & Culture* 19 (1): 61–82. https://doi.org/10.1080/0966369X.2011.617905.

Ramachandran, B. Bindu. 2021. *An Anthropological Study of Marine Fishermen in Kerala: Anxieties, Compromises and Survivals.* Newcastle upon Tyne: Cambridge Scholars Publishing.

Raycraft, Justin. 2019. "Conserving Poverty: Destructive Fishing Gear Use in a Tanzanian Marine Protected Area." *Conservation & Society* 17 (3): 297–309.

Razo, Itsi. 2018. "Se fortalece inspección y vigilancia en el Parque Nacional Bahía de Loreto." *Pronatura Noroeste AC* (blog), February 22, 2018. https://pronatura

-noroeste.org/se-fortalece-inspeccion-y-vigilancia-en-el-parque-nacional-bahia
-de-loreto/.

Réyez, José. 2016. "Áreas naturales protegidas, en el abandono." *Contralínea* (blog), December 11, 2016. https://contralinea.com.mx/portada/areas-naturales -protegidas-en-el-abandono/.

Richardson, Liz, Catherine Durose, Matt Ryan, and Jess Steele. 2024. "Knowledge for the Commons: What Is Needed Now?" *International Journal of the Commons* 18 (1): 218–30. https://doi.org/10.5334/ijc.1250.

Robbins, Joel. 2007. "Between Reproduction and Freedom: Morality, Value, and Radical Cultural Change." *Ethnos* 72 (3): 293–314. https://doi.org/10.1080/00141840701576919.

Roseberry, W. 1988. "Political Economy." *Annual Review of Anthropology* 17:161–85. https://doi.org/10.1146/annurev.an.17.100188.001113.

Rothstein, Frances Abrahamer. 1999. "Declining Odds: Kinship, Women's Employment, and Political Economy in Rural Mexico." *American Anthropologist* 101 (3): 579–93. https://doi.org/10.1525/aa.1999.101.3.579.

Saavedra Gallo, Gonzalo, Karen Mardones Leiva, Gonzalo Saavedra Gallo, and Karen Mardones Leiva. 2021. "Representaciones sociales sobre el mar y la pesca artesanal en el océano del neoliberalismo chileno." *Revista colombiana de sociología* 44 (1): 143–67. https://doi.org/10.15446/rcs.v44n1.87914.

Salas, Silvia, Oswaldo Huchim-Lara, Citlalli Guevara-Cruz, and Walter Chin. 2018. "Cooperation, Competition, and Attitude toward Risk of Small-Scale Fishers as Adaptive Strategies: The Case of Yucatán, Mexico." In *Viability and Sustainability of Small-Scale Fisheries in Latin America and The Caribbean*, edited by Silvia Salas, María José Barragán-Paladines, and Ratana Chuenpagdee, 19:101–23. Cham: Springer.

Scott, James C. 1976. *The Moral Economy of the Peasant: Rebellion and Subsistence in Southeast Asia*. New Haven, Conn.: Yale University Press.

Seckinelgin, Hakan. 2006. "The Multiple Worlds of NGOs and HIV/AIDS: Rethinking NGOs and Their Agency." *Journal of International Development* 18 (5): 715–27. https://doi.org/10.1002/jid.1305.

SECTUR (Secretary of Tourism). 2019. "Loreto, Baja California Sur." https://www.gob .mx/sectur/articulos/loreto-baja-california-sur-210374.

SECTUR. 2024a. "Hotel Room Occupancies in Loreto, BCS." https://datatur.sectur .gob.mx/SitePages/Tableros.aspx.

SECTUR. 2024b. "Passengers Arriving in International Flights by Airport." https:// datatur.sectur.gob.mx/SitePages/TrasnAerea.aspx.

Sewell, William H. 1992. "A Theory of Structure: Duality, Agency, and Transformation." *American Journal of Sociology* 98 (1): 1–29. https://doi.org/10.1086/229967.

Shah, Anuj K., Jiaying Zhao, Sendhil Mullainathan, and Eldar Shafir. 2018. "Money in the Mental Lives of the Poor." *Social Cognition* 36 (1): 4–19. https://doi.org/10 .1521/soco.2018.36.1.4.

Shever, Elana. 2008. "Neoliberal Associations: Property, Company, and Family in the Argentine Oil Fields." *American Ethnologist* 35 (4): 701–16. https://doi.org/10 .1111/j.1548-1425.2008.00106.x.

Simon, Herbert A. 1990. "Invariants of Human Behavior." *Annual Review of Psychology* 41:1–20. https://doi.org/10.1146/annurev.ps.41.020190.000245.

Simonian, Lane. 1995. *Defending the Land of the Jaguar: A History of Conservation in Mexico*. Austin: University of Texas Press.

Sims, Katharine R. E., and Jennifer M. Alix-Garcia. 2017. "Parks versus PES: Evaluating Direct and Incentive-Based Land Conservation in Mexico." *Journal of Environmental Economics and Management* 86:8–28. https://doi.org/10.1016/j.jeem.2016.11.010.

Skidelsky, Robert. 2020. *What's Wrong with Economics?* New Haven, Conn.: Yale University Press.

Song, Andrew M., Ratana Chuenpagdee, and Svein Jentoft. 2013. "Values, Images, and Principles: What They Represent and How They May Improve Fisheries Governance." *Marine Policy* 40:167–75. https://doi.org/10.1016/j.marpol.2013.01.018.

Stamieszkin, Karen, Jeffrey Wielgus, and Leah R. Gerber. 2009. "Management of a Marine Protected Area for Sustainability and Conflict Resolution: Lessons from Loreto Bay National Park (Baja California Sur, Mexico)." *Ocean & Coastal Management* 52 (9): 449–58. https://doi.org/10.1016/j.ocecoaman.2009.07.006.

Stead, Victoria. 2021. "Precarity's Reach: Intersections of History, Life, and Labour in the Australian Horticultural Industry." *Journal of the Royal Anthropological Institute* 27 (2): 303–20. https://doi.org/10.1111/1467-9655.13491.

Stern, Marc J. 2010. "Payoffs versus Process: Expanding the Paradigm for Park/People Studies Beyond Economic Rationality." *Journal of Sustainable Forestry* 29 (2–4): 174–201. https://doi.org/10.1080/10549810903547809.

Stonich, Susan C. 2021. *I Am Destroying the Land! The Political Ecology of Poverty and Environmental Destruction in Honduras*. New York: Routledge.

Stronza, Amanda. 2001. "Anthropology of Tourism: Forging New Ground for Ecotourism and Other Alternatives." *Annual Review of Anthropology* 30:261–83.

Strum, Shirley Carol. 1994. "Lessons Learned." In *Natural Connections: Perspectives in Community-Based Conservation*, edited by David Western, Michael Wright, and Shirley Carol Strum, 512–23. Washington, DC: Island Press.

Sullivan, Sian. 2013. "Banking Nature? The Spectacular Financialisation of Environmental Conservation." *Antipode* 45 (1): 198–217. https://doi.org/10.1111/j.1467-8330.2012.00989.x.

Swyngedouw, Erik. 2004. "Modernity and Hybridity: Nature, Regenerationism, and the Production of the Spanish Waterscapes." In *Reading Economic Geography*, edited by Trevor J. Barnes, Jamie Peck, Eric Sheppard, and Adam Tickell, 188–204. Malden, Mass.: Blackwell.

Talavera Martínez, Irene. 2019. "Reparto desigual de agua en Baja California Sur." In *Nuestros recursos, nuestra vida*, edited by Violeta Núñez and Elsa Guzmán, 1:17–40. Mexico City: Universidad Autónoma Metropolitana. https://www.casadelibrosabiertos.uam.mx/contenido/contenido/Libroelectronico/Nuestros-recursos.pdf.

Talavera Martínez, Irene, and Yolanda Cristina Massieu Trigo. 2021. "Conservación y sustentabilidad en la península de Baja California Sur: Iniciativas comunitarias y políticas erráticas." *HorizonTes territoriales* 1 (1): 1–27.

Tallis, Heather, Peter Kareiva, Michelle Marvier, and Amy Chang. 2008. "An Ecosystem Services Framework to Support Both Practical Conservation and Economic Development." *Proceedings of the National Academy of Sciences* 105 (28): 9457–64.

Tax, Sol. 1953. *Penny Capitalism: A Guatemalan Indian Economy*. Washington, D.C.: U.S. Government Printing Office.

Thompson, E. P. 1971. "The Moral Economy of the English Crowd in the Eighteenth Century." *Past & Present* 50 (1): 76–136. https://doi.org/10.1093/past/50.1.76.

Tiano, Susan. 1994. *Patriarchy on the Line: Labor, Gender, and Ideology in the Mexican Maquila Industry*. Philadelphia: Temple University Press.

Toledo, Víctor M., David Garrido, and Narciso Barrera-Basols. 2013. "Conflictos socioambientales, resistencias ciudadanas y violencia neoliberal en México." *Ecología política* 46:115–24.

Travers, Henry, Lucy J. Archer, Geoffrey Mwedde, Dilys Roe, Julia Baker, Andrew J. Plumptre, Aggrey Rwetsiba, and E.j. Milner-Gulland. 2019. "Understanding Complex Drivers of Wildlife Crime to Design Effective Conservation Interventions." *Conservation Biology* 33 (6): 1296–306. https://doi.org/10.1111/cobi.13330.

Trouillot, Michel-Rolph. 1992. "The Caribbean Region: An Open Frontier in Anthropological Theory." *Annual Review of Anthropology* 21:19–42. https://doi.org/10.1146/annurev.an.21.100192.000315.

Tsing, Anna Lowenhaupt. 2015. *The Mushroom at the End of the World: On the Possibility of Life in Capitalist Ruins*. Princeton: Princeton University Press.

Türken, Salman, Hilde Eileen Nafstad, Rolv Mikkel Blakar, and Katrina Roen. 2016. "Making Sense of Neoliberal Subjectivity: A Discourse Analysis of Media Language on Self-Development." *Globalizations* 13 (1): 32–46. https://doi.org/10.1080/14747731.2015.1033247.

Uphoff, Norman, and Jeff Langholz. 1998. "Incentives for Avoiding the Tragedy of the Commons." *Environmental Conservation* 25 (3): 251–61. https://doi.org/10.1017/S0376892998000319.

Urla, Jacqueline. 2019. "Governmentality and Language." *Annual Review of Anthropology* 48:261–78. https://doi.org/10.1146/annurev-anthro-102317-050258.

Vásquez-León, Marcela. 1994. "Avoidance Strategies and Governmental Rigidity: The Case of the Small-Scale Shrimp Fishery in Two Mexican Communities." *Journal of Political Ecology* 1 (1): 67–82. https://doi.org/10.2458/v1i1.21157.

Vásquez-León, Marcela. 2012. "Policies on Conservation and Sustainable Development: Fishing Communities in the Gulf of California, Mexico." In *Neoliberalism and Commodity Production in Mexico*, edited by Thomas Weaver, James B. Greenberg, William Alexander, and Anne Browning-Aiken, 165–86. Boulder: University Press of Colorado.

Vélez-Ibáñez, Carlos G. 2010. *An Impossible Living in a Transborder World: Culture, Confianza, and Economy of Mexican-Origin Populations.* Tucson: University of Arizona Press.

Viatori, Maximilian, and Héctor Andrés Bombiella Medina. 2019. *Coastal Lives: Nature, Capital, and the Struggle for Artisanal Fisheries in Peru.* Tucson: University of Arizona Press.

Vollan, Björn, and Elinor Ostrom. 2010. "Cooperation and the Commons." *Science* 330 (6006): 923–24. https://doi.org/10.1126/science.1198349.

Walker, Margath, Susan M. Roberts, John Paul Jones, and Oliver Fröhling. 2008. "Neoliberal Development through Technical Assistance: Constructing Communities of Entrepreneurial Subjects in Oaxaca, Mexico." *Geoforum* 39 (1): 527–42. https://doi.org/10.1016/j.geoforum.2007.10.009.

Walley, Christine J. 2004. *Rough Waters: Nature and Development in an East African Marine Park.* Princeton: Princeton University Press.

Weber, Elke U., Ann-Renée Blais, and Nancy E. Betz. 2002. "A Domain-Specific Risk-Attitude Scale: Measuring Risk Perceptions and Risk Behaviors." *Journal of Behavioral Decision Making* 15 (4): 263–90. https://doi.org/10.1002/bdm.414.

Weisgrau, Maxine K. 1997. *Interpreting Development: Local Histories, Local Strategies.* Lanham, Md.: University Press of America.

West, Paige. 2006. *Conservation Is Our Government Now: The Politics of Ecology in Papua New Guinea.* New Ecologies for the Twenty-First Century. Durham, N.C.: Duke University Press.

West, Paige. 2016. *Dispossession and the Environment: Rhetoric and Inequality in Papua New Guinea.* New York: Columbia University Press.

West, Paige, James Igoe, and Dan Brockington. 2006. "Parks and Peoples: The Social Impact of Protected Areas." *Annual Review of Anthropology* 35:251–77. https://doi.org/10.1146/annurev.anthro.35.081705.123308.

Western, David, and Michael Wright. 1994. "The Background to Community-Based Conservation." In *Natural Connections: Perspectives in Community-Based Conservation*, edited by David Western, Michael Wright, and Shirley Carol Strum, 1–14. Washington, D.C.: Island Press.

Western, David, Michael Wright, and Shirley Carol Strum. 1994. *Natural Connections: Perspectives In Community-Based Conservation.* Washington, D.C.: Island Press.

Wilk, Richard R. 1989. "Decision Making and Resource Flows within the Household: Beyond the Black Box." In *The Household Economy: Reconsidering the Domestic Mode of Production*, edited by Richard R. Wilk, 23–52. Boulder, Colo.: Westview.

Wilson, Tamar Diana, Alba Eritrea Gámez Vázquez, and Antonina Ivanova. 2012. "Women Beach and Marina Vendors in Cabo San Lucas, Mexico: Considerations about Their Marginalization." *Latin American Perspectives* 39 (6): 83–95. https://doi.org/10.1177/0094582X12454562.

Worthen, Holly. 2012. "Women and Microcredit: Alternative Readings of Subjectivity, Agency, and Gender Change in Rural Mexico." *Gender, Place & Culture* 19 (3): 364–81. https://doi.org/10.1080/0966369X.2011.624740.

Young, Emily. 2001. "State Intervention and Abuse of the Commons: Fisheries Development in Baja California Sur, Mexico." *Annals of the Association of American Geographers* 91 (2): 283–306. https://doi.org/10.1111/0004-5608.00244.

Young, Iris Marion. 2000. *Inclusion and Democracy*. New York: Oxford University Press.

Zambrano, Andres Felipe, Luis Felipe Giraldo, Monica Tatiana Perdomo, Iván Darío Hernández, and Jesús María Godoy. 2023. "Rotating Savings and Credit Associations: A Scoping Review." *World Development Sustainability* 3:100081. https://doi.org/10.1016/j.wds.2023.100081.

Zelizer, Viviana A. Rotman. 2011. *Economic Lives: How Culture Shapes the Economy*. Princeton, N.J.: Princeton University Press.

INDEX

References to figures and illustrations are indicated by numbers in *italics*. Notes are indicated with page and note references, e.g., 43n6.

9/11 terrorist attacks, 8, 72

agency, 8, 17–20, 25, 124, 128, 150–54
Agrawal, Arun, 18–19
air conditioning, 39, 66
Americanos (U.S. residents), 3–4, 42, 59–
    63, 65–66, 71, 78–79, 103–4, 141–42
appliances and household goods, 38, 39,
    41–42, 49, 61–63, 66, 97
aquaculture, 36, 44, 50, 78, 114, 145,
    146–48
aquarium fish exporting, 36, 50, 78–79,
    79, 145, 147. *See also* Hijas del Mar

beaches, 3–4, 6, 53, 54, 63, 68, *69*
boats, 3–4, 28–29, 30–32, 33–34, 64, 110,
    125, 135–36
boom-and-bust cycles, 8–9, 11–13, 23,
    43–47, 49–50, 156
Bryant, Rebecca, 20
buyers, fish, 4, 28–29, 32, 68

Çalışkan, Koray, 9
Callon, Michel, 9
capacity building, 14, 24–25, 144–50, 152–53
Castillo Velasco Martínez, Iris Aurora
    del, 135

choice, 5–6, 9–14, 20–22, 32–34, 40, 51,
    110–11, 123
Cohen, Erik, 54
Cohen, Scott A., 54
Cole, Michael, 20
compa, compadre, or *compadrazgo*, 53,
    91, 95, 114
Conapesca (La Comisión Nacional de
    Acuacultura y Pesca), 115, 115n4, 125–
    27, 134, 136, 137, 140
conservation, values and assumptions
    of, 12–17, 103–9, 151, 157–61. *See
    also* natural resource management;
    neoliberalism
cooperatives, 30–31, 36, 84–85, 140–41,
    146–48. *See also* Hijas del Mar
Córdoba Azcárate, Matilde, 11–12, 55, 159
corruption, 30, 117, 125–27, 130, 137–38,
    140, 151–52
COVID-19 pandemic, 8, 155
craft-selling, 50, 66, 80, 82, 97, *99*
credit, 29, 32, 33–34, 36–37, 40, 49–50,
    90–91
cruise ships, 55–57, *57*
cudina, 36–37, 90–91. *See also* credit

development, economic. *See* capacity building

dispossession, 15–16, 66–68, *67, 68*, 74, 76, 149–50, 157, 158

diving, 28, 30, 32, 43, 50, 59, 104, 131, 134–35, 140

domestic work: as community activity, 36, 40, 54, 90; as household chores, 36, 54, 94; as source of income, 66, 69–70, 80, 83, 94, 97–98, 145, 146, 149, 152; invisibility of, 84–87, 94; moral value of, 39; baking bread, 36, 37, 50, 80, 83, 85, 89, *93*, 93–94, 145, 146, 149, 152; childcare, 36, 37, 39, 90, 97; cooking, 66, 69–70, 84, 89–90 (*See also* restaurants); dishwashing, 36; embroidery, 36, 54, 80, 82, 97, *99*; housekeeping, 65, 69–70, 99; laundry, 36, 80, 84, *87*, 97; making tortillas, 23, 35, 49, 66, 80, 84, 86, 89–90, 89n2, 91, 96; sewing, 89, 90, 97, 152, 3680

ecology, political, 16–17, 123–24

economies, moral, 9, 15, 24, 39, 52, 80, 87–89, 101, 122, 139, 151, 157–58

"economization," 9, 160

economy, political, 16–17, 158

ecotourism. *See* tourism

education. *See also* skills: elementary and middle school, 36, 130–32; high school, 33, 35, 35n1; higher education, 33, 35, 62, 106, 113, 114, 146, 147, 156; environmental, 105–6, 129–32; gender divisions relative to, 33; outside sponsorship of, 62–63; transportation for, 35, 35n1, 36, 40, 63

electricity, 38, 39, 41–42, 66, 68–69, 99, 114

English, knowledge of, 33, 50, 53, 55–56, 61, 63, 64–65, 70, 74

entrepreneurialism, 14–15, 90, 100, 101, 110, 146, 149. *See also* neoliberalism

environmentalists: attitudes regarding fishers and artisanal fishing, 6, 105–6, 131–33, 151; educational efforts of,

131–32; and the MPA, 6–7, 102–4, 109, 110, 115–16, 130, 136, 151–52; and sportfishing, 73, 151

Escobar, Arturo, 159

ethnography, cognitive, 10, 20–22

family, 8, 30–31, 80, 81–84, 91–94

farming, 48

fish. *See* marine life

fishers: assumed ignorance of, 6, 71, 104–6, 130–32, 152–53; attitudes regarding policing, 133–41, 142; attitudes regarding sportfishers, 107–8, 133; beach access for, 3–4, 68, *69*; daily and seasonal routines of, 27–34; environmental awareness of, 6, 8–9, 32, 104–6, 111, 126, 131–32, 152–53, 157–58; government neglect of, 41, 126, 158; income of, 41; precarity of, 29–34, 40–41, 111, 121 (*See also* boom-and-bust cycles; choice; credit; livelihood); relationships with MPA, 7–8, 102–4, 102n1, 107–9, 114–20, 129–30, 133–50, 143n2; social life of, 3–6, 30, 32 (*See also* social events); use of permits by (*See* permits); values of, 7–9, 30, 33, 34, 111, 126, 157–58; well-being of, 4–6, 8–9, 124, 158, 160–61

fishers, foreign and nonlocal, 19, 32, 46, 103, 104n3, 107–8

fishing, artisanal: alternatives to, 114–15, 144–50; costs associated with, 28–34, 41; equipment used in, 28, 29, 43 (*See also* boats; nets); illegal fishing, 30, 34, 106–7, 110, 125–27, 133, 135–36, 138–40; laws and regulations affecting, 30, 41, 105–7, 108, 120–24, 134–35; line fishing, 28, 32, 64, 106; perceptions of, 6–9, 32–34, 105–7, 120–22, 151, 157–58 (*See also* illegal fishing, above); spearfishing, 28, 30, 106, 125–26, 132, 134–35; and sportfishing, 64, 73, 106, 107–8 (*See also* sportfishing)

INDEX

fishing, industrial, 32, 41, 103–4, 103n2, 104n3, 107, 121, 132–33, 134

fishing, sport. *See* sportfishing

Fox Quesada, Vicente, 130–31

Francisco (resort owner), 68, *69*, 71

Fuentes, Mitchell, 6

gender, 17, 30, 33, 80, 81–84

gifts, 54, 61–63

government. *See also* Conapesca; marine protected area; Profepa; SEMARNAT: corruption in, 117, 125–27, 130, 137–38, 140, 143–44, 151–52; as employer, 38; investment in tourism, 59–60; involvement in conservation and fishing, 41, 108, 115–16, 118, 126, 158

greed, 12–14, 109–12, 122–23

Hardin, Garrett, 12–14, 110–11, 122–23

health care, 5, 38, 70, 71, 75, 90, 90n3, 95, 155

Hijas del Mar (Daughters of the Sea) cooperative, *79*; importance of networking for, 78–79, 98–100; occupational strategies of, 50, 78–79, 84–85, 96–100; reasons for participation in, 83–85, 88–89, 91; spousal attitudes regarding, 78, 82–83

hotel, boutique, 23, 49, 65–66, 82, 93, 97

households, 94. *See also* domestic work; family

housing, 4–5, 49, 77

Hutchins, Edwin, 20

individual rationality, 5–6, 9–20, 24–25, 34, 51–52, 110–112, 123, 150–54, 157. *See also* agency; choice; neoliberalism

infrastructure: airports, 59, 60, 64, 72; electricity, 38, 39, 41–42, 66, 68–69, 99, 114; internet, 39, 62, 66; phone service, 37, 39, 62, 66, 114; roads and highways, 59, 66–68, *67*, 75–76; water system, 42, 68

islands, *7*, 24, 28, 36, 56, 59, 60, 103, 108, 116, 129–30, 132

Kaaristo, Maarja, 54–55

Kaus, Andrea, 119–20

Kincaid, Jamaica, 55, 75

land rights and ownership, 6, 48, 68–69

law, Mexican: regarding beaches and land ownership, 6; regarding fishing and fisheries, 104, 108, 110, 128, 132; unequal application of, 4 (*See also* corruption)

LBNP. *See* marine protected area (MPA)

livelihood: and conservation, 122–28, 144–50; multiple livelihoods, 8, 40–41, 50, 65–66, 69, 70, 75, 97–98 (*See also* microenterprises); strategies of, 8, 47–52, 95–101, 152–53, 156, 160–61; values associated with, 87–94

livestock. *See* ranching

Loreto, *7*; high school in, 35, 35n1; as market for fish, 28; tourism in, 55–60, *57, 58*, 73–74

Loreto Bay National Park (Parque Nacional Bahía de Loreto). *See* marine protected area (MPA)

Loreto residents: Carlos (MPA staff member), 113–14, 115, 147, 148 (*See also* marine protected area (MPA)); Luis, 104, 105; Lupe, 146–47; O'Neil, Ann and Don, 103–4, 134 (*See also Americanos* (U.S. residents)); Pedro (Conapesca official), 125–27; Raul (MPA director), 144–46

mangoes, selling, 77–78

marine life. *See also* aquaculture; aquarium fish exporting; fishing: boom-bust cycles of, 43–45; declines in, 6–7, 43, 45, 103, 104, 105–7, 110, 131–32, 152, 156; increases in, 134; monitoring of, 132; abalone, 30; chocolate clams, 44, 59, 156; clams, 28, 146, 147; lobsters, 30; mano de leon scallops, 146, 147; oysters and pearls, 8, 43, 45; pelicans, 134; rays, 156; sardines, 43, 133, 134;

sea bass, 28; sea cucumbers, 28, 44, 46; sea turtles, 30, 134, 156; sergeant majors *(petaca rayada)*, 156; sharks, 43, 45, 106, 132; shrimp, 104, 133, 134; squid, 29, 44, 46, 134; "trash" fish, 6, 29, 32; triggerfish *(cochi)*, 156; tropical fish *(See* aquarium fish exporting); tuna, 43, 103; whales, 43, 59; yellowtail (amberjack), 28, 103, 134

marine protected area (MPA): capacity-building efforts of, 93, 98–100, 114–15, 121–22, 144–50; constraints on and affordances of, 8, 126–28, 134, 136–40, 142–44, 150–53; creation of, 6–7, 13, 102–3, 112, *113*; educational efforts of, 128, 129–32; meetings and planning activities of, 112–22, *113*, *117*, 128–30, 128n1; monitoring by, 132; regulatory activities of, 7–8, 13, 17, 24–25, 30, 109–12, 120–23, 125–26, 132–44; relationships with environmentalists, 6–7, 102–4, 109, 110, 115–16, 130, 136, 151–52; relationships with fishers, 7–8, 102–4, 102n1, 107–9, 114–24, 126–27, 129–30, 133–50, 143n2; relationships with tourism entrepreneurs, 102–4, 102n1, 115–16, 122, 129, 136, 143–44, 151–52; relationships with women entrepreneurs, 93, 98–100, 145–48, 152; staff of, 8, 112–22, *113*, 128–30, 141–45, 147–53; values of, 13, 24, 110–11, 118–23, 150–53

meetings and planning activities, 102, 112–25, *113*, *117*, 128–30, 128n1, 134, 140, 143, 143n2, 148

microenterprises, 77–80, 84–87, 98–101

migration, 23, 32, 47–48, 48n3, 50, 55, 60, 99, 132, 147

military, 136, 137

Mitchell, Ross E., 119

morality: agency and, 18–19, 25; conflicting values of, 7–8, 15, 74–75, 122, 151, 157–58; economies of, 9, 15, 24, 39, 52, 80, 87–89, 101, 122, 139, 151, 157–58; neoliberal *(See* neoliberalism)

MPA. *See* marine protected area (MPA)

natural resource management, 117–20. *See also* conservation; marine protected area; tragedy of the commons

neoliberalism: alternatives to, 157–61; influence on environmental conservation, 12–17, 24, 110–11, 123; values and assumptions of, 9–18, 54, 55, 110–11, 152–53 *(See also* choice; rationality)

nets, 28–30, *31*, 64, 104, 105–7, 134, 139

networks, social: MPA staff participation in, 114, 125–26, 129–30; as necessary for business success, 78–79, 92–93, 97–101; needed for switch to tourism, 64–65, 73–74; as survival strategy, 8, 89–94, 98–101

Nopoló, 72

Ortner, Sherri, 18

Ostrom, Elinor, 13–14, 111

padrinos (godparents/sponsors), 62, 65, 90

pangas (fishing boats). *See* boats

Parkins, John R., 119

Parque Nacional Bahía de Loreto (Loreto Bay National Park). *See* marine protected area (MPA)

permits, 30, 106, 108, 125–26, 133, 136–42, 146–47

phone service, 37, 39, 62, 66, 114

Playa Tranquilla: beach of, 3–4, 6, 53, 54, 63, 68, *69*; changes in, 3–4, 47–48, 66–72, *67*, *69*, 155–56; map of vicinity, *7*; pseudonym of, 3n1; residents of *(See* Playa Tranquilla residents); rhythms and patterns of, 23, 27–52; tourism in, 4, 7–8, 42, 53–55, 60–76 *(See also* hotel; resorts; sportfishing); uncertainty in *(See* boom-and-bust cycles; precarity)

INDEX 189

Playa Tranquilla residents: Adela, 91, 92–93, 97; Alfonso, 48; *Americano* residents of, 42, 65–66, 71 (*See also Americanos*); doña Ana, 82, 88–89, 155; don Antonio, 106–7, 126–27, 155; Beatrice, 89; Blanca, 61; doña Carmen, 46, 155; Dalia, 77–78, 84, 86; Dan and Jessica (*Americano* residents), 65–66, 71 (*See also* hotel, boutique); Isabel, 63–64, 155; don Javier, 3–6, 9–10, 20–21, 27, 37, 63–64, 68, 125–27, 156–57; Lupita, 82, 83, 92; Magdalena, 27, 35; Maria, 84, 89–90, 97; Mario, 156; Memo, 27, 35; occupations of (*See* domestic work; fishing; livelihood; tourism; women's work and occupations); Paulina, 83, 85, 89, 93–94; doña Rosa, 95; Yvonne, 82, 92

policing, 24–25, 110, 126, 132–44

power, relations of, 9–18, 54–55, 118–20, 150–53, 158–60. *See also* agency; dispossession

precarity. *See also* boom-and-bust cycles; livelihood: of fishers, 29–34, 40–41, 111, 121; strategies for surviving, 8–9, 23, 46–47, 49–50, 52–53

Profepa (La Procuraduría Federal de Proteción al Ambiente), 115, 115n4, 125–27, 134, 137, 140

Program for Regional Sustainable Development (Programa de Desarrollo Regional Sustenable), 145–46

Pronatura Noroeste, 135

pseudonyms, use of, 3n1

Pueblos Mágicos, 73

Puerto Escondido, 72

quinceañeras. *See* social events

ranching, 37, 40, 50, 150

rationality, economic, 9–18, 152–54. *See also* choice; neoliberalism; tragedy of the commons

Reeves, Madeleine, 19

regulation, 7–8, 12–13, 17, 24–25, 30, 41, 105–1112

relationships, 28, 30–31, 46, 48–51, 65–66, 71, 73–75, 153, 157–58; MPA and environmentalists, 6–7, 102–4, 109, 110, 115–16, 130, 136, 151–52; MPA and fishers, 7–8, 102–4, 102n1, 107–9, 114–20, 129–30, 133–50, 143n2; MPA and tourism entrepreneurs, 102–4, 102n1, 115–16, 122, 129, 136, 143–44, 151–52; MPA and women entrepreneurs, 93, 98–100, 145–48, 152; scientists and local community, 79, 91, 98, 108, 114, 116, 146–48; tourists and local communities, 53–54, 56–57, *57*, 60–63, 65–66

resorts, tourist, 4, 23, 42, 47, 49, 55, 66–72, *67*, *69*, *71*, 92

restaurants, 36, 80, 82, 83, 90, 91, 92–93, 97, 98, 145, 146

Richardson, Liz, 19

Saavedra Gallo, Gonzalo, 157

salir adelante (getting ahead, getting by), 50–51, 91, 101, 111, 153

scientists: environmental monitoring by, 132; interactions with local community, 79, 91, 98, 108, *113*, 113–14, 116, 146–48, 159

Semana Santa tourism, 54

SEMARNAT (Secretariat of Environment and Natural Resources), 116, 118, 141

Skidelsky, Robert, 9

skills: acquisition of, 23, 40, 47, 48, 50, 70, 78, 94, 96, 97–99, 150; barriers to using, 64, 150, 153; lack of, 32–33, 34, 73–74

snorkeling, 59, 156

social events, 36, 39, 44, 58, 62, 65, 90. *See also padrinos*

spearfishing, 28, 30, 106, 125–26, 132, 134–35

sportfishing: artisanal fishing and, 73, 106–7, 122, 133; barriers to participating in, 28, 33, 41, 64–65; environmental impact of, 73, 122, 151; as important tourism activity, *58*, 58–59; morality of, 122, 151; relationship with MPA, 104, 109, 120, 136; spearfishing, 106

stores, 36, 37–38, 40, 50, 53, 80

Stronza, Amanda, 55

television, 39. *See also* appliances and household goods

tortillas, 23, 35, 49, 66, 80, 84, 86, 89–90, 89n2, 91, 96

tourism: barriers to participation in, 11–12, 33, 60–61, 70–71, 73–75, 121, 158; boom-and-bust cycle of, 8, 72–73; camping, 53, 54, 60, 62–65, 141–42; cruise ships, 55–57, *57*; economic impact of, 59–60; ecotourism, 41, 65, 72; environmental impact of, 66–68, *67*, 73, 122, 151; MPA engagement with, 102–4, 102n1, 115–16, 121, 122, 129, 136, 143–44, 146, 151–52; as part of multiple livelihoods, 33, 41, 50, 63–66, 69–71; permits for, 133, 136, 141–42; in Playa Tranquilla, 4, 7–8, 23, 42, 53–55, 60–76, 98–100 (*See also* hotel, boutique; resorts; sportfishing); resorts, 4, 23, 42, 47, 49, 66–72, *67*, *69*, *71*; scholarship on, 54–55, 75; snorkeling, 156

tourism entrepreneurs: attitudes regarding artisanal fishing, 105–6, 133, 136, 151; relationships with the MPA, 102–4, 102n1, 115–16, 122, 129, 136, 143–44, 151–52

tourists. *See also Americanos* (U.S. residents): environmental education of, 131; fees for, 141–42; interactions with local communities, 53–54, 56–57, *57*, 60–63, 65–66, 98–99; permits for, 133, 136, 141–42

tragedy of the commons, 12–14, 109–12, 122–24, 128, 133

transportation: air travel, 59, 60, 64, 72; community vans and busses, 35, 35n1, 36, 40, 63; informal systems of, 95–96; lack of, 95, 117

trash, 38, 55, 59, 71, 99, 126, 130, 131, 142, 149

trawlers. *See* fishing, industrial

tropical fish. *See* aquarium fish exporting

uniforms, school, 36, 50, 90, 97

United States. *See also Americanos* (U.S. residents): cheaper prices in, 57; migration to, 48, 48n3, 99

Universidad Autónoma de Baja California Sur, *113*, 113–14

U.S. expatriates. *See Americanos* (U.S. residents)

values: conflicting, 7–8, 14–16, 22, 74–75, 100–101, 122, 151, 157–58; neoliberal, 9–18, 54, 55, 110–11, 152–53; regarding family, 8, 80, 89, 91–92; regarding the environment, 12–17, 100–101, 103–9, 149–50, 151, 157–61; regarding work, 8, 30, 33, 34, 39, 52, 80–84, 87–94, 96–97, 101, 148

vigilancia. See policing

water system, 42, 68. *See also* infrastructure

weddings. *See* social events

well-being, 4–6, 8–9, 124, 158, 160–61

West, Paige, 15, 74, 149–50

women: daily routines and responsibilities, 36–37, 40; education and, 33, 131; gendered constraints on, 23–24, 81–84; strategies of, 95–97, 152–53 (*See also* livelihood); values of, 39, 80, 81, 87–94, 96–97, 101, 148; widows, 28, 65

women's work and occupations. *See also* domestic work; Hijas del Mar: development opportunities for, 93, 98–100,

146, 148, 152 (*See also* aquaculture; capacity building); familial attitudes regarding, 80, 81–84, 92–94; financing of, 38, 49–50, 78, 86, 97–98, 99, 100, 146 (*See also cudina*); invisibility of, 81, 84–87; microbusinesses, 23–24, 36–37, 39, 66, 77–80; motivations behind, 84–94; social aspects of, 89–92; wage labor, 65–66, 69–70

work. *See also* domestic work; fishing, artisanal; tourism; women's work and occupations: familial aspects of, 30–31, 80, 81–84, 91–94; values associated with, 8, 30, 33, 34, 39, 52, 80–84, 87–94, 96–97, 101, 148

Zedillo Ponce de León, Ernesto, 102, 104

ABOUT THE AUTHOR

Nicole D. Peterson is an associate professor of anthropology at the University of North Carolina Charlotte and an applied, environmental, and economic anthropologist. They engage with communities dealing with changes and inequities around food, health, and the environment, with a focus on decision-making. Dr. Peterson has studied natural resource management and economic development in Mexico, decision-making under uncertainty and climate change adaptation in Ethiopia, and Charlotte-area food security, including the State of the Plate food system assessment effort.